1st National Edition

WHO WILL HANDLE YOUR FINANCES IF YOU CAN'T?

By Attorneys Denis Clifford and Mary Randolph

Edited by Attorney Ralph Warner

Illustrated by Mari Stein

NOLO PRESS   BERKELEY

YOUR RESPONSIBILITY WHEN USING A SELF-HELP LAW BOOK

We've done our best to give you useful and accurate information in this book. But laws and procedures change frequently and are subject to differing interpretations. If you want legal advice backed by a guarantee, see a lawyer. If you use this book, it's your responsibility to make sure that the facts and general advice contained in it are applicable to your situation.

KEEPING UP TO DATE

To keep its books up to date, Nolo Press issues new printings and new editions periodically. New printings reflect minor legal changes and technical corrections. New editions contain major legal changes, major text additions or major reorganizations. To find out if a later printing or edition of any Nolo book is available, call Nolo Press at (510) 549-1976 or check the catalog in the *Nolo News*, our quarterly newspaper.

To stay current, follow the "Update" service in the *Nolo News*. You can get the paper free by sending us the registration card in the back of the book. In another effort to help you use Nolo's latest materials, we offer a 25% discount off the purchase of any new Nolo book if you turn in any earlier printing or edition. (See the "Recycle Offer" in the back of the book.)

FIRST EDITION	November 1992
EDITOR	Ralph Warner
ILLUSTRATIONS	Mari Stein
COVER DESIGN	Toni Ihara
INDEX	Sayre Van Young
PRINTING	Delta Lithograph

Clifford, Denis.
     Who will handle your finances if you can't? / by Denis Clifford and
Mary Randolph. -- 1st national ed.
          p. cm.
     Includes index
     ISBN 0-87337-179-8 : $19.95
     1. Power of Attorney--United States--Popular works. 2. Finances
Personal--United States. I. Randolph, Mary. II. Title.
KF1347.Z9C565 1992
346.73'029--dc20
[347.30629]   92-10999
                                            CIP

ACKNOWLEDGMENTS

We'd like to thank:

Jake Warner, who edited all the drafts of the manuscript with his usual insight and energy.

Beverly M. Lyon, an estate planning attorney in Kensington, California; and Mary Willis, an attorney with Consumers' Group Legal Services in El Cerrito, California, who offered helpful information on their experiences with durable powers of attorney.

Ann Heron and Steve Elias of Nolo Press, who also commented on the manuscript.

Lisa Guerin, who once again diligently researched state law from A to W.

Terri Hearsch, who cheerfully designed and formatted the many forms in this book.

Ely Newman, who painstakingly proofread the book, including all those forms.

Toni Ihara, who met the challenge of designing a cover for a book with a title three blocks long.

Amy Ihara, who designed and laid out the book and never, ever lost patience with last-minute changes.

CONTENTS

1 USING A DURABLE POWER OF ATTORNEY FOR FINANCES

2 HOW DURABLE POWERS OF ATTORNEY WORK

3 CHOOSING YOUR ATTORNEY-IN-FACT

4 THE ATTORNEY-IN-FACT'S RESPONSIBILITIES

5 PREPARING A DURABLE POWER OF ATTORNEY

6 STATE-SPECIFIC DURABLE POWER OF ATTORNEY FORMS

7 MAKING IT LEGAL

8 REVOKING A DURABLE POWER OF ATTORNEY

9 LAWYERS AND LEGAL RESEARCH

GLOSSARY

APPENDIX

Nolo Durable Power of Attorney Form

State-Specific Power of Attorney Forms

     Alaska form
     California form
     Colorado form
     Connecticut form
     Illinois form
     Indiana form
     Minnesota form
     New Mexico form
     New York form
     North Carolina form
     Tennessee form

Physician's Determination of Incapacity

Designation of Authority

Resignation of Attorney-in-Fact

Notice of Revocation (Unrecorded Power of Attorney)

Notice of Revocation (Recorded Power of Attorney)

1

USING A DURABLE POWER OF ATTORNEY FOR FINANCES

Many of us feel a well-grounded fear that we may someday become seriously ill and unable to handle our own affairs. Who would step in on our behalf to pay bills, make bank deposits, watch over investments and deal with the paperwork that always accompanies collecting insurance and government benefits? As our lives grow in length (but not always in quality), it's reasonable to plan for such a contingency.

Let's start by asking what happens if you don't do any planning. If you're married, your spouse will have some limited authority over joint finances. But to get legal authority to deal with most financial and property matters, your spouse or other family members would have to hire a lawyer and go to court, where a judge would appoint someone to handle your finances.

Fortunately, you can avoid the intrusiveness and expense of that court proceeding. All you need to do is prepare a document called a "durable power of attorney for finances"—now, while you're still healthy and independent. With a durable power of attorney for finances, you can give a trusted person the authority to handle all your financial matters if it ever becomes necessary. Preparing a durable power of attorney is a simple, inexpensive and reliable way to ensure that your finances stay in the hands of the trusted person you chose. It's also a wonderful thing to do for the family members who otherwise face an unfamiliar and intimidating courtroom proceeding. If you do become incapacitated, the durable power of attorney will likely appear as a minor miracle to those close to you.

Because durable powers of attorney are widely used, the person you choose to act on your behalf should have no trouble getting banks, government agencies and other institutions to accept his or her authority.

A WORD ABOUT PROCRASTINATION

 It's easy to understand why people put off preparing a durable power of attorney. No one likes to consider the possibility of being incapable of handling his or her own affairs. For some, facing the truth that you or someone you care about may become incapacitated is a courageous act.

CHECKLIST: PREPARING A DURABLE POWER OF ATTORNEY

☐ 1. Decide:
   ☐ whether your durable power of attorney will take effect immediately or only if you become incapacitated. (Chapter 2)
   ☐ who you want to have authority to handle some or all of your financial affairs (your attorney-in-fact). (Chapter 3)
   ☐ what authority you want your attorney-in-fact to have. (Chapter 4)

☐ 2. Prepare a durable power of attorney, spelling out the duties of your attorney-in-fact. (Chapter 5 or 6)

☐ 3. Sign the durable power of attorney in front of a notary public (and witnesses, in some states). (Chapter 7)

☐ 4. Record the durable power of attorney at the local land records office, if necessary. (Chapter 7)

☐ 5. Deliver a copy of the durable power of attorney to the attorney-in-fact and institutions that might deal with the attorney-in-fact. (Chapter 7)

☐ 6. Review your durable power of attorney every five to seven years and prepare a new one if your circumstances have changed significantly. (Chapter 8)

A. Durable Powers of Attorney: An Overview

When you create and sign a power of attorney, you give another person legal authority to act on your behalf. The person who is given this authority is called your "attorney-in-fact." The word "attorney" here means anyone authorized to act on another's behalf; it's most definitely not restricted to lawyers.

The power of attorney you create with this book is "durable," which means it stays valid even if you become unable to handle your own affairs (incapacitated). If you don't specify that you want your power of attorney to continue if you become incapacitated, it will automatically end (in almost all states) if you later become incapacitated.

Principal: The person who creates and signs the power of attorney document, authorizing someone else to act for him or her.

Attorney-in-Fact: The person who is authorized to act for the principal. In many states, the attorney-in-fact is also referred to as an "agent" of the principal.

Alternate Attorney-in-Fact: The person who takes over as attorney-in-fact if your first choice cannot or will not serve.

Conventional Power of Attorney: A power of attorney that automatically ends if the principal becomes incapacitated.

Durable Power of Attorney: A power of attorney that states that it will remain valid and in effect even if the principal becomes incapacitated, or will take effect only if the principal becomes incapacitated.

Incapacitated: Unable to handle one's own financial matters or health care decisions. Also called "disabled" in some states. Generally, incapacity isn't precisely defined by state law. Usually, a physician makes the determination.

Springing Durable Power of Attorney: A durable power of attorney that takes effect only if a physician determines that the principal cannot handle his or her own financial affairs.

1. When the Power of Attorney Takes Effect

A durable power of attorney can be drafted so that it goes into effect as soon as you sign it. That is appropriate if you face a serious operation or incapacitating illness.

But it's more common to specify that the durable power of attorney does not go into effect unless a doctor certifies that you have become incapacitated. This is called a "springing" durable power of attorney. It allows you to keep control over your affairs unless and until you become incapacitated, when it springs into effect. The durable power of attorney ends only when you die or revoke it.

Example: As a result of Alzheimer's disease, Fred can no longer manage his finances. Several years ago, however, while his mental faculties were still good, Fred signed a springing durable power of attorney for finances. The document gave his brother Benjamin authority over Fred's finances in the event that Fred's physician signed a statement to the effect that Fred could no longer handle his own affairs.

Benjamin asks Fred's doctor to examine Fred and sign such a statement, which the doctor does. The durable power of attorney springs into effect, which means Benjamin can sign Fred's checks, make bank deposits for him, sell his securities or do whatever else is necessary to manage Fred's finances sensibly.

(Chapter 2, *How Durable Powers of Attorney Work,* Section C, explains this in detail.)

2.   What the Attorney-in-Fact Does

Commonly, people give an attorney-in-fact broad power over their finances. But you can give your attorney-in-fact as much or as little power as you wish. (It's easy to do with the fill-in-the-blanks forms in this book; instructions are in Chapters 5 and 6.) You may want to give your attorney-in-fact authority to do some or all of the following:

- use your assets to pay your everyday expenses and those of your family
- buy, sell, maintain, pay taxes on and mortgage real estate and other property
- collect benefits from social security, Medicare or other government programs or civil or military service
- invest your money in stocks, bonds and mutual funds
- handle transactions with banks and other financial institutions
- buy and sell insurance policies and annuities for you
- file and pay your taxes
- operate your small business

- claim property you inherit or are otherwise entitled to
- represent you in court
- manage your retirement accounts.

These powers are discussed in detail in Chapter 4, *The Attorney-in-Fact's Responsibilities.*

You can tailor your durable power of attorney for finances to fit your needs by limiting the power you grant and placing conditions upon the attorney-in-fact. For example, you might give your attorney-in-fact authority over your real estate, with the express restriction that your house may not be sold.

Whatever powers you give the attorney-in-fact, the attorney-in-fact must act in your best interests, keep accurate records, keep your property separate from his or hers, and avoid conflicts of interest.

You cannot, in most states, give your attorney-in-fact authority to do certain things on your behalf. For the most part, these prohibitions are in areas that you wouldn't want to delegate anyway, so you really don't need to worry about them. Here are the main ones:

Marriage, Adoption, Wills. You cannot authorize your attorney-in-fact to marry, adopt or make a will on your behalf. These acts are considered too personal to delegate to someone else.

Powers You've Already Delegated. If you've already given someone legal authority to manage some or all of your property, you cannot delegate that authority to your attorney-in-fact. Here are two common examples:

- You created a living trust that gives the successor trustee power over trust property if you become incapacitated. (See Section B, below.)
- You signed a partnership agreement that gives your partners authority to manage your interest in the business if you can't. (See Chapter 4, *The Attorney-in-Fact's Responsibilities*, Section D.)

3. Tear-Out Durable Power of Attorney Forms

To create a legally valid durable power of attorney, all you have to do is properly complete and sign a fill-in-the-blanks form that's a few pages long. Some states have their own forms. This book contains all the state forms and a Nolo form, which can be used in any state. There are complete instructions for filling out all each form.

After you fill out the form, you must sign it in front of a notary public. In some states, witnesses must also watch you sign the document. You may also need to put a copy on file at the local land records office. (Chapter 7, *Making It Legal*, explains how to do all this.)

Some banks and brokerage companies have their own durable power of attorney forms. If you want your attorney-in-fact to have an easy time with these institutions, you may need to prepare two (or more) durable powers of attorney: the bank's form and the broader form in this book.

B. What Happens If You Don't Have a Durable Power of Attorney for Finances

If you become incapacitated and you haven't prepared a durable power of attorney for finances, a court proceeding is probably inescapable. Your spouse, closest relatives or companion will have to ask a court for authority over at least some of your financial affairs.

How much court involvement is needed depends on whether or not you are married and whether or not you have done any planning for incapacity at all.

FAKING IT

 If someone becomes incapacitated, panicky family members may consider just faking the signatures necessary to carry on routine financial matters. After all, what's wrong with signing Aunt Amanda's name to a check to pay her phone bill? It's not stealing.

No, it's forgery, which is just as illegal. It can get well-meaning relatives into a lot of trouble. The law is strict in this area to guard against dishonest relatives who might loot a relative's assets.

Forging a signature on checks, bills of sale, tax returns, etc. may work for a while, but it will probably be discovered eventually. The conservatorship proceeding everyone was trying to avoid will still be necessary—and the court will not be eager to put a proven liar in charge of a relative's finances.

---

1. If You Are Married

If you are married, don't assume that your spouse will be able to manage your finances if you can't, without a durable power of attorney.

Your spouse does have some authority over property you own together—to pay bills from a joint bank account or sell stock in a joint brokerage account, for example. There are significant limits, however, on your spouse's right to sell property owned by both spouses. For example, in most states, both spouses must agree to the sale of co-owned real estate or cars. Because an incapacitated spouse can't consent to such a sale, the other spouse's hands are tied.

Example: New York residents Michael and Ellen have been married for 47 years. Their major assets are a home and stock. The home is owned in both their names as joint tenants. The stock was bought only in Michael's name, and the couple has never transferred it into shared ownership.

Michael becomes incapacitated and requires expensive medical treatment. Legally, Ellen cannot sell the stock to pay for medical costs.

She could sell her interest, not Michael's, in the house, or take a loan against it, but doesn't want to. And as a practical matter, a bank would probably be very reluctant to grant a mortgage that wasn't signed by both spouses.

When it comes to property that belongs only to you, your spouse has no legal authority. You must use a durable power of attorney to give your spouse authority over your property.

Example: Courtney's husband, Hal, is incapacitated and living in a nearby nursing home. Courtney wants to raise money by selling Hal's old car, which he can no longer drive, but she can't because the title is in Hal's name.

2. If You Have a Living Trust

A revocable living trust, even though it is created primarily to avoid probate, can also be useful if you become incapable of taking care of your financial affairs. That's because the person who will distribute trust property after your death (the successor trustee) can also, in most cases, take over management of the trust property if you become incapacitated. Usually the trust document gives the successor trustee authority to manage all property in the trust and to use it for your needs.[1]

Example: Jasmine creates a probate-avoidance living trust, appointing herself as trustee (the person in charge of the property that technically is owned by the living trust). The trust document states that if she becomes incapacitated, and a physician signs a statement saying she no longer can manage her own affairs, her daughter Joy will replace her as trustee.

Most people transfer into a living trust assets that are expensive to probate, such as real estate and valuable securities. Few people transfer all their property to a living trust, and the successor trustee has no authority over property that the trust doesn't own. So although it's helpful, a living trust

---

[1] If you're not sure whether or not your living trust gives this power to the successor trustee, read the trust document. (The living trusts produced by *Nolo's Living Trust* software grant this power.)

isn't a complete substitute for a durable power of attorney for finances.

The two documents work well together, however, especially if you name the same trusted person to be your attorney-in-fact and the successor trustee of your living trust. That person will have authority to manage property both in and out of your living trust and be able to handle day-to-day matters such as endorsing checks and paying bills from your checking account.

Example: Consuela, a widow, owns all the stock of a prosperous clothing manufacturing corporation. To avoid probate, she transfers the stock into a living trust, naming her brother, Rodolfo, as successor trustee. If Consuela becomes incapacitated, Rodolfo will become acting trustee, and manage the trust property (the stock) for Consuela's benefit.

Consuela also prepares a durable power of attorney for finances and names Rodolfo as her attorney-in-fact. That gives him authority over whatever assets she does not transfer to the trust—for example, her bank accounts and car.

3.   If You Own Joint Tenancy Property

Joint tenancy is a way that more than one person can own property together. The most notable feature of joint tenancy is that when one owner dies, the other owner(s) automatically own the deceased person's share of the property. But if you become incapacitated, the other owners have very limited authority over your share of the joint tenancy property.

If you and someone else own a bank account in joint tenancy, and one of you becomes incapacitated, the other owner is legally entitled to use the funds. The healthy joint tenant can take care of the financial needs of the incapacitated person simply by paying bills from the joint account. But the other account owner has no legal right to endorse checks made out to the incapacitated person. In

practice, it might be possible—if not technically legal—to get an incapacitated person's checks into a joint account by stamping them with "For Deposit Only."

Matters get more complicated with other kinds of joint tenancy property. Real estate is a good example. If one owner becomes incapacitated, the other has no legal authority to sell or refinance the incapacitated owner's share.

By contrast, with a durable power of attorney, you can give your attorney-in-fact authority over property you own in joint tenancy, including real estate and bank accounts.

4.   If a Court Appoints a Conservator

If you don't have a durable power of attorney for finances, chances are your relatives will have to go to court to get someone appointed to manage your financial affairs. To do this, they must ask a judge to rule that you cannot take care of your own affairs—a public airing of a very private matter. And like any court proceeding, it can be expensive if a lawyer must be hired.[2] Depending on where you live, the person appointed is called a conservator, guardian of the estate, committee or curator; for simplicity, this book uses the common term "conservator." The incapacitated person is known as the "conservatee."

At a court hearing, the judge hears testimony about the need for a conservatorship. If everyone agrees, the hearing can be routine—albeit upsetting and embarrassing. Court proceedings are matters of public record; in some places, a notice may even be published in a local newspaper. If relatives fight

---

[2]In California, most conservatorship proceedings may be handled without an attorney by using *The Conservatorship Book,* by Lisa Goldoftas and Carolyn Farren (Nolo Press).

over who is to be the conservator, matters can be nasty, complicated and expensive.

HOW A DURABLE POWER OF ATTORNEY AVOIDS CONSERVATORSHIP PROCEEDINGS

A conservatorship proceeding is what a durable power of attorney is designed to avoid. If you create a durable power of attorney for finances and later become incapacitated, a conservatorship is unnecessary, because your attorney-in-fact would already have legal authority to handle your financial affairs.

A conservatorship proceeding would be initiated only if no one were willing to serve as attorney-in-fact, the attorney-in-fact wanted guidance from a court or a close relative thought the attorney-in-fact wasn't acting in your best interests.

A court may appoint one person to make both financial and personal decisions, or may appoint different people. Someone who is responsible for making personal (not financial) decisions about the physical care of someone else is often called a "guardian of the person."

A judge who decides that a conservator is needed may ask the conservatee to express a preference for conservator. State law also generally provides a priority list for who is appointed. For example, a number of states make the person's spouse the first choice as conservator, followed by an adult child, parent and brother or sister. The conservator is entitled to payment for his or her services, from the conservatee's assets.

In many states, the law has a loophole, allowing the court to appoint whomever it determines will act in the conservatee's "best interests." It's possible the conservatee will wind up with some crony of the judge managing his finances. If so, there's a distinct possibility that the conservator will pay himself handsomely for less than dedicated service.

When a conservator is appointed, the conservatee loses the right to control his or her own money. If the court also appoints a personal guardian, the conservatee may lose the right to manage even a small allowance, vote, travel or drive a car.

The appointment of a conservator is usually just the beginning of court proceedings. Often the conservator must:

- post a bond—a kind of insurance policy that pays if the conservator steals or misuses property
- prepare (or hire a lawyer or accountant to prepare) detailed financial reports and periodically file them with the court
- get court approval for certain transactions, such as selling real estate or making slightly risky investments.

All of this, of course, costs money—your money. A conservatorship isn't necessarily permanent, but it may be ended only by the court.

C. When You Shouldn't Rely on a Durable Power of Attorney

The expense and intrusion of a conservatorship are rarely desirable. In a few situations, however, special concerns justify the process.

1. You Want Court Supervision of Your Finances

If you can't think of someone you trust enough to appoint as your attorney-in-fact, with broad authority over your property and finances, don't create a durable power of attorney. A conservatorship, with the built-in safeguard of court supervision, is worth the extra cost and trouble.

2. You Fear Family Fights

If you have a considerable amount of property and fear that family members would fight over its management if you appointed an attorney-in-fact, a conservatorship may be preferable. Your relatives may still fight, but at least the court will be there to keep an eye on your welfare and your property.

D. How a Durable Power of Attorney Fits Into an Estate Plan

A durable power of attorney for finances serves a very important purpose by arranging for the management of your finances and avoiding the need for a conservatorship. But it is only part of an estate plan—that is, a plan for taking care of your property and your family at your death or incapacity. You need other documents to accomplish other goals.

This section touches on some of the other basic estate planning tasks you should consider when you create your durable power of attorney. It does not try to consider every aspect of estate planning—reducing estate tax, for example, is not covered.[3]

The chart below summarizes your options for taking care of different estate planning problems. It also shows who will be in charge of carrying out your wishes under each method. To avoid conflicts, it's wise to name the same person to fill as many roles as possible. For example, if you make a will, a durable power of attorney for finances and a revocable living trust, it's often best to name the same person to serve as executor of your will, attorney-in-fact for the durable power of attorney and successor trustee of the living trust.

---

[3]For detailed information on estate planning, see *Plan Your Estate With a Living Trust*, by Denis Clifford (Nolo Press).

BASIC ESTATE PLANNING

Document	Function	Person in charge
Durable power of attorney for finances (effective immediately)	Give someone authority to make personal financial decisions on your behalf immediately.	Attorney-in-fact
Springing durable power of attorney for finances	Give someone authority to make personal financial decisions on your behalf if you become incapacitated.	Attorney-in-fact
Will	Leave property to people and charities you want to inherit it.	Executor
	Nominate personal guardian to care for minor children if you and the other parent can't.	Personal guardian
	Arrange for management of property inherited by minor children.	Custodian or trustee
Durable power of attorney for health care	Give someone authority to make health care decisions, including use of life-prolonging treatment, on your behalf if you become incapacitated.	Attorney-in-fact
Living will	Tell physicians what life-prolonging treatments you do not want to receive in certain circumstances.	Physicians
	In some states, can also give someone you choose authority to make health care decisions on your behalf.	Patient proxy or advocate
Revocable living trust	Avoid probate and give someone authority to manage trust property if you become incapacitated.	Successor trustee

1. Making Medical Decisions

If you become incapacitated, you'll need someone to make medical as well as financial decisions for you. The document you create with this book—a durable power of attorney for finances—does **not** give your attorney-in-fact legal authority to make medical decisions for you.

To make sure that medical decisions, including decisions about the use of life support systems, are in the hands of someone you trust, you should prepare another document: a durable power of attorney for health care. In most states, you'll also want to write out your wishes in a "living will."

a. Durable Powers of Attorney for Health Care

A durable power of attorney for health care lets you choose someone to make medical decisions on your behalf if you can't. People frequently use durable powers of attorney for health care to set out instructions regarding the use, or non-use, of life-sustaining procedures if they become incapacitated and suffer from a terminal illness.

Even if you want the same person to make both financial and medical decisions for you, you should sign two separate powers of attorney: one for finances and one for health care. In many states, separate documents are required by law. But even where it is legally permissible to combine a financial durable power of attorney with a durable power of attorney for health care, it's not a good idea, for several reasons:

- State laws that regulate health care durable powers of attorney are changing rapidly as legislatures strive to keep up with new medical technology and new court decisions; you may want to change your health care durable power of attorney when the laws change.
- Combined (medicial and financial) durable power of attorney forms do not let you be very specific about your wishes regarding medical treatment.
- Health care documents often have different validation requirements—for example, they may have to be signed in front of witnesses, while a financial durable power of attorney doesn't have to be in most states.
- Each durable power of attorney will be used for a very different purpose and presented to different people and organizations, often at different times.
- By using two documents, you don't have to show your medical wishes to people who are concerned only with your finances, and vice versa.

b. Living Wills

A living will, also called a Directive to Physicians, is a statement of your wishes about certain kinds of medical treatment and life-sustaining procedures.[4] It comes into play if you can't communicate decisions. A living will is directed to your doctors; if it is properly prepared, they are legally bound to respect your wishes or to transfer you to a doctor who will. Most states now provide fill-in-the-blanks living will forms; if your state does, use the official form.

Many states now allow you to name a "proxy" or "patient advocate" in a living will. You can give your proxy the same powers as the attorney-in-fact appointed in a durable power of attorney for health care would have. Unless your state allows you to appoint such a proxy, you'll get the best protection by writing both a living will and a durable power of

---

[4]Despite the similar name, a "living will" is not a conventional "will" used to designate how property should be distributed after a person's death. Nor is a "living will" the same as a "living trust," which is an estate planning device used to transfer your property outside of probate after your death.

attorney for health care, which does let you appoint someone to make sure your wishes are respected.

WHERE TO GET LIVING WILL AND HEALTH CARE DURABLE POWER OF ATTORNEY FORMS

 To get a copy of your state's health care durable power of attorney form and living will form, ask at a local hospital. Most large hospitals now stock such forms and give them out for free.

You can also get living will forms from Choice in Dying, a nonprofit organization, at 250 W. 57th St., New York, NY 10107. Send $3 and a self-addressed stamped envelope.

---

2.   Winding Up Your Affairs After Death

All durable powers of attorney end when the principal dies. That means that you can't give your attorney-in-fact authority to handle things after your death, such as paying your debts, making funeral or burial arrangements or transferring your property to the people who inherit it.

If you want your attorney-in-fact to have authority to wind up your affairs after your death, use a will to name that person as your executor. If you also want to avoid probate, you may want to prepare a living trust and name that person as your successor trustee.

3.   Arranging Care for Young Children

You cannot use a durable power of attorney to give anyone authority to care for your minor children. Your attorney-in-fact will have authority over your property, not your family. You can, however, authorize your attorney-in-fact to use your property to pay for your children's needs. (See Chapter 5, *Preparing a Durable Power of Attorney*, Section C.)

If you become incapacitated, the children's other parent will be responsible for caring for them. If he or she cannot care for them, a court will appoint someone—a close family member, if possible—to do it.

If you know who you want to be your minor children's personal guardian if the other parent is out of the picture or couldn't do the job, write down your choice in your will. If anyone is likely to come forward and contest your choice, include a statement of your reasons in your will or in a letter or videotape you leave with your will. This type of statement can be quite persuasive to a court.

4.   Leaving Property to Family, Friends or Charities

Your attorney-in-fact cannot make a will (a document that designates how property should be distributed after your death) for you, or change your existing will. You can, however, give the attorney-in-fact authority to make gifts of your property while you are still alive, including gifts designed to save on estate taxes.

5.   Protecting Assets

Within legal limits, the attorney-in-fact can take action to prevent all of your money from being used up for medical or housing costs, and try to preserve assets for your family. For example, Medicaid rules exempt some property when determining eligibility for benefits, but there are detailed rules about timing and the amount of income and assets. The attorney-in-fact should get advice from an expert before trying asset-saving strategies.

ESTATE PLANNING RESOURCES FROM NOLO PRESS

Plan Your Estate With a Living Trust, by Denis Clifford. A good guide to many aspects of estate planning, including living trusts, pay-on-death bank accounts and estate tax savings.

Nolo's Simple Will Book, by Denis Clifford. Step-by-step instructions on how to prepare a will.

WillMaker, software (Macintosh or DOS) that lets you make your own will.

Nolo's Law Form Kit: Wills. Forms and instructions for preparing a simple will.

Nolo's Living Trust, software (Macintosh) that lets you create a probate-avoidance revocable living trust.

Elder Care: A Consumer's Guide to Choosing and Financing Long-Term Care, by Joseph Matthews. Shows how to evaluate and pay for long-term care, including nursing homes.

E. Helping Someone Prepare a Power of Attorney

If someone close to you—perhaps a parent, relative or friend—appears likely to become incapacitated before too long, it is a kindness to recommend that he or she prepare and sign a durable power of attorney now. (This is true especially if you'll be the one left to deal with a legal tangle if no durable power of attorney is prepared.) You can explain how a durable power works and how it can give the person a say in his or her affairs—now, before it's too late. You can also offer reassurance that the document does not need to take effect until a doctor or someone else the person absolutely trusts decides it's needed.

But if a loved one resists your honest attempts to help, there is nothing you can do. You should never coerce a person into giving up the right to handle his or her own affairs. Problems are especially likely to develop if you both urge an ill person to sign a durable power of attorney and will serve as attorney-in-fact. An angry relative or close friend could file a lawsuit claiming you exerted "undue influence" over the person who signed the durable power of attorney, and a legal battle could ensue.

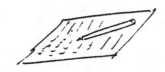

2

HOW FINANCIAL DURABLE POWERS OF ATTORNEY WORK

This chapter explains in more detail how durable powers of attorney for finances work in the real world.

A. Who Can Prepare a Durable Power of Attorney

You can create a valid power of attorney if you are an adult (at least 18 years old in most states) and mentally competent.

No one makes a determination, when you sign the document, about your mental state. The issue will come up later only if someone goes to court and challenges the durable power of attorney, claiming that you weren't mentally competent when you signed it. That kind of lawsuit is very rare.

Even in the highly unlikely event of a court hearing, the competency requirement is not difficult to satisfy. If you understood, when you signed the durable power of attorney, the consequences of your act, then you were legally competent, and the power of attorney is valid. To make this determination, the judge would probably question the witnesses (if any) who watched you sign the document and others who knew you well at the time. There would be no general inquiry into your life. It wouldn't matter, for example, that you might have been forgetful or absent-minded around the time you signed the durable power of attorney.

 Heading off problems. If you think someone is likely to go to court and challenge the legitimacy of your durable power of attorney or claim that you were coerced into signing it, it's wise to see a lawyer. You may be able to minimize the chances of a successful challenge by having witnesses watch you sign the document or videotaping a statement of your intent.

B. The Expense of a Durable Power of Attorney

In most instances, the only expense of creating a durable power of attorney is the price of this book and a few dollars for a notary to verify your signature on the document. In some situations, however, there may be other costs.

1. Up-Front Costs

If you file (record) the power of attorney in the local public land records office, you'll have to pay a small fee. You'll need to record your durable power of attorney if your state requires it (most don't) or if you have given your attorney-in-fact authority to buy, sell or mortgage real estate on your behalf.

Although it's not usually necessary, you may decide that you want a lawyer to review or modify your durable power of attorney. The fee for this service shouldn't be large, at least by lawyers' standards. (Chapter 9, *Lawyers and Legal Research*, discusses how to hire and pay a lawyer.)

2. Ongoing Costs

If you make a springing durable power of attorney, it may never take effect, because you may never become incapacitated. But if it does, there may be additional costs. Remember, though, that the alternative to having your attorney-in-fact take over is to request a court-appointed conservator, which is invariably more costly.

Attorney-in-Fact's Payment. If you decide your attorney-in-fact is to be paid for his or her services, those fees will be paid from your assets. (Chapter 4, *The Attorney-in-Fact's Responsibilities*, discusses payment.)

Fees for Accountants and Experts. If the attorney-in-fact must hire professionals, such as accountants or financial advisers, to help with managing your property and finances, their fees will be paid from your assets.

C. When the Attorney-in-Fact Takes Over

Unlike most legal documents, a durable power of attorney doesn't have to take effect as soon as you sign it. You can sign it but have it take effect only if and when you become incapacitated.

1. Springing Powers of Attorney

A "springing" durable power of attorney takes effect only if you become incapacitated and are unable to handle your financial affairs. When you sign a springing financial durable power of attorney, you do not relinquish any authority over your property. The document has absolutely no effect unless and until you become incapacitated (or "disabled," as some state laws refer to the condition).

Most people prefer this kind of durable power of attorney, because they're not in immediate danger of incapacity. If that's your situation, signing a springing durable power of attorney is simply a sensible precaution—a kind of risk-free legal insurance, which will protect you if you ever need it.

a. Who Decides That You're Incapacitated

Obviously, someone must decide when a springing durable power of attorney should take effect. If you use the Nolo Press durable power of attorney form in this book, one or two doctors (you decide) must determine that you are incapacitated before your attorney-in-fact can take over. This removes the danger that family members or friends will make their own judgment that you are incapacitated—even if you disagree.

HAVING SOMEONE WHO'S NOT A PHYSICIAN MAKE THE DECISION

Because incapacity isn't really a medical condition, logically there's no compelling reason to have a physician make the determination that you are incapacitated. But it's almost always done that way, even though only Alaska and New Mexico require, by law, statements from health care professionals.

We recommend, however, that you do choose a doctor for this task. A doctor's statement is the most familiar and reassuring to the people your attorney-in-fact will have to deal with. Banks and other institutions might be unwilling to rely on a statement by a family member or close friend that you are unable to handle your affairs.

There is a simple way, however, to let your attorney-in-fact to make the decision when to start using the authority granted by the durable power of attorney. See section b, "Letting the Attorney-in-Fact Decide," below.

If you do want someone who is neither a doctor nor the attorney-in-fact to be involved, we recommend that you require statements from that person and a physician. You'll have to change Part 5 (see Chapter 5) of the Nolo form to substitute "persons" for "licensed physicians."

You can name the doctor you want to make the determination, or just say you want your "personal physician" to do it. If the need ever arises, the doctor must certify, in writing, that you are unable to manage your financial affairs. (A form for your physician to sign is included in the Appendix.) Before you sign a springing durable power of attorney, ask the doctor if he or she would be willing to make this determination if it became necessary. Be sure you and the doctor are in basic agreement about what "incapacitated" means in your situation.

If you're comfortable with the idea of a certain doctor, whom you name in the document, making this determination, there's no need to require another physician's statement. If you are concerned about leaving this determination in the hands of just one person, name a second doctor.

Special state requirements. In a state that has its own official durable power of attorney form, you may be required to follow a certain procedure. For example, in Alaska, two doctors must sign affidavits (sworn, notarized statements) that you are incapacitated before your springing durable power of attorney takes effect. Special state requirements are covered in Chapters 5 and 6.

b.   Letting the Attorney-in-Fact Decide

Requiring a physician to rule on your ability to manage your affairs is intended to be a safeguard, to protect you from anyone who might want to take control of your finances when you don't want them to. If you're not at all concerned about that possibility, or you don't know a doctor you feel comfortable asking to make this decision, you can bypass the physician's involvement. Do this by making your durable power of attorney effective as soon as you sign it, but instructing your trusted attorney-in-fact not to exercise his or her authority until it becomes necessary.

Essentially, this means that you leave the decision about your incapacity in the hands of the person you name as attorney-in-fact. If you do that, you must absolutely trust the attorney-in-fact not to abuse his or her authority.

The advantage is that the attorney-in-fact doesn't have to involve a physician to make the power of attorney effective. These days, when many people don't have a close relationship with a personal physician, you may prefer to let the attorney-in-fact, who is someone you trust completely, make the decision.

c.   Defining Incapacity

Incapacity is not a recognized medical condition, and there is no precise legal definition. The general understanding is summed up by the New Mexico durable power of attorney form, which defines incapacity to mean that someone is no longer able "to effectively manage personal care, property or financial affairs." The Missouri law attempts a more in-depth definition of a disabled person: someone who is "unable by reason of any physical or mental condition to receive and evaluate information or to communicate decisions to such an extent that the person lacks ability to manage his financial resources."[1]

Incapacity may mean that you have lost some physical or mental abilities. For example, you may still be in command of your mental faculties, but unable, because of injury, illness, old age or blindness, to care for your property. You might be unable to handle financial matters, but still be able to make personal medical decisions. Or you might be able to handle personal day-to-day finances, but not manage investments.

Common physical causes of incapacity are problems associated with advancing age, such as heart attacks, strokes and Alzheimer's disease. Incapacity can also be caused by serious accidents, drug or alcohol addiction, degenerative diseases such as AIDS or mental illness. People sometimes move in and out of periods of incapacity caused by physical or mental illness.

Once the doctor has signed a statement documenting your incapacity, the attorney-in-fact can attach it to the original power of attorney. Then, if anyone questions the attorney-in-fact's authority to act for you, the attorney-in-fact can produce the statement and confirm his or her authority.

---

[1]Ann. Mo. Stat. § 475.010(4)(a).

2.   Immediately Effective Powers of Attorney

If you know, or reasonably believe, that you are likely to become incapacitated soon, it probably makes the most sense to make your durable power of attorney take effect when you sign it, or on some specified date not far in the future.

For example, if you or someone you love has a serious degenerative disease and is rapidly losing the ability to manage business affairs, a durable power of attorney that is effective immediately would be appropriate. If you are facing major surgery, you could sign a durable power of attorney that will become effective the day of the surgery.

D.   Making Sure Your Power of Attorney Is Accepted

A durable power of attorney won't do you any good if no one will accept your attorney-in-fact's authority to act on your behalf. You want to be sure that your bank will allow the attorney-in-fact to deposit and withdraw money from your account, insurance companies will let your attorney-in-fact collect your benefits, and so on.

Fortunately, durable powers of attorney are in common usage, and financial institutions and government agencies are used to them. Your attorney-in-fact, armed with a signed and notarized power of attorney document (and, if the durable power of attorney is "springing," a signed statement from your physician that you are incapacitated), should have no problem getting people to accept his or her authority.

But certain questions come up regularly when an attorney-in-fact tries to exercise his or her authority. Here's how to deal with a few of the more common ones.

1.   Has the Durable Power of Attorney Been Amended or Revoked?

It's reasonable for someone to want to make sure that the document your attorney-in-fact produces, as evidence of authority, is still valid.

To reassure a third party, your attorney-in-fact can show that person the power of attorney document, which contains language specifically designed to provide this reassurance. The paragraph from the Nolo power of attorney form is shown below; state-specific forms have comparable language.

---

15.   Reliance on this Power of Attorney

I agree that any third party who receives a copy of this document may act under it. Revocation of the power of attorney is not effective as to a third party until the third party has actual knowledge of the revocation. I agree to indemnify the third party for any claims that arise against the third party because of reliance on this power of attorney.

Laws in many states also protect third parties who rely on apparently valid powers of attorney. For example, an Indiana statute states that a written, signed power of attorney is presumed valid, and a third party may rely on it.[2] And in New York, it's unlawful for a bank, trust company, savings and loan, pension fund or retirement system in the state to refuse to honor a statutory power of attorney form that has been properly signed and notarized.[3]

As a last resort, the attorney-in-fact can sign a sworn statement, in front of a notary public, stating

---

[2]Ann. Ind. Code § 30-5-8-2.

[3]N.Y. Gen. Obligations Law § 5-1504.

that as to his or her knowledge, the durable power of attorney has not been revoked and that you are still alive. Most states have laws that make such a statement conclusive proof that the durable power of attorney is in fact still valid.

2.   Does the Attorney-in-Fact Have the Authority He or She Claims?

Any third party who relies on a durable power of attorney must be sure that the attorney-in-fact has the power he or she claims to have. That means the third party must examine the document, to see if it grants the authority in question.

There are two ways to plan for and avoid any problems in this area. First, the durable power of attorney forms in this book are very specific about the attorney-in-fact's powers. For example, if you give your attorney-in-fact authority over your banking transactions, the document expressly states that the attorney-in-fact is empowered to write checks on your behalf. Your attorney-in-fact can point to the paragraph that grants that authority, so a doubting bank official can read it in black and white. And if you use a state-specific form, the forms should be familiar to people in banks and government agencies.

Second, many banks and brokerage houses have their own durable power of attorney forms. If yours does, we recommend that you use it, as well as the broader power of attorney form in this book. You'll head off any problems for your attorney-in-fact, because the bank will have no need to examine and quibble with the power of attorney; it will know exactly what powers its own form grants.

If your attorney-in-fact does run into resistance, the best advice is for him or her to seek, politely but insistently, someone higher up in the bureaucracy.

3.   Was the Principal Mentally Competent When He or She Signed the Durable Power of Attorney?

You must be mentally competent to make a valid durable power of attorney (see Section A, above). If you weren't competent when you signed your durable power, the document has no legal effect.

If you think that someone might raise this issue later, and demand proof that you were competent when you signed your durable power, you may want to get a doctor's statement now. The doctor should state that he or she has seen you recently and believes you to be mentally competent. Later, if necessary, the attorney-in-fact could produce the signed, dated statement.

E.   If You Move to Another State

Although there are broad similarities, state laws on durable powers of attorney for finances differ considerably. If you move to another state after having signed a durable power of attorney in your old state, the old power of attorney should be accepted. Missouri law, for example, states that a durable power of attorney signed in another state, valid under that state's laws, is valid in Missouri.[4] Some other states have similar laws.

Your attorney-in-fact may, however, run into problems that are more practical than legal:

- If the document looks unfamiliar to the forms the people at the bank or other institution are used to seeing, they may be reluctant to accept its authority. This is especially likely if your new state has its own form.
- The document may need to be recorded (put on file) with the local land records office or filed with the local court in the new state. If the

---

[4]Ann. Mo. Stat. § 404.730.

document does not meet certain requirements, the records office in the new state may not accept it.

Because of these potential pitfalls, if you move to another state, it's best to revoke your old durable power of attorney and create a new one, complying with all regulations of your new state. (The process is explained in Chapter 8, *Revoking a Power of Attorney*.)

F.   When the Power of Attorney Ends

A durable power of attorney for finances never expires. It's valid until you revoke it, you die or there is no one to serve as your attorney-in-fact.

1.   You Revoke the Power of Attorney

As long as you are mentally competent, you can revoke a power of attorney for finances at any time, whether or not it has taken effect. All you need to do is fill out a simple form, sign it in front of a notary public, and give copies to the attorney-in-fact and to people or institutions the attorney-in-fact has been dealing with. (Instructions are in Chapter 8, *Revoking a Durable Power of Attorney*.)

> **Example:** Susan prepares a springing durable power of attorney naming her closest friend, Tina, as her attorney-in-fact. Three years later, they have a bitter fight. Susan prepares a one-page document that revokes the durable power of attorney, and gives Tina a copy. She then prepares a new power of attorney, naming her sister Joan as her (new) attorney-in-fact.

2.   A Court Invalidates Your Power of Attorney

Even if you sign a durable power of attorney for finances, if you become incapacitated there is a

remote possibility that a disgruntled relative could ask a court to appoint a conservator to manage your financial affairs. (See Chapter 1, *Using a Durable Power of Attorney*, Section B)

It's rare, but a power of attorney could be ruled invalid if a judge concluded that you were mentally incompetent when you signed the durable power of attorney, or that you were the victim of fraud or undue influence. The power of attorney could also be invalidated for a technical error. If that happens, the judge could appoint a conservator to take over management of your property.

In a few states, if a court appoints a conservator, your durable power of attorney is automatically revoked, and the conservator takes over responsibility for your finances and property. In most states, the attorney-in-fact becomes accountable to the conservator, not just to you, and the conservator has the power to revoke your durable power of attorney. In a few states, the conservator has the power to revoke your durable power of attorney only if the court specifically grants it. (For a list of the rules in each state, see Chapter 8, *Revoking a Durable Power of Attorney*.)

To guard against the possibility that your plans for financial management might be thwarted if a court appoints a conservator, you can provide, in your durable power of attorney, that you want the person you chose to be attorney-in-fact to be named as the conservator. Even if it's not required by law, most courts will honor your request absent a powerful reason not to. (See Chapter 5, *Preparing a Durable Power of Attorney*, Section C.)

3.   After a Divorce

In California, Illinois, Indiana and Missouri, if your spouse is your attorney-in-fact and you divorce, your ex-spouse's authority is immediately terminated. If you named an alternate (successor) attorney-in-fact in your power of attorney, that person takes over as attorney-in-fact.

Regardless of state law, if you get divorced you should revoke your durable power of attorney and make a new one.

4.   No Attorney-in-Fact Is Available

A durable power of attorney must end if there's no one to serve as the attorney-in-fact. To avoid this, you can name a back-up (alternate) attorney-in-fact, who will serve if your first choice can't. (See Chapter 3, *Choosing Your Attorney-in-Fact.*)

For a bit of extra insurance, you can also allow the alternate attorney-in-fact to delegate his or her duties to someone else. (See Chapter 5, *Preparing a Durable Power of Attorney.*)

5.   After Your Death

A durable power of attorney ends when the principal dies. In most states, however, if the attorney-in-fact doesn't know of your death and continues to act on your behalf, his or her actions are still valid.

If you want your attorney-in-fact to have any authority over winding up your affairs after your death, you must grant that authority in your will or living trust. (See Chapter 1, *Using a Durable Power of Attorney*, Section D.)

G.   Re-Doing Your Power of Attorney Periodically

If you make a springing durable power of attorney, it's a good idea to revoke it and create a new one every five to seven years, especially if your circumstances have changed significantly. A durable power of attorney never expires, but if the document was signed many years before it goes into effect, the attorney-in-fact may have more difficulty getting banks, insurance companies or people in government agencies to accept its authority. (See Chapter 8, *Revoking a Durable Power of Attorney.*)

CHOOSING YOUR ATTORNEY-IN-FACT

The most important decision you must make when you create a durable power of attorney is who you want to serve as your attorney-in-fact.

The attorney-in-fact will have tremendous power over your property. You need to choose someone you trust completely. Fortunately, most of us know at least one such person—usually a spouse, relative or close friend. If there's no one you trust completely with this great authority, a durable power of attorney isn't for you. It's foolish to think you can make up for a lack of trust by putting restrictive provisions or controls over the attorney-in-fact in the document itself. Such restrictions can serve as a supplemental check to try to ensure your wishes are carried out, but they're never an adequate substitute for trust.

Nor can you count on anyone to keep an eye on the attorney-in-fact once he or she takes over your finances. If your attorney-in-fact handles your affairs carelessly or dishonestly, the only recourse of your family or friends would be a lawsuit—obviously, not a satisfactory approach. Lawsuits are burdensome and expensive, and would entangle your loved ones in the legal red tape a power of attorney was designed to avoid. And there's no guarantee that money lost by an incompetent attorney-in-fact would ever be recovered.

A.   General Considerations

Any competent adult can serve as your attorney-in-fact; the person most definitely doesn't have to be a lawyer. You may choose whomever you want.

Of course, you shouldn't name someone to serve as your attorney-in-fact without first discussing it with the person and making sure he or she accepts this serious responsibility. If you don't, you may well create grave problems down the line. The person you've chosen may not want to serve, for a variety of reasons. And even if the person would be willing, if he or she doesn't know of his or her responsibilities, confusion and delay are inevitable if you become incapacitated.

For many people, it's obvious who the attorney-in-fact should be. Often a spouse or loved one is the person you most trust to manage your finances. Or perhaps one member of your family is particularly good at managing business affairs and routinely helps you and other family members with them.

In most situations, the attorney-in-fact does not need extensive experience in financial management; common sense, dependability and complete honesty are enough. And your attorney-in-fact can get any reasonably necessary professional help—from an accountant, lawyer or tax preparer, perhaps—and pay for it out of your assets. If, however, you want the attorney-in-fact to help run your small business or manage extensive investments, be sure you choose someone with enough experience to handle the job.

For some people, the choice of who you want to be your attorney-in-fact may not be so clear. Perhaps your mate is old or ill, and wouldn't be a good choice for attorney-in-fact. Or you may have no mate, and no one you feel entirely comfortable asking to take over your financial affairs. Or if you have an active, complex investment portfolio or own a business, you might decide that your attorney-in-fact needs business skills, knowledge or management abilities beyond those of the people closest to you.

If you're not sure who to choose, read the rest of this chapter and discuss the issue with those close to you. Keep in mind that it's better not to establish a durable power of attorney than to entrust your affairs to someone in whom you don't have complete confidence.

⚠ Avoidiing Family Conflict. If there are long-standing feuds among family members, they may object to your choice of attorney-in-fact or the extent of the authority delegated. If you foresee any such personal conflicts, it's wise to try to defuse them in advance. A discussion with the people who are leery of the power of attorney might help.

B.   If You're Married

If you're married, you'll probably want to make your spouse your attorney-in-fact unless there is a compelling reason not to. There are powerful legal and practical reasons, in addition to the emotional ones, for appointing your spouse. The main one is that naming anyone else creates the risk of conflicts between the attorney-in-fact and your spouse over how to manage property that belongs to both spouses. It's the last thing that your spouse needs at such a time. (A spouse's authority over an incapacitated spouse's property is discussed in Chapter 1, *Using a Durable Power of Attorney*, Section B.)

> **Example:** Henry and Amelia, a married couple, each create a durable power of attorney for finances. Henry names Amelia as his attorney-in-fact, but Amelia names her sister Anna. Later, Amelia becomes unable to manage her affairs, and Anna takes over as her attorney-in-fact. Soon Anna and Henry are arguing bitterly over what should be done with the house and investments that Henry and Amelia own together. If they can't resolve their differences, Henry or Anna may have to go to court and ask a judge to determine what is in Amelia's best interests.

If your spouse is ill, quite elderly or simply not equipped to manage your financial affairs, you may have to name someone else as attorney-in-fact. The wisest course is for you and your spouse to agree on who the attorney-in-fact should be, perhaps one of your grown children.

NOTE FOR MINNESOTA READERS

In Minnesota, if your attorney-in-fact is your spouse, he or she cannot transfer (give away or sell) real estate that belongs to you. (Minn. Stat. § 519.06.)

 Divorce does not end your spouse's authority in most states. If your spouse is your attorney-in-fact, that designation does not automatically end if you get divorced, except in California, Illinois, Indiana and Missouri.[1] In any state, after a divorce you should revoke the power of attorney and create a new one, naming someone else as your new attorney-in-fact. (See Chapter 8, *Revoking a Durable Power of Attorney*.)

C.   If You Have a Living Trust

If you have created a revocable living trust to avoid probate or minimize estate taxes, you have already arranged for someone to have power over the property you have transferred to the trust if you become incapacitated. (Living trusts are discussed in Chapter 1, *Using a Durable Power of Attorney*, Section D.) If you and your spouse made a living trust together, the trust document almost certainly gives your spouse authority over trust property if you become incapacitated. If you made an individual trust, the person you named to be successor trustee probably has that power.

The fact that you create a durable power of attorney doesn't change any of this. Your attorney-in-fact will not have authority over property in your living trust. To avoid conflicts, it's advisable to have the same person managing both trust property and non-trust property if you become incapacitated. So

---

[1]Cal. Civ. Code § 2355(f); Ill. Rev. Stat. § Ch. 110 1/2, § 802-6; Ann. Ind. Code § 30-5-4-4; Mo. Rev. Stat. § 404.717.

normally, you'll name the same person as successor trustee and as your attorney-in-fact.

Example: Carlos, a widower, prepares a revocable living trust to avoid probate and a durable power of attorney for finances in case he becomes incapacitated. He names his son, Jeffrey, as successor trustee of the living trust and attorney-in-fact under the durable power of attorney.

Several years later Carlos has a stroke and is temporarily unable to handle his everyday finances. Jeffrey steps in to deposit his father's pension checks and pay his monthly bills, using his authority as attorney-in-fact. As successor trustee, he also has legal authority over the property Carlos transferred to his living trust, including Carlos's house.

D. Appointing More Than One Person

In general, it's better to have just one attorney-in-fact. If more than one person has to share the responsibility, conflicts between them could disrupt the handling of your finances. Also, some banks and other financial institutions prefer to deal with a single attorney-in-fact rather than joint ones.

But it's legal (in almost all states) and may be desirable to name more than one person. (If you use the Illinois durable power of attorney form, however, you can name only one attorney-in-fact.) For example, you might name two or more of your children, if you don't expect any disagreements between them and you think one of them might feel hurt and left out if passed over.

But carefully consider the possibility of conflicts. It's usually a bad idea to name more than one child, for example, if they don't get along and you're just trying to avoid hurt feelings. In extreme situations, the attorneys-in-fact might even have to go to court to resolve disputes. The result might be more bad feeling than if you had just picked one person to be attorney-in-fact (and explained your reasoning to your offspring) in the first place.

If you name more than one attorney-in-fact, you can give each of them authority to act independently on your behalf or require all of them to agree before they can act. There's no hard and fast rule on which strategy is better. Allowing each to act separately makes it more convenient for them to get things done. But recordkeeping will be messier if you have two (or more) people managing your property—independently taking money out of your bank account or selling stock, for example.

If you name more than one attorney-in-fact, and one of them can't serve, the others will serve. If none of them can serve, the alternate you named will take over. (See Section G, below.)

E. Poor Choices for Attorney-in-Fact

Here are some suggestions on who to avoid when you're choosing an attorney-in-fact.

1. Someone Who Lives Far Away

To carry out duties and responsibilities properly and promptly, it's best that the attorney-in-fact live nearby. Although overnight mail, faxes and other technological wonders have made it easier to conduct business long-distance, it's still best to be close at hand. After all, this is the person who will be responsible for day-to-day details of your finances: opening your mail, paying bills, looking after property and so on.

But many families, of course, are spread across the country these days. If there's only one person you trust enough to name as attorney-in-fact, and he or she lives far away, you may have to settle for the less than ideal situation.

2.   An Institution

Don't name an institution, such as a bank, as attorney-in-fact. It isn't legal in some states, and is definitely not desirable. Serving as attorney-in-fact is a personal responsibility, and there should be personal connection and trust between you and your attorney-in-fact. If the person you trust most happens to be your banker, appoint that person, not the bank.

F.   If You Can't Think of Anyone To Name

If you can't come up with a family member or close friend to name, you may want to consider asking your lawyer, business partner or banker to serve as attorney-in-fact. If you really know and trust the person, it may be a good option for you.

G.   Naming an Alternate Attorney-in-Fact

You should name at least one alternate (successor) attorney-in-fact in case your first choice can't serve or needs to resign after serving for a period of time. You may want to name your spouse as attorney-in-fact and your adult daughter as alternate, for example.

As a further precaution, you can authorize an attorney-in-fact to name additional successors to serve if all those you named cannot. That eliminates the minimal risk that the position might become vacant because of the original attorney-in-fact's death, disability or resignation. If this occurs, and you haven't named a successor, your durable power of attorney would be useless. There would have to be a court action, such as a full-scale conservatorship proceeding, to find someone to manage your affairs.

4

THE ATTORNEY-IN-FACT'S RESPONSIBILITIES

How much authority you want to give your attorney-in-fact is up to you. But whatever the attorney-in-fact's duties, he or she must always act in your best interests.

This chapter discusses the specific responsibilities you can give your attorney-in-fact and the attorney-in-fact's obligation to act honestly and prudently on your behalf.

A.   Basic Responsibilities: Honesty and Prudence

The attorney-in-fact you appoint in your durable power of attorney is a "fiduciary"—someone who holds a position of trust and must act in your best interests. What the law requires of your attorney-in-fact can be summed up as follows:

- Manage your property honestly and prudently.
- Avoid conflicts of interest.
- Keep your property completely separate from his or her own.
- Keep adequate records.

These standards do not present problems in most simple situations. For example, if you just want your attorney-in-fact to sign for your retirement check, deposit it in your bank account and pay for your basic needs, there is slight possibility of uncertainty or dispute.

If any of these rules would impose unnecessary hardships on your attorney-in-fact, you can insert clauses in your durable power of attorney letting the attorney-in-fact deviate from them, so that the attorney-in-fact's freedom isn't unnecessarily fettered.

Each of these rules is discussed below.

1.   Managing Your Property Prudently

The attorney-in-fact must be careful with your money and other property. State laws require an attorney-in-fact to act as a "prudent person" would under the circumstances. That means the attorney-in-fact has no obligation to make canny investment moves with your cash. The primary goal is not to lose your money.

The attorney-in-fact may, however, take cautious actions on your behalf. For example, if your money is in a low-interest bank account, the attorney-in-fact might invest the money in government bonds, which pay higher interest but are still very safe.

2.   Avoiding Conflicts of Interest

Normally, an attorney-in-fact has no right to engage in activities where he or she personally stands to benefit. Such activities, which create conflicts of interest between the principal and attorney-in-fact, are called "self-dealing." The attorney-in-fact's motive is irrelevant. If the transaction is challenged in court, it is presumed fraudulent until the attorney-in-fact proves otherwise.

> **Example:** David is the attorney-in-fact for his elderly mother, Irene. After Irene's failing eyesight makes it impossible for her to drive, David decides to buy her car from her. He looks up the car's fair market value to make sure he is paying a fair amount, writes a check and deposits it in her bank account.
>
> This transaction is forbidden, even though David isn't cheating Irene, unless Irene's power of attorney specifically allows David to benefit from his management of her property and finances.

The ban on self-dealing is intended to protect you—after all, the attorney-in-fact is supposed to be acting on your behalf. It's quite sensible, however, to give the attorney-in-fact permission for self-dealing if your attorney-in-fact is your spouse, a close family member, a business partner or other person whose affairs are already intertwined with yours. You can grant permission in the power of attorney document. (See Chapter 5, *Preparing a Power of Attorney*, Section C, Part 10.)

Example 1: Maurice wants Alice, his best friend, to serve as his attorney-in-fact. They have been involved in many real estate transactions together: shared ownerships and sales to each other. Currently they are involved in several projects together. Maurice doesn't want to risk disrupting these projects or curtailing Alice's ability to do business, so he specifically states in his durable power of attorney that Alice may benefit from transactions she undertakes on Maurice's behalf as his attorney-in-fact.

Example 2: Art appoints his son, Michael, as his attorney-in-fact for finances. Art knows his summer home may have to be sold to raise cash, and he wants Michael to have the first chance to buy it. He specifically provides in his durable power of attorney that Michael has first choice to buy Art's summer home at the fair market price if Michael, as attorney-in-fact, determines it should be sold.

3.   Keeping Funds Separate

An attorney-in-fact is never allowed to mix (commingle) your funds with his or her own unless the power of attorney specifically authorizes it. You will probably want to grant that authority if you appoint your spouse, mate or immediate family member as attorney-in-fact, and your finances are already thoroughly mixed together in joint bank or security accounts.

Example: Jim and Eduardo have been living together for 25 years. They have a joint checking account and share all basic living expenses. Each names the other as his attorney-in-fact in springing durable power of attorney documents. If one actually serves as the other's attorney-in-fact, technically, he wouldn't be allowed to mix the principal's funds with his own. But this is exactly what they have been doing all along.

To avoid any possible problems, Jim and Eduardo both include, in their powers of attorney, specific provisions that allow commingling of funds.

(Chapter 5, *Preparing a Durable Power of Attorney*, Section C, Part 11 explains how to include this provision.)

4.   Keeping Separate Records

Your attorney-in-fact is legally required to keep accurate and separate records for all transactions made on your behalf. This is true whether or not the attorney-in-fact is paid to serve as attorney-in-fact. Good records are particularly important if the attorney-in-fact ever wants to resign and turn the responsibility over to a successor.

This isn't an onerous requirement. All the attorney-in-fact must be able to do is show where and how your money has been spent. In most instances, it's enough to have a balanced checkbook and receipts for bills paid and claims made. And because the attorney-in-fact will probably file tax returns on your behalf, income and expense records may be necessary.

Example: Keiji appoints Kathryn, his niece, to serve as his uncompensated attorney-in-fact. Keiji receives income from his savings, two IRAs, Social Security and stock dividends. Kathryn will have to keep records of the income for bank and tax purposes.

You and your prospective attorney-in-fact should discuss and agree on what recordkeeping is appropriate. The attorney-in-fact may also want to review your current records now to make sure they're in order.[1] If you don't have clear records, the attor-

---

[1]If, like most people, your records are in haphazardly-labeled shoe boxes and file folders, this may be a good time to get organized. One way to start is with a computer program called *Nolo's Personal RecordKeeper*. It helps you organize family, medical, financial and insurance records and inventory your property.

ney-in-fact may have to sort out needless complications later.

As part of managing your finances, the attorney-in-fact may hire a bookkeeper, accountant or other financial advisor and pay for the services from your property.

B.   Powers Granted to the Attorney-in-Fact

The power of attorney forms in this book contain a list of powers, and you can give your attorney-in-fact some or all of them. (Either way, you can put very specific limitations on powers that you grant. See Section C, below.)

Many people choose to give all the powers, so their attorney-in-fact will have authority to handle whatever might come up concerning their property or finances.

If you do grant all the powers, your attorney-in-fact should have the legal authority to take care of whatever financial matters come up if you became incapacitated. He or she will be able to handle your investments, real estate, banking and so on. The attorney-in-fact can use your assets to pay for any of your debts and expenses, including home maintenance, taxes, insurance premiums, wage claims, medical care, child support, alimony and your personal allowance. The attorney-in-fact can sign deeds, make gifts, pay school expenses, and endorse and deposit checks.

On the power of attorney forms, the powers are listed in a kind of shorthand way—for example, "real estate transactions" or "taxes." (The first page of the North Carolina form is shown below.) Each of the powers is explained in the document or, if you use a state-specific form, in your state's statutes. Here is a general explanation of each of the powers, as they're listed on the Nolo power of attorney form.

NORTH CAROLINA STATUTORY SHORT FORM OF GENERAL POWER OF ATTORNEY

NOTICE: THE POWERS GRANTED BY THIS DOCUMENT ARE BROAD AND SWEEP-ING. THEY ARE DEFINED IN CHAPTER 32A OF THE NORTH CAROLINA GENERAL STATUTES WHICH EXPRESSLY PERMITS THE USE OF ANY OTHER OR DIFFERENT FORM OF POWER OF ATTORNEY DESIRED BY THE PARTIES CONCERNED.

State of _____

County of _____

I _____, the undersigned, hereby appoint _____ my attorney-in-fact for me and give such person full power to act in my name, place and stead in any way which I myself could do if I were personally present with respect to the following matters as each of them is defined in Chapter 32A of the North Carolina General Statutes to the event that I am permitted by law to act through an agent. (DIRECTIONS: Initial the line opposite any one or more of the subdivisions as to which the principal desires to give the attorney-in-fact authority.)

(1) Real property transactions; .... _____

(2) Personal property transactions; .... _____

(3) Bond, share and commodity transactions; .... _____

(4) Banking transactions; .... _____

(5) Safe deposits; .... _____

(6) Business operating transactions; .... _____

(7) Insurance transactions; .... _____

(8) Estate transactions; .... _____

(9) Personal relationships and affairs; .... _____

(10) Social security and unemployment; .... _____

(11) Benefits from military service; .... _____

(12) Tax; .... _____

(13) Employment of agents; .... _____

(If power of substitution and revocation is to be given, add: 'I also give to such person full power to appoint another to act as my attorney-in-fact and full power to revoke such appointment.')

_____

_____

(If period of power of attorney is to be limited, add: 'This power terminates _____, 19 ___.')

_____

(If power of attorney is to be a durable power of attorney under the provision of Article 2 of Chapter 32A and is to continue in effect after the incapacity or mental incompetence of the principal, add: 'This power of attorney shall not be affected by my subsequent incapacity or mental incompetence.')

Page 1

! Read the statute if you have questions. This section should give you a good idea of what your attorney-in-fact is allowed to do on your behalf when you grant certain powers. But it doesn't cover every detail of the attorney-in-fact's authority, and state laws vary. If you need to know whether or not your attorney-in-fact can take a specific action on your behalf, read your state's statutes (if you use a state-specific form) or the detailed description of the powers in Part 17 of the Nolo power of attorney form.

1. Real Estate Transactions

This gives your attorney-in-fact broad power to buy, sell, mortgage or lease real estate on your behalf. It makes the attorney-in-fact in charge of managing any real estate you own—responsible for paying any mortgage and taxes (with your assets) and making necessary repairs and maintenance. Most important, the attorney-in-fact may sell, mortgage, partition or lease your real property. The attorney-in-fact may also take any other action connected to real estate. For example, the attorney-in-fact may:

- buy or lease real estate for you
- refinance your mortgage to get a better interest rate
- pay off liens (legal claims) on your property
- buy insurance for your property
- build, remodel or remove structures on your property
- grant easements over your property
- bring or defend lawsuits over real estate.

The attorney-in-fact has a legal obligation, remember, to take only those actions that are in your best interests.

NOTE FOR DISTRICT OF COLUMBIA AND MINNESOTA READERS

These states limit an attorney-in-fact's authority when it comes to selling your property:

District of Columbia law does not allow an attorney-in-fact to sell the principal's real estate. (D.C. Code § 45-601.)

In Minnesota, if your attorney-in-fact is your spouse, he or she cannot transfer (give away or sell) real estate that belongs to you. (Minn. Stat. § 519.06.)

---

2. Personal Property Transactions

This allows your attorney-in-fact to buy, sell, rent or exchange personal property—that is, anything but real estate—on your behalf. The attorney-in-fact can also insure, use, move, store, repair or pawn your items of personal property.

Example: Paul names his wife, Gloria, as his attorney-in-fact for financial matters. When he later goes into a nursing home, his old car, which he can no longer use, becomes an expense Gloria cannot afford. As Paul's attorney-in-fact, she has legal authority to sell the car.

Most power of attorney forms restrict this power to "tangible" personal property—that is, physical items of property. Intangible property includes stock certificates, bonds, promissory notes and other items that have no value in themselves but represent items of value. (Authority over such property is covered in other categories on the form, such as "bond, shares, and commodity transactions.")

NOTE FOR DISTRICT OF COLUMBIA READERS

District of Columbia law does not allow an attorney-in-fact to sell personal property of the principal. (D.C. Code § 45-601.)

---

3. Stock, Bond, Commodity and Option Transactions

This lets your attorney-in-fact manage all your securities, including stocks, bonds, mutual funds, commodities and call and put options. The attorney-in-fact can buy or sell securities, accept or transfer certificates or other evidence of ownership and exercise voting rights.

4. Banking and Other Financial Institution Transactions

A main reason many people create durable powers of attorney is so they can arrange for someone to handle their banking transactions. If you give your attorney-in-fact authority to handle your bank accounts, your bills can be paid, and pension or other checks can be deposited in your accounts even if you can no longer take care of these matters yourself.

> **Example:** Virginia, who is in her 70s, is admitted to the hospital for emergency surgery. She's too weak to even think about paying her bills or depositing her social security check—and anyway, she can't get to the bank. Fortunately, she earlier created a durable power of attorney for finances, naming her niece Marianne as her attorney-in-fact. Marianne can deposit Virginia's check and sign checks to pay the bills that come while Virginia is in the hospital.

Your attorney-in-fact may open and close accounts with banks, savings and loans, credit unions or other financial institutions on your behalf. The attorney-in-fact may write checks on these accounts, endorse checks you receive, and receive account statements. The attorney-in-fact also has access to

your safe deposit box, to withdraw or add to its contents.

In most states, the attorney-in-fact may also borrow money on your behalf, and pledge your assets as security for the loan.

5. Business Operating Transactions

This clause gives your attorney-in-fact authority to act for you in operating a business that you own yourself or that you run with partners or as a corporation. Subject to the terms of a partnership agreement or corporate rules (bylaws and shareholders' agreements), the attorney-in-fact may:

- sell or liquidate the business
- merge with another company
- prepare, sign and file reports, information and returns with government agencies
- pay business taxes
- enforce the terms of a partnership agreement, if any, in court
- exercise any power or option you have under a partnership agreement.

If your business is a sole proprietorship, the attorney-in-fact may also:

- hire and fire employees
- move the business
- change the nature of the business or its methods of operation, including selling, marketing, accounting and advertising
- change the name of the business
- change the form of the business's organization—that is, enter into a partnership agreement or incorporate the business
- continue or renegotiate the business's contracts
- contract with lawyers, accountants or others
- collect and spend money on behalf of the business.

If you're a sole proprietor, a durable power of attorney is a very useful way to let someone else run the business if you become incapacitated. Because no court proceedings are required, if you become incapacitated, there should be no disruption of your business—your attorney-in-fact steps in right away. Obviously, you should work out a plan with the person you plan to appoint as your attorney-in-fact.

⚠ Check your partnership agreement or corporate bylaws and shareholders' agreements. If you operate your business with other people as a partnership or closely-held corporation, the partnership agreement or corporate bylaws or shareholders' agreements should cover what happens if a partner or shareholder becomes incapacitated. Typically, the other business owners can operate the business during the incapacitated person's absence or even buy out his or her share. These rules can't be overridden by a durable power of attorney.

Example: Mike wants his wife, Nancy, to be his attorney-in-fact to manage his finances if he becomes incapacitated. Mike, a house painter, runs the M-J Painting Co. with his equal partner, Jack. Mike and Jack's partnership agreement provides that if one partner becomes incapacitated, the other has exclusive authority to operate the business. To prevent misunderstanding and conflict, Mike puts a clause in his durable power of attorney expressly excluding Nancy from having any authority over operations of M-J Painting.

If Jack and Nancy have conflicts over money, however, there still could be problems. Mike, Jack and Nancy should think through the arrangement carefully, and may want to consult a lawyer. Whatever they decide on should be spelled out in detail in the partnership agreement and Mike's durable power of attorney.

6.   Insurance and Annuity Transactions

This clause allows the attorney-in-fact to buy, borrow against, cash in or cancel insurance policies or annuity contracts for you and your spouse, children and other dependent family members. The attorney-in-fact's authority extends to all your policies and contracts, whether they name you or someone else as the beneficiary.[2]

If you already have an insurance policy or annuity contract, the attorney-in-fact can keep paying the premiums or cancel it, whichever he or she decides is in your best interests.

When it comes to allowing the attorney-in-fact to name beneficiaries of your insurance policies, state laws differ. Here are the rules:

- **Nolo form (Chapter 5) and California, Indiana, Minnesota or Tennessee forms:** The attorney-in-fact cannot name himself or herself as beneficiary on a renewal, extension or substitute for an existing policy unless he or she was already the beneficiary before you signed the power of attorney.
- **Alaska, Connecticut, New York and North Carolina forms:** The attorney-in-fact can name himself or herself the beneficiary of a new insurance policy only if the attorney-in-fact is your spouse, child, grandchild, parent brother or sister.
- **Illinois form:** There are no special restrictions on who the attorney-in-fact can name as a beneficiary, but the rule against self-dealing (see Section A, above) would seem to forbid the attorney-in-fact from naming himself or herself.

---

[2]If, however, you and your spouse own a policy, and your attorney-in-fact is not your spouse, your spouse will have to consent to any transaction that affects the policy. Especially in community property states, policies that are in one spouse's name may in fact be owned by both spouses.

7.   Estate, Trust and Other Beneficiary Transactions

This clause authorizes your attorney-in-fact to act on your behalf to claim property you inherit or are entitled to from any other source. For example, if you were entitled to money from a trust fund, your attorney-in-fact could go to the trustee (the person in charge of the trust) and press your claim on your behalf.

If you use the Nolo power of attorney form or the California, Illinois, Indiana, Minnesota or Tennessee form, this clause also allows your attorney-in-fact to transfer items of your property to a revocable living trust you have already established. (Probate-avoidance living trusts are discussed in Chapter 1, *Using a Durable Power of Attorney*, Section D.)

If you use the Alaska, Connecticut, New York or North Carolina form and want to give your attorney-in-fact this power, you will have to add it to your power of attorney. (See instructions in Chapter 6, *State-Specific Durable Power of Attorney Forms*.)

Example: Maureen, an Illinois resident, sets up a revocable living trust to avoid probate at her death, and transfers her house and some valuable antiques to the trust. Years later, when Maureen becomes incapacitated from a stroke, her son Paul takes over her finances as her attorney-in-fact. While she is incapacitated, Maureen inherits a house from her elder sister. Paul, as attorney-in-fact, is able to transfer the house to Maureen's living trust—avoiding a substantial probate bill for Maureen's heirs when she dies.

8.   Claims and Litigation

This provision allows your attorney-in-fact to represent you in all matters that involve courts or government agencies. The attorney-in-fact can bring or settle a lawsuit on your behalf. The attorney-in-fact can accept court papers intended for you (this is called accepting "service of process"), and go to court

on your behalf, including bankruptcy or tax court. If you lose a lawsuit, the attorney-in-fact can use your assets to pay the winner whatever you are obligated to pay.

9.   Personal and Family Maintenance

Terminology note: This clause is called "Personal Relationships" or "Personal Relationships and Affairs" on some state forms.

This is an important clause. It gives the attorney-in-fact power to use your assets to pay your everyday expenses and those of your family.

It authorizes the attorney-in-fact to spend your money for your family's food, living quarters, education, cars, medical and dental care, membership dues (for churches, clubs or other organizations) vacations and travel. The attorney-in-fact is allowed to spend as much as it takes to maintain your customary standard of living and that of your spouse, children and anyone else you normally support.

In some states, this clause also authorizes the attorney-in-fact to claim salary, commissions or wages owed you.

Alaska, Connecticut and New York forms: This clause also gives the attorney-in-fact power to file tax returns on your behalf. (See section 12, below.)

10.   Government Benefits

This allows your attorney-in-fact to apply for and collect any government benefits you may be entitled to from social security, Medicare, Medicaid or other governmental programs, or civil or military service. Your attorney-in-fact must send the government office a copy of the durable power of attorney to prove his or her authority.

Terminology note: State-specific forms don't have a "government benefits" provision; they cover these topics in clauses called "Benefits from military service," "Social Security, employment and military service benefits" or other similar-sounding names.

SOCIAL SECURITY CHECKS

If you want your social security checks paid directly to a person or business, not your attorney-in-fact, you may appoint that person or business to be your "representative payee." This practice is common when the recipient of the check is in a nursing home and would just pay it over to the home anyway.

---

11.   Retirement Plan Transactions

This gives your attorney-in-fact authority over retirement plans such as individual retirement accounts (IRAs) and Keogh plans. The attorney-in-fact may select payment options, designate beneficiaries (the people who will inherit any money left in the fund at your death) and change current designations, make voluntary contributions to your plan, change the way the funds are invested and roll over plan benefits into other retirement plans. If authorized by the plan, the attorney-in-fact may borrow from, sell assets to and buy assets from the plan.

12.   Tax Matters

This provision gives your attorney-in-fact authority to act for you in all state, local and federal tax matters. The attorney-in-fact can prepare and file tax returns and other documents, pay tax due, contest tax bills and collect refunds. (To file a tax return on your behalf, the attorney-in-fact must include a copy of the power of attorney with the return.[3]) The

---

[3]Treas. Reg. § 1.6012-1(5).

attorney-in-fact is also authorized to receive confidential information from the IRS.

Alaska form: Authority over tax matters is given in the "Personal affairs" and "Records, reports, and statements" section.

Connecticut and New York forms: Authority over tax matters is given in the "Personal relationships and affairs" section.

Indiana and Minnesota forms: Authority over tax matters is given in the "Records, reports, and statements" section.

13.   Delegation

If you expect the attorney-in-fact to be out of town or unavailable for periods of time, you can allow the attorney-in-fact to delegate his or her authority temporarily. (Part 3 of the durable power of attorney.) In other words, you permit the attorney-in-fact to create a secondary power of attorney for you.

Example 1: Caroline names her son, Eugene, as her attorney-in-fact for finances, effective immediately. She names a close friend, Nicole, as alternate attorney-in-fact. A year later, Eugene goes to Europe for three weeks' vacation, so he delegates his authority over Caroline's bank accounts to Nicole until he returns.

Example 2: Anthony names his wife, Rosa, as his attorney-in-fact; his son Michael is the alternate attorney-in-fact. When Rosa declines to serve because of her own ill health, Michael takes over, but soon finds that other responsibilities make it impossible to continue. He delegates all his authority to his sister, Theresa.

C.   Restrictions on Your Attorney-in-Fact

Powers of attorney are flexible tools. If you aren't satisfied with granting some or all of the powers discussed in Section B, above, you can tailor your power of attorney to your needs. This section sets out some provisions you may want to consider adding to your power of attorney. (How to add clauses to your power of attorney is explained in Chapter 5, *Preparing a Durable Power of Attorney* and Chapter 6, *State-Specific Durable Power of Attorney Forms.*)

1.   Restricting the Sale of Your Home

Losing your home, especially if you've lived there many years, can be a disturbing prospect. If you want to forbid your attorney-in-fact from selling or mortgaging your home, you can include a provision like the one below.

"My attorney-in-fact shall have no authority to engage in any transaction to sell, convey, exchange, transfer, partition, lease or encumber the real property, or any rights or security interest therein, of my principal place of residence located at *street address city, state, zip code* ."

Think carefully before you include such a restriction, however. Of course you don't want to lose your home—but if a financial emergency makes it necessary, you may not want to tie the hands of your attorney-in-fact. Especially if your spouse or other co-owner of your home will be your attorney-in-fact, you probably want to trust that person to make a decision that's in your best interests.

2.   Restrictions on Running Your Small Business

If you have given your attorney-in-fact power over your small business interests but want to restrict the attorney-in-fact's freedom to sell or encumber the business, include a clause like this one:

"My attorney-in-fact shall have no authority to sell, transfer, or otherwise exchange or encumber my business, *business name* at *street city, state, zip code* ."

If you don't want to include an outright ban on selling the business, you may still want someone—your spouse or financial advisor, perhaps—notified if the attorney-in-fact wants to sell it. If that's the case, include a clause like this:

"If my attorney-in-fact deems it necessary to sell *whatever you specify,* he or she shall give written notice of that intent to sell, before the sale and as soon as reasonably possible, to: *names and addresses* ."

3.   Requiring Periodic Reports

Unless you require it, your attorney-in-fact doesn't have to report to anyone about his or her handling of your finances. Usually, that's fine. In unusual circumstances, though, you may want to require reports. For example, if the attorney-in-fact is in charge of your business, investors may need to receive a quarterly or semi-annual financial statement, audited or reviewed by an accountant. Or perhaps you want to diffuse a potentially explosive personal conflict by reassuring mistrustful family members that they'll receive regular reports about your finances.

Example: Theodore, who is ill, appoints his son, Jason, as his attorney-in-fact for finances. Theodore's two other children, Nancy and Ed, live out of state and aren't on the best of terms with Jason.

To prevent suspicion or conflict between his children over Jason's handling of Theodore's finances, Theodore decides to require Jason to give Nancy and Ed semi-annual reports of all financial transactions he engages in as attorney-in-fact.

Here is a clause you can adapt and add to your power of attorney:

"My attorney-in-fact shall prepare written, semi-annual reports regarding my finances, including the income received and expenses incurred by my attorney-in-fact for me during the previous six-month period. These reports shall be mailed within 30 days of the end of each six-month period to: ___names and addresses___."

D. Payment of the Attorney-in-Fact

In family situations, an attorney-in-fact is normally not paid if the duties won't be complicated or burdensome.

If your property and finances are extensive, however, and the attorney-in-fact is likely to devote significant time and effort managing them, compensation seems fair—after all, you can afford it. Certainly, you should discuss and resolve this issue with the proposed attorney-in-fact before you finalize your document.

Whatever payment arrangement you settle on should be included in the durable power of attorney itself. If you don't specify something, the attorney-in-fact may or may not be entitled to "reasonable" compensation for services rendered, depending on state law.

You can be definite or vague about amounts. For example, you can say that the attorney-in-fact is entitled to a set hourly rate or just to "reasonable compensation, as determined by the attorney-in-fact." (See Chapter 5, *Preparing a Durable Power of Attorney*, Section C.)

Example 1: Alfreda, a widow, owns a substantial amount of property: a house, a small apartment building and several bank and mutual fund accounts. In declining health, she appoints her nephew Hector as her attorney-in-fact for finances. Hector has helped her look after her apartment building for several years already. In the power of attorney document, which takes effect immediately, she agrees to pay Hector $10,000 a year for his services as attorney-in-fact.

Example 2: Martin creates a springing durable power of attorney naming his brother, Andrew, as attorney-in-fact. Martin has many stocks and other investments, and the brothers agree that Andrew should be paid if he has to manage Martin's finances. They consider an hourly wage, but decide not to be that specific now. Martin checks the box that lets Andrew pay himself "reasonable" fees for his services.

E. Supervision of the Attorney-in-Fact

An attorney-in-fact is not directly supervised by a court; that's the whole point of appointing one and avoiding a conservatorship. The attorney-in-fact is not required to file reports with any courts or government agencies.

A court may become involved only if someone close to you fears that the attorney-in-fact is acting dishonestly or not in your best interests. It's rare, but close relatives or friends may ask a court to order the attorney-in-fact to take certain actions. Or they may ask the court to terminate the power of attorney and appoint a conservator to look after your affairs. If a conservator is appointed for you, the attorney-in-fact will have to account to the conservator. (Conservatorships are discussed in Chapter 1, *Using a Durable Power of Attorney*, Section B.) Or they may challenge the durable power of attorney itself, on the ground that you weren't mentally competent when you signed it or were the victim of some kind of fraud.

Some states have statutes that set out specific procedures for such court actions. For example, a California statute authorizes certain people—the principal, the attorney-in-fact, a spouse or child of the principal, and any person who would inherit property from the principal if he or she died without a will (close family members, in most cases)—to ask a court to resolve questions relating to the durable power of attorney.[4] In Tennessee, state law provides that the next of kin can petition a court to require an attorney-in-fact to post a bond (basically, an insurance policy, generally issued by a surety company).[5]

If your state doesn't have such a statute, someone interested in your welfare and upset with the attorney-in-fact could still go to court and ask for a conservator to be appointed. If you wish, in your durable power of attorney you can nominate your attorney-in-fact to serve as conservator or guardian if a court appoints one. (See Chapter 5, *Preparing a Durable Power of Attorney*, Section C.)

---

[4]Cal. Civ. Code § 2411..

[5]Tenn. Code Ann. § 34-6-106.

CALIFORNIA: PREVENTING CHALLENGES TO A POWER OF ATTORNEY

In a California durable power of attorney, you may eliminate the authority of any person (except the conservator of your estate, if one is appointed) to petition the court under the California durable power of attorney statute. Before doing this, you must, by law, be advised of your rights by a lawyer, who must sign a statement to that effect.

If, for example, you wanted to appoint a friend as attorney-in-fact but feared a court challenge from one of your adult children, you might restrict that child's ability to challenge your power of attorney.

Unfortunately, such a restriction probably doesn't accomplish much. There are many ways to litigate. Even if you prevent someone from suing under the California durable power of attorney statute, a determined challenger can surely find another method for getting to court. Phrased more precisely, such a person can surely find a lawyer who'll get to court, if the lawyer is paid well enough.

F.   Liability for Mistakes or Dishonesty

Under state law, an attorney-in-fact may be financially liable to the principal even for a careless mistake in handling the principal's property—for example, making an investment that seemed safe but turned out to be a loser.

You can, however, change this rule in your durable power of attorney. Because most people choose a spouse, close relative or friend to be attorney-in-fact, the Nolo durable power of attorney form (Chapter 5) makes the attorney-in-fact liable only for losses resulting from willful misconduct or gross negligence—not for a well-meaning decision that turned out badly. Essentially, that means that the attorney-in-fact is liable only for intentional wrongdoing or extreme carelessness with your assets. If you use a state-specific form, you can add such a provision. (See Chapter 6, *State-Specific Power of Attorney Forms*.)

G.   Resignation

No one can be forced to serve as an attorney-in-fact—it's a voluntary job, and in theory, the attorney-in-fact can legally resign at any time.

Resignation is simplest when the durable power of attorney names a successor to take over as attorney-in-fact, and the successor is willing and able to serve. If the document doesn't name a successor, or the successor cannot serve, a conservatorship proceeding may be necessary. (Conservatorships are discussed in Chapter 1, *Using a Durable Power of Attorney*, Section B.) Leaving a disabled principal in the lurch without a good reason could be considered a breach of duty, and a court might order an attorney-in-fact to continue serving until a conservator can be appointed and take over.

A tear-out resignation form, which your attorney-in-fact can sign and send to the successor, is included in the Appendix.

H.   The Alternate Attorney-in-Fact's Duties

In case your attorney-in-fact becomes unable to serve, you should name an alternate attorney-in-fact (also called successor attorney-in-fact). The person you name as alternate takes over only if your first choice (or all of them, if you named more than one person as attorney-in-fact) cannot or will not serve.

Someone who is asked to serve as a successor attorney-in-fact may be worried about possible liability for the acts of the original attorney-in-fact. To protect against this, the Nolo durable power of attorney form (Chapter 5) states that a successor attorney-in-fact is not liable for any acts of a prior attorney-in-fact.

I.   If You're Asked To Serve as an Attorney-in-Fact

Serving as attorney-in-fact is a serious responsibility, not one that should be assumed because of obligation or guilt. But in most situations, it involves little legal risk and is a loving and generous thing to do for a close relative or friend.

If you take on the role of attorney-in-fact, however, it won't be easy to change your mind. Before you accept, talk to the principal and ask yourself some questions:

- Will others close to the principal support you, or will they be jealous and suspicious? Can you deal with whatever conflict and tension are involved?
- If you would become attorney-in-fact only if the principal becomes incapacitated (a "springing" durable power of attorney), do you know how this determination will be made, and by whom? Are you comfortable with the process?
- Do you feel confident that you know how the principal would want you to make decisions about his or her finances?
- Do you have the expertise to manage the principal's financial holdings and keep necessary records? Can you hire someone to help you?
- Would you be liable to the principal if you made mistakes when handling the principal's finances? Read the durable power of attorney to find out.
- How much time will your duties require? Will you be paid for your time?

5

PREPARING A DURABLE POWER OF ATTORNEY

Once you understand what you want to accomplish with your durable power of attorney for finances—you've chosen your attorney-in-fact and thought about what powers to give him or her—preparing the durable power itself is easy.

All you have to do is tear out the appropriate form from the back of the book and follow the instructions in this chapter. It probably won't take you more than an hour.

A.   What Forms To Use

The forms in this book are called "general" powers of attorney, because they can be used to give your attorney-in-fact a broad range of powers. A limited power of attorney, on the other hand, grants a much narrower authority to your attorney-in-fact.

1.   The General Power of Attorney

The Appendix of this book contains two kinds of tear-out durable power of attorney forms:

- the Nolo form, good in all states
- state-specific forms for these states:

Alaska	New Jersey (modify Nolo form)
California	New Mexico
Colorado	New York
Connecticut	North Carolina
Illinois	Pennsylvania (modify Nolo form)
Indiana	Tennessee
Minnesota	

These states have enacted laws that recommend the use of certain forms or language to create durable powers of attorney. The state-specific forms aren't mandatory; you can use the Nolo form if you decide it better meets your needs. But if you stick to the familiar official language, banks, brokers, title companies and others your attorney-in-fact will deal with are less likely to object to the legality of your form. Chapter 6 contains instructions for each of the state forms.

2.   Limited Powers of Attorney

As mentioned earlier, many banks and brokerage houses have their own durable power of attorney forms. If yours does, we recommend that you use it, as well as the broader power of attorney form in this book. If, for example, your bank has its own form, using it will head off any problems for your attorney-in-fact, because the bank will have no need to examine and quibble with the power of attorney. The bank will already have its form on file and know exactly what authority it grants.

B.   How To Fill Out the Form

It's not hard to prepare a durable power of attorney correctly, but it's important to follow the instructions carefully. If you don't, your attorney-in-fact might not be able to get a bank, title company, insurance company or government agency to accept his or her authority. Remember, if your durable power of attorney is in effect, it means you will have become incapacitated, and you won't be able to fix any mistakes in the document.

1. **Make copies of the blank form.** Tear out the form you want to use and make a few photocopies. You can use one for a draft and save a clean one for the final document—the one you will sign and have notarized.

2. **Type the document.** It's not a legal requirement that a durable power of attorney be typed, but your attorney-in-fact is much less likely to run into trouble if it is. People expect legal documents to be typed and may be suspicious of handwritten ones.

3. **Don't erase anything.** Your final form should not contain any words that have been erased or whited-out. If the instructions tell you to cross out something, type a string of x's through the words.

 Get help if you need it. A durable power of attorney can transfer tremendous power either now or, in the case of a springing durable power of attorney, sometime in the future. Even though you can revoke it at any time (as long as you are mentally competent), never create a durable power of attorney unless you thoroughly understand the authority you plan to transfer. If you have questions, see an expert.

C. Step-by-Step Instructions

Here are instructions for filling in each part of the Nolo durable power of attorney form. You may want to refer to the discussions in earlier chapters as you make the choices necessary to fill out the form. At the beginning of the instructions for each item, look for this icon.

 Next to it will be the name of the chapter that discusses the topic in more detail.

Part 1. Attorney-in-Fact

 Chapter 3, *Choosing Your Attorney-in-Fact*.

In the first two blanks on the form, fill in your name and the city and state where you live. Enter your name the way it appears on formal business documents, such as your driver's license, deeds to real estate or bank accounts. This may or may not be the name on your birth certificate.

> **Example:** Your birth certificate lists your name as Rose Mary Green. But you've always gone by Mary, and always sign documents as Mary McNee, your married name. You would use Mary McNee on your durable power of attorney.

If your important documents refer to you by different names, you can enter the various versions of your name, joined by "aka" (also known as). But a better strategy would be to settle on one name, use it here, and change your other documents to conform. You'll save your attorney-in-fact some hassles.

IF YOU LIVE IN MORE THAN ONE STATE

If during the course of a year you live in more than one state, your residence is the state with which you have the most significant contacts—where you vote, register vehicles, own valuable property, have bank accounts or run a business. If you have a will or living trust, be consistent: use the address in the state you declared as your residence in those documents.

Next, type in the name of the person (or persons) you've chosen and who have agreed to serve, if necessary, as your attorney-in-fact for finances. Choosing your attorney-in-fact is the most important decision you make when preparing a durable power of attorney.

You may also, in the next sentence on the form, name an alternate (successor) attorney-in-fact. You don't have to name an alternate, but it's a good idea. If you named more than one attorney-in-fact, the successor will serve only if all the people you named first cannot serve.

Part 2.   More Than One Attorney-in-Fact

If you named only one person as your attorney-in-fact, skip Part 2 (don't check either box) and go on to Part 3.

Chapter 3, *Choosing Your Attorney-in-Fact*, Section D.

a.   Authorization of Each Attorney-in-Fact

If you named more than one person to serve as attorney-in-fact or successor attorney-in-fact, choose whether or not you want to allow each one to act separately on your behalf. If you check the box in front of "jointly," each attorney-in-fact will have to sign all documents and approve all decisions made on your behalf.

b.   Resolution of Disputes

If you named more than one attorney-in-fact, it's a good idea to specify a method for resolving any intractable disputes. If you check the box, disputes must be submitted to an arbitrator, who will make a binding decision. You can name anyone you want to be the arbitrator.

If you don't choose this clause, the attorneys-in-fact are free to resolve disputes any way they want.

But if they don't agree on mediation or arbitration, they may end up in court.

Part 3.   Delegation of Authority

Chapter 4, *The Attorney-in-Fact's Responsibilities*, Section B.

This clause lets your attorney-in-fact delegate some or all of his or her authority to someone else. If you allow it (by checking the "may" box), your attorney-in-fact can name someone else to act as your attorney-in-fact, temporarily or permanently.

Part 4.   Effective Date

Chapter 2, *How Durable Powers of Attorney Work*, Section B.

Here, you must specify whether you want your durable power of attorney to become effective:

- as soon as you sign it, or
- only if you become incapacitated (a springing durable power).
  You must check one of the boxes.

DURABLE POWER OF ATTORNEY FOR FINANCIAL MANAGEMENT

WARNING TO PERSON EXECUTING THIS DOCUMENT

This is an important legal document. It creates a durable power of attorney. Before executing this document, you should know these important facts:

This document may provide the person you designate as your attorney-in-fact with broad powers to manage, dispose, sell and convey your real and personal property and to borrow money using your property as security for the loan.

These powers will exist for an indefinite period of time unless you limit their duration in this document. These powers will continue to exist notwithstanding your subsequent disability or incapacity.

This document does not authorize anyone to make medical or other health care decisions for you.

You have the right to revoke or terminate this power of attorney.

If there is anything about this form that you do not understand, you should ask a lawyer to explain it to you.

1. Attorney-in-Fact

I, _Iris L. Rodham-Carter_ of _Seattle, Washington_, appoint _William C. Carter_ as my attorney-in-fact to act for me in any lawful way with respect to the powers delegated in Part 6 below. If that person (or all of those persons, if more than one is named) does not serve or ceases to serve as attorney-in-fact, I appoint _Hillary A. Yeung_ to serve as attorney-in-fact.

2. More Than One Attorney-in-Fact

a. Authorization

If more than one attorney-in-fact is designated, they are authorized to act:

☐ jointly. ☐ independently.

b. Resolution of Disputes

☐ If my attorneys-in-fact cannot agree on a decision or action under the authority delegated to them in this durable power of attorney, that dispute shall be resolved by binding arbitration. The arbitration shall be carried out by a single arbitrator, who shall be _____ _____, if available. The arbitration shall begin within five days of written notice by any attorney-in-fact to the arbitrator that a dispute between the attorneys-in-fact has arisen. The details of the arbitration shall be determined by the arbitrator. The written decision of the arbitrator shall be binding on all my attorneys-in-fact.

3. Delegation of Authority

My attorney-in-fact ☒ may ☐ may not   delegate, in writing, any authority granted under this durable power of attorney to a person he or she selects. Any such delegation shall state the period during which it is valid and specify the extent of the delegation.

Page 1

Part 5.   Determination of Incapacity

If you made your durable power of attorney effective immediately, skip Part 5 (don't check boxes or fill in blanks).

Chapter 2, *How Durable Powers of Attorney Work*, Section C.

If you are creating a springing power of attorney, you must state here who you want to determine, if it becomes necessary, that you have become incapacitated and that the durable power of attorney is in effect. You can have one or two physicians make this determination and sign statements, under penalty of perjury, to that effect.[1] (A statement for a physician to sign is included in the Appendix.)

NOTE FOR ALASKA AND NEW MEXICO READERS

Alaska law requires sworn statements from two physicians to make a springing durable power of attorney take effect.

New Mexico law requires notarized statements from two qualified health care professionals.

You can fill in the name of the physician(s) you want to make the determination. Or, if you don't want to name a specific person, you can put "my personal physician" or "my attending physician." Then, if it becomes necessary, the doctor who is caring for you at the time will make a determination about your ability to manage your financial affairs.

---

[1] It's possible to designate someone who's not a physician to be one of the persons who rules on your incapacity. See Chapter 2, *How Durable Powers of Attorneys Work*, Section C.

Part 6.   Powers of the Attorney-in-Fact

Chapter 4, *The Attorney-in-Fact's Responsibilities*, Sections B and C.

The power of attorney form contains a list of powers; you can give the attorney-in-fact all of them or only some. Either way, you can put specific limitations on the powers that you grant. For example, if you give your attorney-in-fact authority over your real estate, later in the document you can still put in a provision forbidding the attorney-in-fact from selling your residence.

• To give your attorney-in-fact all of the listed powers, initial the blank in front of the first item in the list:

_____ a. ALL POWERS (b THROUGH m) LISTED BELOW.

Most people choose to give the broadest possible authority to their attorney-in-fact. As discussed in Chapter 4, generally that's a good strategy, unless you have a particular reason for not granting a certain power.

Scanning the list of powers, you may think that it's not necessary to grant some of them—after all, why give your attorney-in-fact authority over "claims and litigation" when you aren't involved in any lawsuits? What you should keep in mind is that even though you aren't involved in a lawsuit now, you could be later. For example, your power of attorney might spring into effect because you're in the hospital, seriously injured in a car accident, and you can't take care of your financial affairs. Your attorney-in-fact might need authority to settle a claim on your behalf.

• To grant only specific powers to the attorney-in-fact, initial the blank in front of each power you want to grant. If you wish, you can also line out the other powers.

(In the Nolo power of attorney form, each of the listed powers is defined in Part 17.)

NOTES FOR DISTRICT OF COLUMBIA, MINNESOTA AND NEW JERSEY READERS

District of Columbia law does not allow an attorney-in-fact to sell real estate or any other property of the principal. (D.C. Code § 45-601.)

In Minnesota, if your attorney-in-fact is your spouse, he or she cannot convey real estate that belongs to you. (Minn. Stat. § 519.06.)

In New Jersey, you may want to make a slight modification to the Nolo form to use special New Jersey rules for banking transactions. (See Chapter 6, *State-Specific Durable Power of Attorney Forms*, Section J for instructions.)

Part 7. Special Instructions to the Attorney-in-Fact

 Chapter 4, *The Attorney-in-Fact's Responsibilities*, Section C.

Here, you can qualify the powers you granted in Part 6 with your own instructions or restrictions. The list of possible additions, of course is nearly endless; a few examples are discussed in Chapter 4. Whatever you add, be sure it doesn't contradict something already in the form; you could create confusion and problems down the road.

• If you don't want to add any restrictions here, type "None" in the space provided.

Because most people don't need to add to the Nolo form, Part 7 contains room to add only one or two extra clauses. If you want to add more words than will fit in the space we've left, you'll have to retype the whole form.

 Not enough room? If you start making too many additions, it's an indication that the Nolo durable power of attorney may not be appropriate in your circumstances. You may want to see a lawyer about drafting a truly personalized document. (Chapter 9, *Lawyers and Legal Research*, discusses how to find and hire a lawyer.)

DURABLE POWER OF ATTORNEY FOR FINANCIAL MANAGEMENT

4. Effective Date

This power of attorney is effective:

☒ immediately, and shall continue in effect if I become incapacitated or disabled.

☐ only if I become incapacitated or disabled and unable to manage my financial affairs.

5. Determination of Incapacity

For purposes of this durable power of attorney, my incapacity or disability shall be determined by written declarations by ☐ one ☐ two licensed physician(s). Each declaration shall be made under penalty of perjury and shall state that in the physician's opinion I am substantially unable to manage my financial affairs. If possible, the declaration(s) shall be made by _____ _____. No licensed physician shall be liable to me for any actions taken under this part which are done in good faith.

6. Powers of Attorney-in-Fact

I hereby grant to my attorney-in-fact power to act on my behalf in the following matters, as indicated by my initials by each granted power or on line a, granting all the listed powers. Powers that are not initialed are not granted.

INITIALS

_I.L.RC._ a. ALL POWERS (b THROUGH m) LISTED BELOW.

_____ b. Real estate transactions.

_____ c. Tangible personal property transactions.

_____ d. Stock and bond, commodity and option transactions.

_____ e. Banking and other financial institution transactions.

_____ f. Business operating transactions.

_____ g. Insurance and annuity transactions.

_____ h. Estate, trust, and other beneficiary transactions.

_____ i. Claims and litigation.

_____ j. Personal and family maintenance.

_____ k. Benefits from social security, Medicare, Medicaid, or other governmental programs, or civil or military service.

_____ l. Retirement plan transactions.

_____ m. Tax matters.

Note: These powers are defined in Part 17, below.

7. Special Instructions to the Attorney-in-Fact

_____

_____

_____

_____

_____

Page 2

Part 8.   Compensation and Reinbursement of the Attorney-in-Fact

Chapter 4, *The Attorney-in-Fact's Responsibilities*, Section D.

Whether or not your attorney-in-fact is paid usually depends on your relationship to each other and the extent of the attorney-in-fact's responsibilities.

- If you decide not to pay your attorney-in-fact, check the first box.
- If you want to provide for payment, check one of the last two boxes. It's common to simply give the attorney-in-fact the right to reasonable compensation and let him or her determine an amount. Or you can check the third box and fill in an hourly, monthly or yearly fee.

Part 9.   Nomination of Conservator or Guardian

Chapter 2, *How Durable Powers of Attorney Work*, Section G.

It's possible, though highly unlikely, that a court proceeding could be brought to set aside or override your durable power of attorney.

If the durable power of attorney is declared invalid, the court will appoint someone (usually called a conservator or guardian) to handle your financial affairs. In this clause, you ask the court to name your attorney-in-fact to that post. In many states, a court must, by law, follow your recommendation unless there is a good reason not to; in other states, your wishes will generally be honored.

Part 10.   Personal Benefit by Attorney-in-Fact

Chapter 4, *The Attorney-in-Fact's Responsibilities*, Section A.

Unless you say otherwise, your attorney-in-fact is not permitted to profit or benefit personally from any transaction he or she engages in as your representative. This restriction is designed to protect you, but in some instances it's not necessary or desirable. For example, if your attorney-in-fact is also your wife, or your child who will someday inherit most or all of your property, you don't want her to have to worry because selling an item of property you own jointly will benefit her as well as you.

- If you want to leave the attorney-in-fact free to benefit personally from any acts he or she does as your attorney-in-fact, check the first box.
- If you want this general rule to apply except for a specific circumstance or two, check the second box and write in the exceptions.
- If you don't want to allow the attorney-in-fact to benefit personally from any action taken on your behalf, check the third box.

DURABLE POWER OF ATTORNEY FOR FINANCIAL MANAGEMENT

8. Compensation and Reimbursement of the Attorney-in-Fact

☒ The attorney-in-fact shall not be compensated for services, but shall be entitled to reimbursement, from the principal's assets, for reasonable expenses. Reasonable expenses include reasonable fees for information or advice from accountants, lawyers or investment experts relating to the attorney-in-fact's responsibilities under this power of attorney.

☐ The attorney-in-fact shall be entitled to reimbursement for reasonable expenses and reasonable compensation for his or her services. Reasonable compensation shall be determined exclusively by the attorney-in-fact.

☐ The attorney-in-fact shall be entitled to reimbursement for reasonable expenses and compensation for his or her services of $_____ per _____ .

9. Nomination of Conservator or Guardian

If, in a court proceeding, it is ever resolved that I need a conservator, guardian or other person to administer and supervise my estate or person, I nominate my attorney-in-fact to serve in that capacity. If my attorney-in-fact cannot serve, I nominate the successor attorney-in-fact nominated in Part 1 to serve.

10. Personal Benefit to Attorney-in-Fact

☒ My attorney-in-fact may buy any assets of mine or engage in any transaction he or she deems in good faith to be in my interest, no matter what the interest of or benefit to my attorney-in-fact.

☐ My attorney-in-fact may not be personally involved in or benefit personally from any transaction he or she engages in on my behalf, except _____
_____ .

☐ My attorney-in-fact may not be personally involved in or benefit personally from any transaction he or she engages in on my behalf.

11. Commingling by Attorney-in-Fact

My attorney-in-fact ☒ may ☐ may not   mix (commingle) any of my funds with any funds of his or hers.

12. Bond

The attorney-in-fact shall serve without bond.

13. Liability of Attorney-in-Fact

My attorney-in-fact shall not incur any liability to me, my estate, my heirs, successors or assigns for acting or refraining from acting under this document, except for willful misconduct or gross negligence. My attorney-in-fact is not required to make my assets produce income, increase the value of my estate, diversify my investments or enter into transactions authorized by this document, as long as my attorney-in-fact believes his or her actions are in my best interests or in the best interests of my estate and of those interested in my estate. A successor attorney-in-fact shall not be liable for acts of a prior attorney-in-fact.

Page 3

Part 11.   Commingling by the Attorney-in-Fact

 Chapter 4, *The Attorney-in-Fact's Responsibilities*, Section A.

Legally, the attorney-in-fact cannot mix (commingle) your monies with his own. But if your attorney-in-fact is your spouse or long-term lover, your funds may have been commingled for a long time. You should authorize this commingling by checking the second box in this part.

> When you've completed Part 11 of the Nolo form, you've completed your power of attorney. The rest of the form is standard language. You should read and understand it, but you don't need to fill in any more blanks.

Part 12.   Bond

Your attorney-in-fact is not required to post a bond. A bond is an insurance policy, generally issued by a surety company, that protects against losses caused by the attorney-in-fact's improper actions. If you trust your attorney-in-fact, the expense of a bond isn't justified; if you don't, a durable power of attorney doesn't make sense. And it can be difficult for an individual (as opposed to a financial institution) to buy a bond.

 If you want a bond. If for some reason you want to require a bond, see a lawyer. You may want court supervision of the person in charge of your finances, and a conservator might be more appropriate for your situation. (See Chapter 1, *Using a Durable Power of Attorney*, Section C.)

Part 13.   Liability of the Attorney-in-Fact

 Chapter 4, *The Attorney-in-Fact's Responsibilities*, Section F.

This clause makes the attorney-in-fact liable for losing your money or other property only if the loss was caused by willful misconduct or gross negligence—that is, intentional wrongdoing or extremely careless behavior. Without this clause, the attorney-in-fact might be (depending on state law) liable to you for losses caused by any negligence (unreasonable carelessness) committed while acting as attorney-in-fact. That could make your attorney-in-fact subject to liability for a good faith mistake—a result you probably don't want, given that you're choosing a close relative or friend to be attorney-in-fact.

Part 14.   Gifts to the Attorney-in-Fact

This clause states that the attorney-in-fact has no authority to give your property to himself or herself. It avoids a potential tax problem: If the attorney-in-fact's authority over your property is extremely broad, there's a minor risk that the value of that property would be included in the attorney-in-fact's taxable estate, if the attorney-in-fact died before you (not likely, but it could happen).

If you want the attorney-in-fact to have authority to give your property to himself, see a lawyer.

Part 15.   Reliance on This Power of Attorney

This clause expressly exonerates from liability people or institutions who rely on the attorney-in-fact's authority when shown a copy of the durable power. Even if the durable power has been revoked, a third party can rely on it unless he or she has actually received notice of a revocation. It can work wonders when it comes to getting banks, brokers and others with whom your attorney-in-fact may deal to relax.

 If you do revoke your power of attorney. This clause helps your attorney-in-fact get his or her authority accepted, but it also means that if you do revoke the power of attorney, you must give copies of the revocation to anyone you think the attorney-in-fact might try to deal with. It's also wise to record it in the land records office of any county in which you own real estate. If you don't, you could be on the hook for the former attorney-in-fact's actions. (See Chapter 8, *Revoking a Durable Power of Attorney*.)

Part 16.   Severability

This is a standard clause in all kinds of legal documents. It ensures that even in the unlikely event that some part of your power of attorney is declared invalid by a court, the rest of the document is still valid.

Part 17.   Specific Powers of the Attorney-in-Fact

This part spells out the details of the attorney-in-fact's powers, which you granted in Part 6. You don't have to check any boxes or fill in any information here.

D.   What's Next?

Once you've filled out the power of attorney, you must sign it in front of a notary public. Instructions are in Chapter 7, *Making It Legal*.

DURABLE POWER OF ATTORNEY FOR FINANCIAL MANAGEMENT

14. Gifts by Attorney-in-Fact

My attorney-in-fact may not (i) appoint, assign or designate any of my assets, interests or rights directly or indirectly to himself or herself, or estate, creditors, or the creditors of his or her estate, (ii) disclaim assets to which I would otherwise be entitled if the effect of the disclaimer is to cause such assets to pass directly or indirectly to my attorney-in-fact or his or her estate, or (iii) use my assets to discharge any of his or her legal obligations, including any obligation of support owed to others (excluding me and those whom I am legally obligated to support).

15. Reliance on this Power of Attorney

I agree that any third party who receives a copy of this document may rely on and act under it. Revocation of the power of attorney is not effective as to a third party until the third party has actual knowledge of the revocation. I agree to indemnify the third party for any claims that arise against the third party because of reliance on this power of attorney.

16. Severability

If any provision of this document is ruled unenforceable, the remaining provisions shall stay in effect.

17. Construction of Powers Granted to the Attorney-in-Fact

The powers granted in Part 6 above authorize the attorney-in-fact to do the following.

b. Real estate transactions

Act for the principal in any manner to deal with all or any part of any interest in real property that the principal owns at the time of execution or thereafter acquires, under such terms, conditions and covenants as the attorney-in-fact deems proper. The attorney-in-fact's powers include but are not limited to the power to:

(1) Accept as a gift, or as security for a loan, reject, demand, buy, lease, receive or otherwise acquire ownership of possession of any estate or interest in real property.

(2) Sell, exchange, convey with or without covenants, quitclaim, release, surrender, mortgage, encumber, partition or consent to the partitioning of, grant options concerning, lease, sublet or otherwise dispose of any interest in real property.

(3) Maintain, repair, improve, insure, rent, lease, and pay or contest taxes or assessments on any estate or interest in real property owned, or claimed to be owned, by the principal.

(4) Prosecute, defend, intervene in, submit to arbitration, settle and propose or accept a compromise with respect to any claim in favor of or against the principal based on or involving any real estate transaction.

c. Tangible personal property transactions

Act for the principal in any manner to deal with all or any part of any interest in personal property that the principal owns at the time of execution or thereafter acquires, under such terms as the attorney-in-fact deems proper. The attorney-in-fact's powers include but are not limited to the power to:

Lease, buy, exchange, accept as a gift or as security for a loan, acquire, possess, maintain, repair, improve, insure, rent, lease, sell, convey, mortgage, pledge, and pay or contest taxes and assessments

Page 4

(Pages 5 to 8 of the form are in the Appendix.)

STATE-SPECIFIC DURABLE POWER OF ATTORNEY FORMS

The states listed below have enacted laws that recommend the use of certain forms or language to create durable powers of attorney for finances. If you live in one of these states, you'll probably want to use the state-specific form. Instructions are in this chapter; a tear-out copy of each form is included in the Appendix.

STATES WITH THEIR OWN DURABLE POWER OF ATTORNEY FORMS OR LANGUAGE

Alaska	New Jersey (modify Nolo form)
California	New Mexico
Colorado	New York
Connecticut	North Carolina
Illinois	Pennsylvania (modify Nolo form)
Indiana	Tennessee
Minnesota	

The state-specific forms are often called "short forms," because they don't include all the details of the authority granted to the attorney-in-fact. Instead, the form contains only a list of broad powers. You choose the ones you want the attorney-in-fact to have; the details are spelled out in your state's statutes.

For example, on the form you might check a box to give your attorney-in-fact power over your "real estate transactions." Your state's statutes—but not the power of attorney document itself—contain a lengthy explanation of exactly what authority that gives your attorney-in-fact. As you can see from the example below, giving your attorney-in-fact power over "real estate transactions" grants the power to conduct all common transactions and many that aren't so common.

CALIFORNIA UNIFORM STATUTORY FORM POWER OF ATTORNEY
(California Civil Code § 2475)

NOTICE: THE POWERS GRANTED BY THIS DOCUMENT ARE BROAD AND SWEEPING. THEY ARE EXPLAINED IN THE UNIFORM STATUTORY FORM POWER OF ATTORNEY ACT (CALIFORNIA CIVIL CODE SECTIONS 2475-2499.5, INCLUSIVE). IF YOU HAVE ANY QUESTIONS ABOUT THESE POWERS, OBTAIN COMPETENT LEGAL ADVICE. THIS DOCUMENT DOES NOT AUTHORIZE ANY-ONE TO MAKE MEDICAL AND OTHER HEALTH CARE DECISIONS FOR YOU. YOU MAY REVOKE THIS POWER OF ATTORNEY IF YOU LATER WISH TO DO SO.

I, _Eli Bernstein, 1785 Townsend Ave., San Francisco, CA 94111_ [your name and address] appoint _Rochelle Grant, 311 Parker St., San Rafael, CA 95182_ [name and address of the person appointed, or of each person appointed if you want to designate more than one] as my agent (attorney-in-fact) to act for me in any lawful way with respect to the following initialed subjects:

TO GRANT ALL OF THE FOLLOWING POWERS, INITIAL THE LINE IN FRONT OF (N) AND IGNORE THE LINES IN FRONT OF THE OTHER POWERS.

TO GRANT ONE OR MORE, BUT FEWER THAN ALL, OF THE FOLLOWING POWERS, INITIAL THE LINE IN FRONT OF EACH POWER YOU ARE GRANTING.

TO WITHHOLD A POWER, DO NOT INITIAL THE LINE IN FRONT OF IT. YOU MAY, BUT NEED NOT, CROSS OUT EACH POWER WITHHELD.

INITIAL
_eb_ (A) Real property transactions.
_____ (B) Tangible personal property transactions.
_____ (C) Stock and bond transactions.
_____ (D) Commodity and option transactions.
_____ (E) Banking and other financial institution transactions.
_____ (F) Business operating transactions.
_____ (G) Insurance and annuity transactions.
_____ (H) Estate, trust, and other beneficiary transactions.
_____ (I) Claims and litigation.
_____ (J) Personal and family maintenance.
_____ (K) Benefits from social security, medicare, medicaid, or other governmental pro-grams, or civil or military service.
_____ (L) Retirement plan transactions.
_____ (M) Tax matters.
_____ (N) ALL OF THE POWERS LISTED ABOVE.

YOU NEED NOT INITIAL ANY OTHER LINES IF YOU INITIAL LINE (N).

SPECIAL INSTRUCTIONS:

ON THE FOLLOWING LINES YOU MAY GIVE SPECIAL INSTRUCTIONS LIMITING OR EXTENDING THE POWERS GRANTED TO YOUR AGENT. _____

Page 1

CALIFORNIA STATUTE EXPLAINING REAL ESTATE TRANSACTIONS

~2486. Powers Granted—Real Property Transactions.

In a statutory form power of attorney, the language granting power with respect to real property transactions empowers the agent to do all of the following:

(a) Accept as a gift or as security for a loan, reject, demand, buy, lease, receive, or otherwise acquire, an interest in real property or a right incident to real property.

(b) Sell, exchange, convey with or without covenants, quitclaim, release, surrender, mortgage, encumber, partition, consent to partitioning, subdivide, apply for zoning, rezoning, or other governmental permits, plat or consent to platting, develop, grant options concerning, lease, sublease, or otherwise dispose of, an interest in real property or a right incident to real property.

(c) Release, assign, satisfy, and enforce by litigation or otherwise, a mortgage, deed of trust, encumbrance, lien, or other claim to real property which exists or is asserted.

(d) Do any act of management or of conservation with respect to an interest in real property, or a right incident to real property, owned, or claimed to be owned, by the principal, including all of the following:

(1) Insuring against a casualty, liability, or loss.

(2) Obtaining or regaining possession, or protecting the interest or right, by litigation or otherwise.

(3) Paying, compromising, or contesting taxes or assessments, or applying for and receiving refunds in connection with them.

(4) Purchasing supplies, hiring assistance or labor, and making repairs or alterations in the real property.

(e) Use, develop, alter, replace, remove, erect, or install structures or other improvements upon real property in or incident to which the principal has, or claims to have, an interest or right.

(f) Participate in a reorganization with respect to real property or a legal entity that owns an interest in or right incident to real property and receive and hold shares of stock or obligations received in a plan of reorganization, and act with respect to them, including all of the following:

(1) Selling or otherwise disposing of them.

(2) Exercising or selling an option, conversion, or similar right with respect to them.

(3) Voting them in person or by proxy.

(g) Change the form of title of an interest in or right incident to real property.

(h) Dedicate to public use, with or without consideration, easements or other real property in which the principal has, or claims to have, an interest or right.

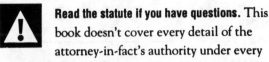 **Read the statute if you have questions.** This book doesn't cover every detail of the attorney-in-fact's authority under every state's law. If you need to know whether or not your attorney-in-fact can take a specific action on your behalf, read your state's statutes. Citations to the statutes are on the form. (Chapter 9, *Lawyers and Legal Research*, explains how to find your state's statutes in a law library.)

A.   What Form To Use

The state-specific forms aren't mandatory; you can use the Nolo form in Chapter 5 if you decide that it better suits your needs. But if you stick to the familiar official language, banks, brokers, title companies and others your attorney-in-fact will deal with are less likely to object to the legality of your form.

If your bank or brokerage house has its own durable power of attorney form, you may also want to use that form in addition to one of the general forms in this book. (See Chapter 5, Section A.)

B.   Modifying a State-Specific Form

Unfortunately, most of the state forms don't cover a number of issues that the Nolo form does. For example, some of them don't even provide a place to indicate that you don't want the durable power of attorney to take effect unless you become incapacitated (a "springing" power of attorney).

You can, however, add clauses to a state-specific form, as long as you don't contradict any of the preprinted language on the form. The instructions for each state's form list important clauses that aren't included in the state form. The most important ones, which you should consider adding to your form, have a checkmark next to them. You can copy the clauses from the Nolo power of

attorney in Chapter 5 and type them on your state's form.

We have left space on each state-specific form for adding such extra instructions. If you want to make substantial modifications to a form and you run out of room, you have three choices:

- Type the entire form over. If you do this, you must be extremely careful to TYPE ALL WARNINGS WORD-FOR-WORD AND EXACTLY AS THEY APPEAR ON THE FORM, IN CAPITAL LETTERS OR BOLDFACE TYPE. If you don't, your power of attorney might be invalid.
- Type the extra information on a sheet labeled "attachment" and staple it to the power of attorney. An example is shown below. You must refer to the attachment on the power of attorney form itself, by typing "see attachment." The attachment should be signed and notarized.
- Use the Nolo form in Chapter 5 instead of the state-specific form.

SAMPLE ATTACHMENT PAGE

Attachment 1

<u>Alternate Attorney-in-Fact</u>. If the person (or all of those persons, if more than one is named) named in this document to serve as attorney-in-fact does not serve or ceases to serve as attorney-in-fact, I appoint Andrew L. Duong to serve as attorney-in-fact.

<u>Effective Date and Determination of Incapacity</u>. This power of attorney is effective only if I become incapacitated or disabled and unable to manage my financial affairs.

For purposes of this durable power of attorney, my incapacity or disability shall be determined by written declaration by a licensed physician. The declaration shall be made under penalty of perjury and shall state that in the physician's opinion I am substantially unable to manage my financial affairs. If possible, the declaration shall be made by Dr. Elizabeth Walton. No licensed physician shall be liable to me for any actions taken under this part which are done in good faith.

Zoë M. Osterman

State of ___California___)
) ss.
County of ___Alameda___   )

On ___March 17___, 19_93_, before me, ___Emma P. Quinn___, a notary public, personally appeared ___Zoe M. Osterman___, personally known to me or proved to me on the basis of satisfactory evidence to be the person whose name is subscribed to this instrument, and acknowledged that he or she executed it.

[NOTARY SEAL]   _Emma P. Quinn_____
                          signature of notary public

C.   How To Fill Out the Form

It's not hard to prepare a durable power of attorney correctly, but it's important to follow the instructions carefully. If you don't, and your attorney-in-fact can't get a bank, title company, insurance company or government agency to accept his or her authority, you will have wasted your effort and opened up the possibility of court proceedings. Remember, if you become incapacitated, you won't be able to fix the document.

Follow these steps:

1. **Make copies of the blank form.** Tear out the form you want to use and make a few extra copies. You can use a copy for drafts and save a clean one for the final document—the one you will sign and have notarized.

2. **Type the document.** It's not a legal requirement that a durable power of attorney be typed, but your attorney-in-fact is much less likely to run into trouble if it is. People expect legal documents to be typed and may be suspicious of handwritten ones.

3. **Don't erase anything.** Your final form should not contain any words that have been erased or whited-out. If the instructions tell you to cross out something, type a string of x's through the words.

 Get help if you need it. A durable power of attorney can transfer tremendous power either now or, in the case of a springing durable power of attorney, possibly sometime in the future. Even though you can revoke it at any time (as long as you are mentally competent), never create a durable power of attorney unless you thoroughly understand the authority you plan to transfer. If you have questions, see an expert.

The state-specific power of attorney forms are very similar to the Nolo form in Chapter 5. To avoid repeating information unnecessarily, the instructions in this chapter contain state-specific information but refer to sections of Chapter 5 for basic instructions. You may also want to refer to earlier chapters as you make the choices that are necessary to fill out your durable power. At the beginning of the instructions for each item, look for this icon:

 Next to it will be the name of the chapter that discusses the topic in more detail.

D.   Alaska

Alaska's short form truly is short and easy to fill out. A completed sample is shown below.

Attorney-in-Fact

 Chapter 5, Section C, Part 1.
Chapter 3, *Choosing Your Attorney-in-Fact*.

In the first two blanks on the form, type your name and address. In the next blank, type in the name and address of the person (or persons) you've chosen and who has agreed to serve as your attorney-in-fact for finances. (You can name an alternate attorney-in-fact later in the form.)

Choosing your attorney-in-fact is the most important decision you make when preparing your durable power of attorney.

Powers

Chapter 4, *The Attorney-in-Fact's Responsibilities*, Section B.

Next, decide what powers to give your attorney-in-fact. You must choose from the list of powers on the form.

- If you, like most people, want to give your attorney-in-fact every power on the list, you don't need to do anything in this section. All powers are granted unless you indicate otherwise.

- If you don't want to grant some of the powers, draw a line through each one you don't want and write your initials in the parentheses at the end of the line. (This is the opposite of the way it's done on the Nolo form in Chapter 5, where you must initial each power that you *do* want the attorney-in-fact to have.)

Most of the powers are explained in Chapter 4, *The Attorney-in-Fact's Responsibilities.* ("Personal relationships and affairs" on the Alaska form corresponds to "personal and family maintenance" in Chapter 4. "Records, reports, and statements" grants the powers given under "Tax matters" on the Nolo form and also gives your attorney-in-fact authority to file documents required by the Social Security Administration or other similar government agency. "Delegation (N)" is covered in Part 3 of the Nolo form; see Chapter 5.)

One power on the Alaska form, however, doesn't appear on the Nolo form:

Health care services (L). We don't recommend it, but you can give your attorney-in-fact the authority to consent to or refuse medical care for you. (This does not give your attorney-in-fact authority to authorize termination of life-sustaining procedures.) But it's usually better to cover your medical and financial matters in separate documents. (See Chapter 1, *Using a Durable Power of Attorney,* Section D.)

If you want to give your attorney-in-fact this authority, Alaska law states that you should add other language, stating whether or not you have also signed a living will, to your durable power of attorney. You can look up the language in the Alaska statutes. (Alaska Stat. § 13.26.335.)

Authority of More Than One Attorney-in-Fact

 Chapter 3, *Choosing Your Attorney-in-Fact,* Section D.

If you named more than one person to serve as attorney-in-fact or successor attorney-in-fact, you must state whether or not you want to allow each one to act separately (independently) on your behalf (the first option listed). If you require them to act jointly (the second option), each attorney-in-fact will have to sign all documents and approve all decisions made on your behalf.

Effective Date

 Chapter 2, *How Durable Powers of Attorney Work,* Section B.

Indicate when you want the durable power of attorney to go into effect: as soon as you sign it, or only if you become incapacitated (a springing durable power). In Alaska, affidavits (notarized statements) from two physicians are required for a springing durable power of attorney to go into effect. You must check one of the choices. If you're not sure which you want, reread the discussion in Chapter 2.

If the power of attorney is to be effective immediately, also check the first choice in the next paragraph to make the power "durable"—that is, valid even if you later become incapacitated.

Termination Date

It's unusual, but you can specify a date that your durable power of attorney will terminate.

- If you want the power of attorney to continue until revocation or your death, leave this paragraph blank.
- If you want the power of attorney to end on a certain date, enter that date in the appropriate paragraph.

Alternate Attorneys-in-Fact

Chapter 3, *Choosing Your Attorney-in-Fact*.

It's a good idea to name an alternate attorney-in-fact to take over if your first choice cannot serve.

Nomination of Conservator or Guardian

Chapter 2, *How Durable Powers of Attorney Work*, Section G.

In this part of the form, you can ask the court to appoint your attorney-in-fact as your conservator, in the unlikely event the issue ever arises. The court must follow your recommendation unless there is a good reason not to.

- If you want to do this, type the name of your attorney-in-fact in the appropriate sentence.

Additional Clauses

Here you can add clauses to customize your durable power. (See Section B, above.) The list below shows the clauses you should consider copying from the Nolo form in Chapter 5 and adding to the Alaska form. The Part number after the name of each clause shows you where to find it in the Nolo form.

Notices

The rest of the form (Notice of Revocation and Notice to Third Parties) states that you can revoke the power of attorney at any time. It also reassures people and institutions your attorney-in-fact will deal with that the attorney-in-fact really does have legal authority to act for you.

CLAUSES NOT INCLUDED IN THE ALASKA SHORT FORM

Determination of Incapacity (Part 5)
Compensation and Reimbursement of Attorney-in-Fact (Part 8)
Personal Benefit by Attorney-in-Fact (Part 10)
Commingling by Attorney-in-Fact (Part 11)
Liability of Attorney-in-Fact (Part 13)
Gifts to Attorney-in-Fact (Part 14)

Signature and Notarization

Sign the power of attorney in the presence of a notary public. Instructions are in Chapter 7, *Making It Legal*.

ALASKA GENERAL POWER OF ATTORNEY

THE POWERS GRANTED FROM THE PRINCIPAL TO THE AGENT OR AGENTS IN THE FOLLOWING DOCUMENT ARE VERY BROAD. THEY MAY INCLUDE THE POWER TO DISPOSE, SELL, CONVEY, AND ENCUMBER YOUR REAL AND PERSONAL PROPERTY, AND THE POWER TO MAKE YOUR HEALTH CARE DECISIONS. ACCORDINGLY, THE FOLLOWING DOCUMENT SHOULD ONLY BE USED AFTER CAREFUL CONSIDERATION. IF YOU HAVE ANY QUESTIONS ABOUT THIS DOCUMENT, YOU SHOULD SEEK COMPETENT ADVICE.

YOU MAY REVOKE THIS POWER OF ATTORNEY AT ANY TIME.

Pursuant to AS 13.26.338—13.26.353, I, _Conrad S. Garcia_ (Name of principal), of _83 Baranoff Lane, Anchorage, AK_ (Address of principal), do hereby appoint _Ramona M. Garcia, 83 Baranoff Ln, Anchorage_ (Name and address of agent or agents), my attorney(s)-in-fact to act as I have checked below in my name, place, and stead in any way which I myself could do, if I were personally present, with respect to the following matters, as each of them is defined in AS 13.26.344, to the full extent that I am permitted by law to act through an agent:

THE AGENT OR AGENTS YOU HAVE APPOINTED WILL HAVE ALL THE POWERS LISTED BELOW UNLESS YOU DRAW A LINE THROUGH A CATEGORY; AND INITIAL THE BOX OPPOSITE THAT CATEGORY.

(A)   real estate transactions .... (   )
(B)   transactions involving tangible personal property, chattels, and goods .... (   )
(C)   bonds, shares, and commodities transactions .... (   )
(D)   banking transactions .... (   )
(E)   business operating transactions .... (   )
(F)   insurance transactions .... (   )
(G)   estate transactions .... (   )
(H)   gift transactions .... (   )
(I)   claims and litigation .... (   )
(J)   personal relationships and affairs .... (   )
(K)   benefits from government programs and military service .... (   )
~~(L)~~   health care ~~services~~ .... (CSG)
(M)   records, reports, and statements .... (   )
(N)   delegation .... (   )
(O)   all other matters, including those specified as follows: .... (   )

_____

_____

IF YOU HAVE APPOINTED MORE THAN ONE AGENT, CHECK ONE OF THE FOLLOWING:

(   )   Each agent may exercise the powers conferred separately, without the consent of any other agent.

(   )   All agents shall exercise the powers conferred jointly, with the consent of all other agents.

TO INDICATE WHEN THIS DOCUMENT SHALL BECOME EFFECTIVE, CHECK ONE OF THE FOLLOWING:

(x)   This document shall become effective upon the date of my signature.

(   )   This document shall become effective upon the date of my disability and shall not otherwise be affected by my disability.

IF YOU HAVE INDICATED THAT THIS DOCUMENT SHALL BECOME EFFECTIVE ON THE DATE OF YOUR SIGNATURE, CHECK ONE OF THE FOLLOWING:

Page 1

(x) This document shall not be affected by my subsequent disability.

(   ) This document shall be revoked by my subsequent disability.

IF YOU HAVE INDICATED THAT THIS DOCUMENT SHALL BECOME EFFECTIVE UPON THE DATE OF YOUR SIGNATURE AND WANT TO LIMIT THE TERM OF THIS DOCUMENT, COMPLETE THE FOLLOWING:

This document shall only continue in effect for _____ (   ) years from the date of my signature.

YOU MAY DESIGNATE AN ALTERNATE ATTORNEY-IN-FACT. ANY ALTERNATE YOU DESIGNATE WILL BE ABLE TO EXERCISE THE SAME POWERS AS THE AGENT(S) YOU NAMED AT THE BEGINNING OF THIS DOCUMENT. IF YOU WISH TO DESIGNATE AN ALTERNATE OR ALTERNATES, COMPLETE THE FOLLOWING:

If the agent(s) named at the beginning of this document is unable or unwilling to serve or continue to serve, then I appoint the following agent to serve with the same powers:

First alternate or successor atttorney-in-fact:____Paul J. Johnson, Fairbanks____.
(Name and address of alternate)

Second alternate or successor atttorney-in-fact:_____.
(Name and address of alternate)

YOU MAY NOMINATE A GUARDIAN OR CONSERVATOR. IF YOU WISH TO NOMINATE A GUARDIAN OR CONSERVATOR, COMPLETE THE FOLLOWING:

In the event that a court decides that it is necessary to appoint a guardian or conservator for me, I hereby nominate _Ramona M. Garcia, Anchorage_ (name and address of person) to be considered by the court for appointment to serve as my guardian or conservator, or in any similar representative capacity.

_____

_____

_____

NOTICE OF REVOCATION OF THE POWERS GRANTED IN THIS DOCUMENT.

You may revoke one or more of the powers granted in this document. Unless otherwise provided in this document, you may revoke a specific power granted in this power of attorney by completing a special power of attorney that includes the specific power in this document that you want to revoke. Unless otherwise provided in this document, you may revoke all the powers granted in this power of attorney by completing a subsequent power of attorney.

NOTICE TO THIRD PARTIES

A third party who relies on the reasonable representations of an attorney-in-fact as to a matter relating to a power granted by a properly executed statutory power of attorney does not incur any liability to the principal or to the principal's heirs, assigns, or estate as a result of permitting the attorney-in-fact to exercise the authority granted by the power of attorney. A third party who fails to honor a properly executed statutory form power of attorney may be liable to the principal, the attorney-in-fact, the principal's heirs, assigns, or estate for a civil penalty, plus damages, costs, and fees associated with the failure to comply with the statutory form power of attorney. If the power of attorney is one which becomes effective upon the disability of the principal, the disability of the principal is established by an affidavit, as required by law.

IN WITNESS WHEREOF, I have hereunto signed my name this ____27th____ day of ____October____, 1992.

_____
Signature of Principal

Subscribed and sworn to or affirmed before me at __Anchorage, Alaska__
on __October 27, 1992__   _____
Signature of Officer or Notary

Page 2

E. California

The California short form contains its own instructions and is fairly straightforward. A completed sample is shown below.

Attorney-in-Fact

 Chapter 5, Section C, Part 1.

In the first blank on the form, type your name and address. In the next blank, type the name and address of the person (or persons) you've chosen and who has agreed to serve as your attorney-in-fact for finances.

Chapter 3, *Choosing Your Attorney-in-Fact*, discusses how to pick an attorney-in-fact. It's the most important decision you make when preparing your durable power of attorney.

Powers

 Chapter 4, *The Attorney-in-Fact's Responsibilities*, Section B.

Next, decide what powers to give your attorney-in-fact. You must choose from the list of powers on the form.

- If you, like most people, want to give your attorney-in-fact every power on the list, initial the blank in front of line (N).
- If you want to give only some powers, initial the blank in front of each power you want to grant. You can cross out the others, but it's not required.

Special Instructions

Here you can add clauses to customize your durable power. (See Section B, above.) The list below shows the clauses you should consider copying from the Nolo form in Chapter 5 and adding to the California short form. The Part number after the name of each clause shows you where to find it in the Nolo form.

The most important of these are the first two. It's always a good idea to name an alternate attorney-in-fact. And you must include the clause in Part 4 if you want a springing durable power of attorney. Unless you add it, your durable power of attorney will take effect as soon as you sign it.

CLAUSES NOT INCLUDED IN THE CALIFORNIA SHORT FORM

✓ Alternate Attorney-in-Fact (Part 1)

✓ Effective Date (Part 4)

Determination of Incapacity (Part 5)

Compensation and Reimbursement of Attorney-in-Fact (Part 8)

Nomination of Conservator or Guardian (Part 9)

Personal Benefit by Attorney-in-Fact (Part 10)

Commingling by Attorney-in-Fact (Part 11)

Liability of Attorney-in-Fact (Part 13)

Gifts to Attorney-in-Fact (Part 14)

Exercise of Power of Attorney Where More Than One Agent Designated

 Chapter 5, Section C, Part 2.

If you named more than one person to serve as attorney-in-fact, you must state whether or not you want to allow each one to act separately (independently) on your behalf.

- If you do, type "separately" in the blank.
- If you want them to act jointly, type "jointly" in the blank. Each attorney-in-fact will have to sign all documents and approve all decisions made on your behalf.

Reliance of Third Parties

 Chapter 5, Section C, Part 15.

This clause tells a third party that it's safe to rely on the attorney-in-fact's authority when shown a copy of the durable power.

Certificate of Acknowledgement

Sign the power of attorney in the presence of a notary public. Instructions are in Chapter 7, *Making It Legal.*

Attorney-in-Fact's Acceptance of Responsibility

The sentence at the bottom of the form means that if your attorney-in-fact exercises any authority under the power of attorney, he or she must act as your "fiduciary." A fiduciary must always act in your best interests. (See Chapter 4, *The Attorney-in-Fact's Responsibilities,* Section A.)

CALIFORNIA UNIFORM STATUTORY FORM POWER OF ATTORNEY
(California Civil Code § 2475)

NOTICE: THE POWERS GRANTED BY THIS DOCUMENT ARE BROAD AND SWEEPING. THEY ARE EXPLAINED IN THE UNIFORM STATUTORY FORM POWER OF ATTORNEY ACT (CALIFORNIA CIVIL CODE SECTIONS 2475-2499.5, INCLUSIVE). IF YOU HAVE ANY QUESTIONS ABOUT THESE POWERS, OBTAIN COMPETENT LEGAL ADVICE. THIS DOCUMENT DOES NOT AUTHORIZE ANY-ONE TO MAKE MEDICAL AND OTHER HEALTH CARE DECISIONS FOR YOU. YOU MAY REVOKE THIS POWER OF ATTORNEY IF YOU LATER WISH TO DO SO.

I, _Lillian L. Woo, 8892 Grant St., Sacramento, CA_

_____ [your name and address] appoint _Robert M. Woo, 8892 Grant St., Sacramento, CA_

_____ [name and address of the person appointed, or of each person appointed if you want to designate more than one] as my agent (attorney-in-fact) to act for me in any lawful way with respect to the following initialed subjects:

TO GRANT ALL OF THE FOLLOWING POWERS, INITIAL THE LINE IN FRONT OF (N) AND IGNORE THE LINES IN FRONT OF THE OTHER POWERS.

TO GRANT ONE OR MORE, BUT FEWER THAN ALL, OF THE FOLLOWING POWERS, INITIAL THE LINE IN FRONT OF EACH POWER YOU ARE GRANTING.

TO WITHHOLD A POWER, DO NOT INITIAL THE LINE IN FRONT OF IT. YOU MAY, BUT NEED NOT, CROSS OUT EACH POWER WITHHELD.

INITIAL

_____ (A) Real property transactions.

_____ (B) Tangible personal property transactions.

_____ (C) Stock and bond transactions.

_____ (D) Commodity and option transactions.

_____ (E) Banking and other financial institution transactions.

_____ (F) Business operating transactions.

_____ (G) Insurance and annuity transactions.

_____ (H) Estate, trust, and other beneficiary transactions.

_____ (I) Claims and litigation.

_____ (J) Personal and family maintenance.

_____ (K) Benefits from social security, medicare, medicaid, or other governmental pro-grams, or civil or military service.

_____ (L) Retirement plan transactions.

_____ (M) Tax matters.

LLW (N) ALL OF THE POWERS LISTED ABOVE.

YOU NEED NOT INITIAL ANY OTHER LINES IF YOU INITIAL LINE (N).

SPECIAL INSTRUCTIONS:

ON THE FOLLOWING LINES YOU MAY GIVE SPECIAL INSTRUCTIONS LIMITING OR EXTENDING THE POWERS GRANTED TO YOUR AGENT. _____

Page 1

<u>If Robert M. Woo does not or ceases to serve as attorney-in-fact, I</u>
<u>appoint Elaine P. Woo to serve as attorney-in-fact.</u>

UNLESS YOU DIRECT OTHERWISE ABOVE, THIS POWER OF ATTORNEY IS EFFEC-TIVE IMMEDIATELY AND WILL CONTINUE UNTIL IT IS REVOKED.

This power of attorney will continue to be effective even though I become incapacitated.

STRIKE THE PRECEDING SENTENCE IF YOU DO NOT WANT THIS POWER OF ATTORNEY TO CONTINUE IF YOU BECOME INCAPACITATED.

EXERCISE OF POWER OF ATTORNEY WHERE
MORE THAN ONE AGENT DESIGNATED

If I have designated more than one agent, the agents are to act _____.
IF YOU APPOINTED MORE THAN ONE AGENT AND YOU WANT EACH AGENT TO BE ABLE TO ACT ALONE WITHOUT THE OTHER AGENT JOINING, WRITE THE WORD "SEPARATELY" IN THE BLANK SPACE ABOVE. IF YOU DO NOT INSERT ANY WORD IN THE BLANK SPACE, OR IF YOU INSERT THE WORD "JOINTLY," THEN ALL OF YOUR AGENTS MUST ACT OR SIGN TOGETHER.

I agree that any third party who receives a copy of this document may act under it. Revocation of the power of attorney is not effective as to a third party until the third party has actual knowledge of the revocation. I agree to indemnify the third party for any claims that arise against the third party because of reliance on this power of attorney.

Signed this ___16th___ day of ___September___, 19_92_

___Lillian L Woo___   ___343-54-1291___
           (your signature)   (your social security number)

State of ___California___, County of ___Sacramento___,

CERTIFICATE OF ACKNOWLEDGEMENT OF NOTARY PUBLIC

State of California
County of ___Sacramento___   } ss

On this _17th_ day of _September_, 19_92_ before me, ___Julia O'Hara___,
(name of notary public) personally appeared ___Lillian L. Woo___, (name of principal)
personally known to me (or proved to me on the basis of satisfactory evidence) to be the person whose name is subscribed to this instrument, and acknowledged that he or she executed it.

[NOTARY SEAL]   ___Julia O'Hara___
                              (signature of notary public)

BY ACCEPTING OR ACTING UNDER THE APPOINTMENT, THE AGENT ASSUMES THE FIDUCIARY AND OTHER LEGAL RESPONSIBILITIES OF AN AGENT.

Page 2

F. Colorado

Colorado's short form truly is short and easy to fill out. A completed sample is shown below.

Attorney-in-Fact

Chapter 5, Section C, Part 1.
Chapter 3, *Choosing Your Attorney-in-Fact*.

In the first blank on the form, type your name and address. In the next blank, type in the name and address of the person (or persons) you've chosen and who has agreed to serve as your attorney-in-fact for finances.

Choosing your attorney-in-fact is the most important decision you make when preparing your durable power of attorney.

Powers

Chapter 4, The Attorney-in-Fact's Responsibilities, Section B.

Next, decide what powers to give your attorney-in-fact. You must choose from the list of powers on the form.

• If you, like most people, want to give your attorney-in-fact every power on the list, initial all the powers.

• If you don't want to grant some of the powers, don't initial the ones you don't want, and draw a line through them.

The powers are explained in Chapter 4, *The Attorney-in-Fact's Responsibilities*.

Special Instructions

Here you can add clauses to customize your durable power. (See Section B, above.) The list below shows the clauses you should consider copying from the Nolo form in Chapter 5 and adding to the Colorado form. The Part number after the name of each clause shows you where to find it in the Nolo form.

The most important of these are the first two. It's always a good idea to name an alternate attorney-in-fact. And you must include the clause in Part 4 if you want a springing durable power of attorney. Unless you add it, your durable power of attorney will take effect as soon as you sign it.

CLAUSES NOT INCLUDED IN THE COLORADO SHORT FORM

✓ Alternate Attorney-in-Fact (Part 1)

✓ Effective Date (Part 4)

Determination of Incapacity (Part 5)

Compensation and Reimbursement of Attorney-in-Fact (Part 8)

Nomination of Conservator or Guardian (Part 9)

Personal Benefit to Attorney-in-Fact (Part 10)

Commingling by Attorney-in-Fact (Part 11)

Liability of Attorney-in-Fact (Part 13)

Gifts by Attorney-in-Fact (Part 14)

Notices

The rest of the form reassures people and institutions your attorney-in-fact will deal with that the attorney-in-fact really does have legal authority to act for you.

Signature and Notarization

You must sign the power of attorney in the presence of a notary public. Instructions are in Chapter 7, *Making It Legal.*

COLORADO STATUTORY POWER OF ATTORNEY

Notice: The powers granted by this document are broad and sweeping. They are explained in the Uniform Statutory Power of Attorney Act. If you have any questions about these powers, obtain competent legal advice. This document does not authorize anyone to make medical and other health-care decisions for you. You may revoke this power of attorney if you later wish to do so.

You may have other rights or powers under Colorado law not contained in this form.

I, _____Jonathon S. Campbell, 6641 Boulder Dr., Arvada, CO_____, (insert your name and address) appoint _Suzanne M. Campbell, 6641 Boulder Dr._ _Arvada, CO_____ (insert the name and address of the person appointed) as my agent (attorney-in-fact) to act for me in any lawful way with respect to the following initialed subjects:

To grant one or more of the following powers, initial the line in front of each power you are granting.

To withhold a power, do not initial the line in front of it. You may, but need not, cross out each power withheld.

Initial

JSC (A) Real estate transactions (when properly recorded).

JSC (B) Tangible personal property transactions.

JSC (C) Stock and bond transactions.

JSC (D) Commodity and option transactions.

JSC (E) Banking and other financial institution transactions.

_____ (F) Business operating transactions.

JSC (G) Insurance and annuity transactions.

JSC (H) Estate, trust and other beneficiary transactions.

JSC (I) Claims and litigation.

JSC (J) Personal and family maintenance.

JSC (K) Benefits from social security, medicare, medicaid, or other governmental programs, or military service.

JSC (L) Retirement plan transactions.

JSC (M) Tax matters.

SPECIAL INSTRUCTIONS

On the following lines you may give special instructions limiting or extending the powers granted to your agent.

This power of attorney is effective only if I become incapacitated or disabled and unable to manage my financial affairs. For purposes of this durable power of attorney, my incapacity or disability shall be determined by written declaration by a licensed physician. The declaration shall be made under penalty of perjury and shall state that in the physician's opinion I am substantially

unable to manage my financial affairs. If possible, the declaration

shall be made by Dr. Hannah A. Baldwin. No licensed physician shall be

liable to me for any action taken under this part which are done in

good faith.

_____

_____

Unless you direct otherwise above, this power of attorney is effective immediately and will continue until it is revoked.

This power of attorney will continue to be effective even though I become disabled, incapacitated, or incompetent.

Strike and initial the preceding sentence if you do not want this power of attorney to continue if you become disabled, incapacitated, or incompetent.

I agree that any third party who receives a copy of this document may act under it. Revocation of the power of attorney is not effective as to a third party until the third party learns of the revocation. I agree to indemnify the third party for any claims that arise against the third party because of reliance on this power of attorney.

Signed this _22_ day of _June_, 19 _92_.

_____Jonathon S. Campbell_____
(Your signature)
_____629-42-1340_____
(Your social security number)

State of ____Colorado____

County of ____Denver____

This document was acknowledged before me on
_____June 2, 1992_____ (Date) by

____JONATHON S. CAMPBELL____
(Name of principal)
____Melissa H. Wong____
(Signature of notarial officer)
____Notary Public____
(Title (and rank))

(Seal, if any)

(My commission expires: _January 14, 1993_)

By accepting or acting under the appointment, the agent assumes the fiduciary and other legal responsibilities of an agent.

Page 2

G. Connecticut

The Connecticut short form power of attorney contains its own instructions and is for the most part self-explanatory. A completed sample is shown below.

Attorney-in-Fact

Chapter 3, *Choosing Your Attorney-in-Fact*. Chapter 5, Section C, Part 1.

In the first blank on the form, type your name and address. In the second blank, type in the name and address of the person (or persons) you've chosen and who has agreed to serve as your attorney-in-fact for finances.

Choosing your attorney-in-fact is the most important decision you make when preparing your durable power of attorney.

If you named more than one person to serve as attorney-in-fact or successor attorney-in-fact, you must next state whether or not you want to allow each one to act separately on your behalf.

- If you want to allow each attorney-in-fact to act independently, type "severally" in the blank at the end of the paragraph.
- If you want to require your attorneys-in-fact to act jointly, type "jointly" in the blank at the end of the paragraph. Each attorney-in-fact will have to sign all documents and approve all decisions made on your behalf.

Powers

Chapter 4, *The Attorney-in-Fact's Responsibilities*, Section B.

Next, decide what powers to give your attorney-in-fact. You must choose from the list of powers on the form. If you want to give your attorney-in-fact **every** power on the list, you don't need to do anything in this section. If you don't, draw a line through any power you don't want to grant and write your initials in the space after it. (This is the opposite of the Nolo form in Chapter 5, where you must initial each power that you *do* want the attorney-in-fact to have.)

Most of the powers are explained in Chapter 4. "Personal relationships and affairs" on the Connecticut form is equivalent to "personal and family maintenance" on the form in Chapter 5. "Records, reports, and statements" grants the powers given under "Tax matters" and also gives your attorney-in-fact authority to file documents required by the Social Security Administration or other similar government agency.

One power on the Connecticut form, however, doesn't appear on the Nolo form:

Health care decisions (L). We don't recommend it, but you can give your attorney-in-fact the authority to consent to or refuse medical care, including life support systems, for you. But it's usually better to cover your medical and financial matters in separate documents. (See Chapter 1, *Using a Durable Power of Attorney*, Section D.)

Additional Clauses

On the blank lines after the list of powers, you can add clauses to customize your durable power. (See Section B, above.) The list below shows the clauses you should consider copying from the Nolo form in Chapter 5 and adding to the Connecticut form. The Part number after the name of each clause shows you where to find it in the Nolo form.

The most important of these are the first two. It's always a good idea to name an alternate attorney-in-fact. And you must include the clause in Part 4 if you want a springing durable power of attorney. Unless you add it, your durable power of attorney will take effect as soon as you sign it.

CLAUSES NOT INCLUDED IN THE CONNECTICUT SHORT FORM

✓ Alternate Attorney-in-Fact (Part 1)

✓ Effective Date (Part 4)

  Determination of Incapacity (Part 5)

  Compensation and Reimbursement of Attorney-in-Fact (Part 8)

  Nomination of Conservator or Guardian (Part 9)

  Personal Benefit by Attorney-in-Fact (Part 10)

  Commingling by Attorney-in-Fact (Part 11)

  Liability of Attorney-in-Fact (Part 13)

  Gifts to Attorney-in-Fact (Part 14)

Delegation

 Chapter 5, Section C, Part 3.

This allows your attorney-in-fact to delegate any or all of his or her responsibilities to someone else.

Signature and Notarization

In Connecticut, you must have two witnesses watch you sign your durable power of attorney. Sign the power of attorney in the presence of the witnesses and a notary public, who will fill out the "Acknowledgement" at the bottom of the form. Instructions are in Chapter 7, *Making It Legal*.

CONNECTICUT STATUTORY SHORT FORM DURABLE POWER OF ATTORNEY

Notice: The powers granted by this document are broad and sweeping. They are defined in Connecticut Statutory Short Form Power of Attorney Act, sections 1-42 to 1-56, inclusive, of the general statutes, which expressly permits the use of any other or different form of power of attorney desired by the parties concerned.

Know All Men by These Presents, which are intended to constitute a GENERAL POWER OF ATTORNEY pursuant to Connecticut Statutory Short Form Power of Attorney Act:

That I _Grace E. Laforge, 992 W. Griswold Ave., Hartford, CN_

(insert name and address of the principal) do hereby appoint _Evelyn L. Keeler,_

1803 N. 6th Street, Hartford, CN (insert name and address of the agent, or each agent, if more than one is designated) my attorney(s)-in-fact TO ACT _____.

If more than one agent is designated and the principal wishes each agent alone to be able to exercise the power conferred, insert in this blank the word 'severally'. Failure to make any insertion or the insertion of the word 'jointly' shall require the agents to act jointly.

First: In my name, place and stead in any way which I myself could do, if I were personally present, with respect to the following matters as each of them is defined in the Connecticut Statutory Short Form Power of Attorney Act to the extent that I am permitted by law to act through an agent:

(Strike out and initial in the opposite box any one or more of the subdivisions as to which the principal does NOT desire to give the agent authority. Such elimination of any one or more of subdivisions (A) to (L), inclusive, shall automatically constitute an elimination also of subdivision (M).)

To strike out any subdivision the principal must draw a line through the text of that subdivision AND write his initials in the box opposite.

(A) real estate transactions; ....( )
(B) chattel and goods transactions; ....( )
(C) bond, share and commodity transactions; ....( )
(D) banking transactions; ....( )
(E) business operating transactions; ....( )
(F) insurance transactions; ....( )
(G) estate transactions; ....( )
(H) claims and litigation; ....( )
(I) personal relationships and affairs; ....( )
(J) benefits from military service; ....( )
(K) records, reports and statements; ....( )
(L) ~~health care decisions;~~ ....*(G.E.L)*
(M) all other matters; ....( )

_____

_____

_____

_____

_____

Page 1

If Evelyn L. Keeler does not or ceases to serve as attorney-in-fact, I nominate Richard Keeler, 87 Pine St., Greenwich, CN, to serve as attorney-in-fact.

This power of attorney is effective immediately.

(Special provisions and limitations may be included in the statutory short form power of attorney only if they conform to the requirements of the Connecticut Statutory Short Form Power of Attorney Act.)

Second: With full and unqualified authority to delegate any or all of the foregoing powers to any person or persons whom my attorney(s)-in-fact shall select;

Third: Hereby ratifying and confirming all that said attorney(s) or substitute(s) do or cause to be done.

In Witness Whereof I have hereunto signed my name and affixed my seal this _____23d_____ day of ____March_____, 19_92_.

_____Grace E. Laforge_____ (Signature of Principal) (Seal)

On the date written above, _____Grace E. Laforge_____ declared to us that this instrument was [his/her] durable power of attorney, and requested us to act as witnesses to it. [He/She] signed it in our presence, all of us being present at the same time. We now sign this instrument as witnesses.

_____Hunter Ricard_____, Witness   _____Hartford, Hartford County_____
witness signature   city and county

_____Dana Marie Davidson_____, Witness   _____Hartford, Hartford County_____
witness signature   city and county

ACKNOWLEDGMENT

State of _____CONNECTICUT_____ }
County of _____HARTFORD_____ } ss

On _____MARCH 25_____, 19_92_, before me, _____ROSEMARY SHAPIRO_____ _____, a notary public for the State of _____CONNECTICUT_____, personally appeared _____GRACE E. LAFORGE_____,

personally known to me or proved to me on the basis of satisfactory evidence to be the person whose name is subscribed to this instrument, and acknowledged that he or she executed it.

_____Rosemary Shapiro_____
signature of notary public

[NOTARY SEAL]

My commission expires: _____February 1, 1993_____

Page 2

H.   Illinois

The Illinois short form durable power of attorney contains its own instructions and is for the most part self-explanatory. A completed sample is shown below.

First, after you've read all the warnings at the top of the form, enter the date.

Part 1: Attorney-in-Fact and Powers

 Chapter 5, Section C, Part 1.
Chapter 3, *Choosing Your Attorney-in-Fact*.
Chapter 4, *The Attorney-in-Fact's Responsibilities*, Section B.

Type your name and address in the first blank. In the second blank, type the name and address of the person you've chosen and who has agreed to serve as your attorney-in-fact for finances. The Illinois short form allows you to choose only one person. You can,

however, choose an alternate attorney-in-fact in Part 8, below.

Choosing your attorney-in-fact is the most important decision you make when preparing your durable power of attorney.

In the next part of the form, indicate the powers you want your attorney-in-fact to have. Each of the powers on the list is explained in Chapter 4; the complete text of the attorney-in-fact's powers, from the Illinois statute, is included on the back of the form.

• If, like most people, you want to give your attorney-in-fact every power on the list, you don't need to do anything in this section. All powers are granted unless you indicate otherwise.

• If you don't want to grant some of the powers, cross them out. (This is the opposite of the way it's done on the Nolo form in Chapter 5, where you must initial each power that you *do* want the attorney-in-fact to have.)

Parts 2 and 3: Other Powers and Restrictions

Here, you may give your attorney-in-fact other powers or put restrictions on his or her authority. (See Section B, above.)

Part 4: Delegation

 Chapter 5, Section C, Part 3.

This clause gives your attorney-in-fact the power to delegate any or all of his or her responsibilities to someone else. If you don't want to grant this power, you must cross out the whole paragraph.

Part 5: Payment of the Attorney-in-Fact

 Chapter 5, Section C, Part 8.

This authorizes your attorney-in-fact to "reasonable" payment, from your assets, for his or her duties. If you decide you don't want or need the attorney-in-fact to be paid, you must cross out the paragraph.

Part 6: Effective Date

 Chapter 2, *How Durable Powers of Attorney Work*, Section B.

Here, you must specify whether you want your durable power of attorney to become effective as soon as you sign it, or only if you become incapacitated (a springing durable power). If you're not sure which you want, reread the discussion in Chapter 2.

- If you want the durable power to become effective immediately, enter the date you will sign the power of attorney and have your signature notarized.
- If you want it to take effect only if you become incapacitated, type this language:

        "my incapacity or disability."

Part 7: Termination Date

Most people will leave Part 7 blank. If, for some unusual reason, you don't want the durable power of attorney to last until your death, you may limit its duration. Just fill in the date.

Part 8: Successor Attorney-in-Fact

 Chapter 3, *Choosing Your Attorney-in-Fact*, Section F.

Here, enter the name and address of the person you want to take over as attorney-in-fact if your first choice (Part 1) can't serve. If you list more than one person (called a "successor agent" in the legalese the form uses), they will take over one at a time, in the order you list them.

Part 9: Nomination of Conservator

 Chapter 2, *How Durable Powers of Attorney Work*, Section G.

In this part of the form, you can ask the court to appoint your attorney-in-fact as the guardian of your estate, in the unlikely event the issue ever arises. The court must follow your recommendation unless there is a good reason not to.

If you don't want to do this, you must cross out the paragraph.

Additional Clauses

You can add clauses to customize your durable power. (See Section B, above.) The list below shows the clauses you should consider copying from the Nolo form in Chapter 5 and adding to the Illinois form. The Part number after the name of each clause shows you where to find it in the Nolo form.

CLAUSES NOT INCLUDED IN THE ILLINOIS SHORT FORM

Determination of Incapacity (Part 5)

Personal Benefit by Attorney-in-Fact (Part 10)

Commingling by Attorney-in-Fact (Part 11)

Liability of Attorney-in-Fact (Part 13)

Gifts to Attorney-in-Fact (Part 14)

Signature and Notarization

You must sign the form in the presence of a notary public; instructions are in Chapter 7, *Making It Legal*. The Illinois form also includes spaces for your attorney-in-fact's signature and that of any successor attorneys-in-fact you named, but they're not required; the purpose is to have the attorney-in-fact's signature on record so that people the attorney-in-fact deals with later can verify it.

At the very end of the form, after the notarization, there is a place to fill in the name of the person who prepared the form. You did it yourself, so put your own name.

ILLINOIS STATUTORY SHORT FORM POWER OF ATTORNEY FOR PROPERTY

(NOTICE: THE PURPOSE OF THIS POWER OF ATTORNEY IS TO GIVE THE PERSON YOU DESIGNATE (YOUR "AGENT") BROAD POWERS TO HANDLE YOUR PROPERTY, WHICH MAY INCLUDE POWERS TO PLEDGE, SELL OR OTHERWISE DISPOSE OF ANY REAL OR PERSONAL PROPERTY WITHOUT ADVANCE NOTICE TO YOU OR APPROVAL BY YOU. THIS FORM DOES NOT IMPOSE A DUTY ON YOUR AGENT TO EXERCISE GRANTED POWERS; BUT WHEN POWERS ARE EXERCISED, YOUR AGENT WILL HAVE TO USE DUE CARE TO ACT FOR YOUR BENEFIT AND IN ACCORDANCE WITH THIS FORM AND KEEP A RECORD OF RECEIPTS, DISBURSEMENTS AND SIGNIFICANT ACTIONS TAKEN AS AGENT. A COURT CAN TAKE AWAY THE POWERS OF YOUR AGENT IF IT FINDS THE AGENT IS NOT ACTING PROPERLY. YOU MAY NAME SUCCESSOR AGENTS UNDER THIS FORM BUT NOT CO-AGENTS. UNLESS YOU EXPRESSLY LIMIT THE DURATION OF THIS POWER IN THE MANNER PROVIDED BELOW, UNTIL YOU REVOKE THIS POWER OR A COURT ACTING ON YOUR BEHALF TERMINATES IT, YOUR AGENT MAY EXERCISE THE POWERS GIVEN HERE THROUGHOUT YOUR LIFETIME, EVEN AFTER YOU BECOME DISABLED. THE POWERS YOU GIVE YOUR AGENT ARE EXPLAINED MORE FULLY IN SECTION 3-4 OF THE ILLINOIS "STATUTORY SHORT FORM POWER OF ATTORNEY FOR PROPERTY LAW" OF WHICH THIS FORM IS A PART (SEE THE BACK OF THIS FORM). THAT LAW EXPRESSLY PERMITS THE USE OF ANY DIFFERENT FORM OF POWER OF ATTORNEY YOU MAY DESIRE. IF THERE IS ANYTHING ABOUT THIS FORM THAT YOU DO NOT UNDERSTAND, YOU SHOULD ASK A LAWYER TO EXPLAIN IT TO YOU.)

POWER OF ATTORNEY made this <u>15th</u> day of <u>October</u> (month) <u>1992</u> (year)

1. I, <u>Ruby Louise Staff, 3320 Jefferson St., Galesburg, IL</u>
<u> </u> (insert name and address of principal) hereby
appoint: <u>Anne Marie Colfax, 42 Lakewood Dr., Galesburg, IL</u>
<u> </u> (insert name and address of agent) as my attorney-in-fact (my "agent") to act
for me and in my name (in any way I could act in person) with respect to the following powers, as defined in
Section 3-4 of the "Statutory Short Form Power of Attorney for Property Law" (including all amendments),
but subject to any limitations on or additions to the specified powers inserted in paragraph 2 or 3 below:

(YOU MUST STRIKE OUT ANY ONE OR MORE OF THE FOLLOWING CATEGORIES OF POWERS YOU DO NOT WANT YOUR AGENT TO HAVE. FAILURE TO STRIKE THE TITLE OF ANY CATEGORY WILL CAUSE THE POWERS DESCRIBED IN THAT CATEGORY TO BE GRANTED TO THE AGENT. TO STRIKE OUT A CATEGORY YOU MUST DRAW A LINE THROUGH THE TITLE OF THAT CATEGORY.)

   (a) Real estate transactions.
   (b) Financial institution transactions.
   (c) Stock and bond transactions.
   (d) Tangible personal property transactions.

(e) Safe deposit box transactions.
(f) Insurance and annuity transactions.
(g) Retirement plan transactions.
(h) Social Security, employment and military service benefits.
(i) Tax matters.
(j) Claims and litigation.
(k) Commodity and option transactions.
(l) Business operations.
(m) Borrowing transactions.
(n) Estate transactions.
(o) All other property powers and transactions.

(LIMITATIONS ON AND ADDITIONS TO THE AGENT'S POWERS MAY BE INCLUDED IN THIS POWER OF ATTORNEY IF THEY ARE SPECIFICALLY DESCRIBED BELOW.)

2. The powers granted above shall not include the following powers or shall be modified or limited in the following particulars (here you may include any specific limitations you deem appropriate, such as a prohibition or conditions on the sale of particular stock or real estate or special rules on borrowing by the agent):

_____

_____

3. In addition to the powers granted above, I grant my agent the following powers (here you may add any other delegable powers including, without limitation, power to make gifts, exercise powers of appointment, name or change beneficiaries or joint tenants or revoke or amend any trust specifically referred to below):

_____

_____

YOUR AGENT WILL HAVE AUTHORITY TO EMPLOY OTHER PERSONS AS NECESSARY TO ENABLE THE AGENT TO PROPERLY EXERCISE THE POWERS GRANTED IN THIS FORM, BUT YOUR AGENT WILL HAVE TO MAKE ALL DISCRETIONARY DECISIONS. IF YOU WANT TO GIVE YOUR AGENT THE RIGHT TO DELEGATE DISCRETIONARY DECISION-MAKING POWERS TO OTHERS, YOU SHOULD KEEP THE NEXT SENTENCE, OTHERWISE IT SHOULD BE STRUCK OUT.)

4. My agent shall have the right by written instrument to delegate any or all of the foregoing powers involving discretionary decision-making to any person or persons whom my agent may select, but such delegation may be amended or revoked by any agent (including any successor) named by me who is acting under this power of attorney at the time of reference.

(YOUR AGENT WILL BE ENTITLED TO REIMBURSEMENT FOR ALL REASONABLE EXPENSES INCURRED IN ACTING UNDER THIS POWER OF ATTORNEY. STRIKE OUT THE NEXT SENTENCE IF YOU DO NOT WANT YOUR AGENT TO ALSO BE ENTITLED TO REASONABLE COMPENSATION FOR SERVICES AS AGENT.)

5. My agent shall be entitled to reasonable compensation for services rendered as agent under this power of attorney.

(THIS POWER OF ATTORNEY MAY BE AMENDED OR REVOKED BY YOU AT ANY TIME

Page 3

AND IN ANY MANNER. ABSENT AMENDMENT OR REVOCATION, THE AUTHORITY GRANTED IN THIS POWER OF ATTORNEY WILL BECOME EFFECTIVE AT THE TIME THIS POWER IS SIGNED AND WILL CONTINUE UNTIL YOUR DEATH UNLESS A LIMITATION ON THE BEGINNING DATE OR DURATION IS MADE BY INITIALING AND COMPLETING EITHER (OR BOTH) OF THE FOLLOWING:)

6. (   ) This power of attorney shall become effective on <u>my incapacity or dis-</u> <u>ability.</u> _____ (insert a future date or event during your lifetime, such as court determination of your disability, when you want this power to first take effect)

7. (   )This power of attorney shall terminate on _____ _____ (insert a future date or event, such as court determination of your disability, when you want this power to terminate prior to your death)

(IF YOU WISH TO NAME SUCCESSOR AGENTS, INSERT THE NAME(S) AND ADDRESS(ES) OF SUCH SUCCESSOR(S) IN THE FOLLOWING PARAGRAPH.)

8. If any agent named by me shall die, become incompetent, resign or refuse to accept the office of agent, I name the following (each to act alone and successively, in the order named) as successor(s) to such agent: <u>William A. Staff, Matthew C. Staff.</u> _____

For purposes of this paragraph 8, a person shall be considered to be incompetent if and while the person is a minor or an adjudicated incompetent or disabled person or the person is unable to give prompt and intelligent consideration to business matters, as certified by a licensed physician.

(IF YOU WISH TO NAME YOUR AGENT AS GUARDIAN OF YOUR ESTATE, IN THE EVENT A COURT DECIDES THAT ONE SHOULD BE APPOINTED, YOU MAY, BUT ARE NOT REQUIRED TO, DO SO BY RETAINING THE FOLLOWING PARAGRAPH. THE COURT WILL APPOINT YOUR AGENT IF THE COURT FINDS THAT SUCH APPOINTMENT WILL SERVE YOUR BEST INTERESTS AND WELFARE. STRIKE OUT PARAGRAPH 9 IF YOU DO NOT WANT YOUR AGENT TO ACT AS GUARDIAN.)

9. If a guardian of my estate (my property) is to be appointed, I nominate the agent acting under this power of attorney as such guardian, to serve without bond or security.

10. I am fully informed as to all the contents of this form and understand the full import of this grant of powers to my agent.

<u>For purposes of this power of attorney, my incapacity or disability</u> <u>shall be determined by a written declaration by a licensed physician,</u> <u>made under penalty of perjury. The declaration shall state that in the</u> <u>physician's opinion I am substantially unable to manage my financial</u> <u>affairs. If possible, the declaration shall be made by Dr. Benjamin</u> <u>Johnson. No licensed physician shall be liable to me for any action</u> <u>taken under this part which is done in good faith.</u>

Signed _<u>Ruby Louise Staff</u>_
(principal)

(YOU MAY, BUT ARE NOT REQUIRED TO, REQUEST YOUR AGENT AND SUCCESSOR AGENTS TO PROVIDE SPECIMEN SIGNATURES BELOW. IF YOU INCLUDE SPECIMEN SIGNATURES IN THIS POWER OF ATTORNEY, YOU MUST COMPLETE THE CERTIFI-CATION OPPOSITE THE SIGNATURES OF THE AGENTS.)

Specimen signatures of agent
(and successors)

Anne Marie O'Gay
(agent)

William A. Staff
(successor agent)

Matthew C. Staff
(successor agent)

I certify that the signatures of my
agent (and successors) are correct.

Ruby Louise Staff
(principal)

Ruby Louise Staff
(principal)

Ruby Louise Staff
(principal)

(THIS POWER OF ATTORNEY WILL NOT BE EFFECTIVE UNLESS IT IS NOTARIZED, USING THE FORM BELOW.)

State of ____Illinois____

County of ____Knox____ } ss

The undersigned, a notary public in and for the above county and state, certifies that _____
_____Ruby Louise Staff_____ , known
to me to be the same person whose name is subscribed as principal to the foregoing power of attorney, appeared before me in person and acknowledged signing and delivering the instrument as the free and voluntary act of the principal, for the uses and purposes therein set forth (, and certified to the correct-ness of the signature(s) of the agent(s)).

Dated: ____Oct. 15, 1992____ (SEAL)

____Eva T. Hegenberger____
Notary Public

My commission expires _Dec. 2, 1993_

(THE NAME AND ADDRESS OF THE PERSON PREPARING THIS FORM SHOULD BE INSERTED IF THE AGENT WILL HAVE POWER TO CONVEY ANY INTEREST IN REAL ESTATE.)

This document was prepared by: _Ruby Louise Staff_

Page 7

I. Indiana

Indiana doesn't have a fill-in-the-blanks form for durable powers of attorney, but its statutes do contain a list of powers that you can grant your attorney-in-fact. The Indiana form in this book incorporates those powers and other aspects of Indiana's law with respect to durable powers of attorney.

The form is almost identical to the general form in Chapter 5. To complete it, follow the instructions in Chapter 5 and these special notes:

Part 2. More Than One Attorney-in-Fact

Chapter 3, *Choosing Your Attorney-in-Fact*, Section D.

If you name more than one person to serve as attorney-in-fact and don't check any of the boxes in Part 2, each attorney-in-fact may act independently.

Part 6. Powers of Attorney-in-Fact

Chapter 4, *The Attorney-in-Fact's Responsibilities*, Section B.

Most of the powers listed on the Indiana form correspond to the powers explained in Chapter 4: "Records, reports, and statements" (item m) grants the powers given under "Tax matters" on the Nolo form and also gives your attorney-in-fact authority to file documents required by the Social Security Administration or other similar government agency.

Two powers don't directly correspond to the powers explained in Chapter 4:

Gift transactions (i). This authorizes the attorney-in-fact to make gifts to your spouse, children and other descendants, and organizations (charitable or otherwise) to which you've made gifts. The attorney-

in-fact may not give more than $10,000 in one year to himself or to anyone he has a legal obligation to support.

Fiduciary transactions (j). This formally acknowledges that the attorney-in-fact is a "fiduciary"—someone who has a legal responsibility to act in your best interests and has legal authority to sign all kinds of documents, such as checks, releases or waivers, on your behalf.

Part 8. Compensation of the Attorney-in-Fact

Chapter 4, *The Attorney-in-Fact's Responsibilities*, Section D.

If you don't check any of the boxes, your attorney-in-fact is entitled to reimbursement for all reasonable expenses and a reasonable fee for services rendered.

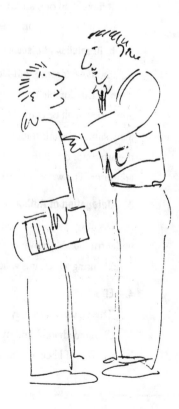

DURABLE POWER OF ATTORNEY FOR FINANCIAL MANAGEMENT: INDIANA

THE POWERS GRANTED BY THIS DOCUMENT ARE BROAD AND SWEEPING. IF YOU HAVE ANY QUESTIONS ABOUT THESE POWERS, GET COMPETENT LEGAL ADVICE.

THIS DOCUMENT DOES NOT AUTHORIZE ANYONE TO MAKE MEDICAL OR OTHER HEALTH CARE DECISIONS FOR YOU.

YOU MAY REVOKE THIS POWER OF ATTORNEY IF YOU LATER WISH TO DO SO.

1. Attorney-in-Fact

I, _Kurt Michael Schneider_ of _Indianapolis_, Indiana, appoint _Jean Nelson-Schneider_ _____ as my attorney-in-fact to act for me in any lawful way with respect to the powers delegated in Part 6 below. If that person (or all those persons, if more than one is named) does not serve or ceases to serve as attorney-in-fact, I appoint _____ to serve as attorney-in-fact.

2. More Than One Attorney-in-Fact

a. Authorization

If more than one attorney-in-fact is designated, they are authorized to act:

☐ jointly. ☐ independently.

b. Resolution of Disputes

☐ If my attorneys-in-fact cannot agree on a decision or action under the authority delegated to them in this durable power of attorney, that dispute shall be resolved by binding arbitration. The arbitration shall be carried out by a single arbitrator, who shall be _____, if available. The arbitration shall begin within five days of written notice by any attorney-in-fact to the arbitrator that a dispute has arisen. The details of the arbitration shall be determined by the arbitrator. The written decision of the arbitrator shall be binding on all my my attorneys-in-fact.

3. Delegation of Authority

My attorney-in-fact ☒ may ☐ may not delegate, in writing, any authority granted under this durable power of attorney to a person he or she selects. Any such delegation shall state the period during which it is valid and specify the extent of the delgation.

4. Effective Date

This power of attorney is effective:

☒ immediately, and shall continue in effect if I become incapacitated or disabled.

☐ only if I become incapacitated or disabled and unable to manage my financial affairs.

5. Determination of Incapacity

For purposes of this durable power of attorney, my incapacity or disability shall be determined by written declarations by ☐ one ☐ two licensed physician(s). Each declaration shall be made under penalty of perjury and shall state that in the physician's opinion I am substantially unable to manage my financial affairs. If possible, the declaration(s) shall be made by _____ _____. No licensed physician shall be liable to me for any actions taken by them under this part which are done in good faith.

6. Powers of Attorney-in-Fact

I hereby grant to my attorney-in-fact power to act on my behalf in the following matters, as indicated by my initials by each granted power. Powers that are not initialed are not granted. The Indiana Code sections noted below are hereby incorporated by reference.

INITIALS

*KMS*   a.   ALL POWERS (b THROUGH o) LISTED BELOW.

_____   b.   Real property transactions. (Ann. Ind. Code § 30-5-5-2)

_____   c.   Tangible personal property transactions. (Ann. Ind. Code § 30-5-5-3)

_____   d.   Bond, share and commodity transactions. (Ann. Ind. Code § 30-5-5-4)

_____   e.   Banking transactions. (Ann. Ind. Code § 30-5-5-5)

_____   f.   Business operating transactions. (Ann. Ind. Code § 30-5-5-6)

_____   g.   Insurance transactions. (Ann. Ind. Code § 30-5-5-7)

_____   h.   Beneficiary transactions. (Ann. Ind. Code § 30-5-5-8)

_____   i.   Gift transactions. (Ann. Ind. Code § 30-5-5-9)

_____   j.   Fiduciary transactions. (Ann. Ind. Code § 30-5-5-10)

_____   k.   Claims and litigation. (Ann. Ind. Code § 30-5-5-11)

_____   l.   Family maintenance. (Ann. Ind. Code § 30-5-5-12)

_____   m.   Benefits from military service. (Ann. Ind. Code § 30-5-5-13)

_____   n.   Records, reports, and statements. (Ann. Ind. Code § 30-5-5-14)

_____   o.   Estate transactions. (Ann. Ind. Code § 30-5-5-15)

7. Special Instructions to the Attorney-in-Fact

_____

_____

_____

_____

8. Compensation and Reimbursement of the Attorney-in-Fact

☒ The attorney-in-fact shall not be compensated for services, but shall be entitled to reimbursement, from the principal's assets, for reasonable expenses. Reasonable expenses include reasonable fees for information or advice from accountants, lawyers or investment experts relating to the attorney-in-fact's responsibilities under this power of attorney.

☐ The attorney-in-fact shall be entitled to reimbursement for reasonable expenses and reasonable compensation for his or her services. Reasonable compensation shall be determined exclusively by the attorney-in-fact.

☐ The attorney-in-fact shall be entitled to reimbursement for reasonable expenses and compensation for his or her services of $_____ per _____ .

9. Nomination of Conservator or Guardian

If, in a court proceeding, it is ever resolved that I need a conservator, guardian or other person to administer and supervise my estate or person, I nominate my attorney-in-fact to serve in that capacity. If my attorney-in-fact cannot serve, I nominate the sucessor attorney-in-fact named in Part 1 to serve.

10. Personal Benefit to Attorney-in-Fact

☐ My attorney-in-fact may buy any assets of mine or engage in any transaction he or she deems in good faith to be in my interest, no matter what the interest of or benefit to my attorney-in-fact.

☒ My attorney-in-fact may not be personally involved in or benefit personally from any transaction he or she engages in on my behalf, except _____

_____

_____ .

☐ My attorney-in-fact may not be personally involved in or benefit personally from any transaction he or she engages in on my behalf.

11. Commingling by Attorney-in-Fact

My attorney-in-fact ☒ may ☐ may not commingle any of my funds with any funds of his or hers.

12. Bond

The attorney-in-fact shall serve without bond.

13. Liability of Attorney-in-Fact

Neither my attorney-in-fact nor any successor attorney-in-fact shall incur any liability to me, my estate, my heirs, successors or assigns for acting or refraining from acting under this document, except for willful misconduct or gross negligence. Neither my attorney-in-fact nor any successors shall be required to make my assets productive of income, increase the value of my estate, diversify my investments or enter into transactions authorized by this document, as long as my attorney-in-fact or successor believes his or her actions are in my best interests or in the best interests of my estate and of those interested in my estate.

14. Gifts by Attorney-in-Fact

a. My attorney-in-fact shall have no incidents of ownership over any life insurance policy in which I may own an interest and which insures his or her life.

b. My attorney-in-fact may not (i) appoint, assign or designate any of my assets, interests or rights directly or indirectly to himself or herself, or estate, creditors, or the creditors of his or her estate, (ii) disclaim assets to which I would otherwise be entitled if the effect of the disclaimer is to cause such assets to pass directly or indirectly to my attorney-in-fact or his or her estate, or (iii) use my assets to discharge any of his or her legal obligations, including any obligation of support owed to others (excluding me and those whom I am legally obligated to support).

c. My attorney-in-fact shall not hold or exercise any powers I may have over assets he or she has given to me or over assets held in an irrevocable trust of which he or she is a grantor.

15. Reliance on this Power of Attorney

I agree that any third party who receives a copy of this document may act under it. Revocation of the power of attorney is not effective as to a third party until the third party has actual knowledge of the revocation. I agree to indemnify the third party for any claims that arise against the third party because of reliance on this power of attorney.

16. Severability

If any provision of this document is ruled unenforceable, the remaining provisions shall stay in effect.

I understand the importance of the powers I delegate to my attorney-in-fact in this document. I recognize that the document gives my attorney-in-fact broad powers over my assets, and that these powers shall become effective as of the date of my incapacity (or sooner if specified in this document) and shall continue indefinitely unless I revoke this durable power of attorney.

Signed this ___14th___ day of ___April___, 19_92_.

State of ___Indiana___   County of ___Marion___

___Kurt Michael Schneider___   ___371-26-5015___
your signature   your social security number

CERTIFICATE OF ACKNOWLEDGMENT OF NOTARY PUBLIC

State of ___Indiana___
County of ___Marion___ } ss

On ___April 14___, 19_92_, before me, ___Jennifer Toohey___,
a notary public, personally appeared ___Kurt Michael Schneider___
_____, personally known to me or proved to me on the basis of satisfactory evidence to be the person whose name is subscribed to this instrument, and acknowledged that he or she executed it.

[NOTARY SEAL]   ___Jennifer Toohey___
                                signature of notary public

Page 4

J.   Minnesota

Minnesota's short form truly is short and easy to fill out. A completed sample is shown below.

Attorney-in-Fact

Chapter 5, Section C, Part 1.
Chapter 3, *Choosing Your Attorney-in-Fact*.

In the first blank on the form, type your name and address. In the next blank, type the name and address of the person (or persons) you've chosen and who has agreed to serve as your attorney-in-fact for finances.

Choosing your attorney-in-fact is the most important decision you make when preparing your durable power of attorney.

If you name more than one person to serve as attorney-in-fact, you must state whether or not you want to allow each one to act separately on your behalf. If you require them to act jointly, each attorney-in-fact will have to sign all documents and approve all decisions made on your behalf.

- If you want each one to be able to act independently, cross out the word "jointly" at the end of the sentence.

Powers

Chapter 4, *The Attorney-in-Fact's Responsibilities*, Section B.

Next, decide what powers to give your attorney-in-fact. You must choose from the list of powers on the form.

- If you, like most people, want to give your attorney-in-fact every power on the list, place an x on line (O), at the bottom of the list.

- To give your attorney-in-fact only certain powers, put an x on the line in front of each one. You may, but are not required to, cross out powers you don't grant.

Most of the powers listed on the Minnesota form correspond to the powers explained in Chapter 4.

"Records, reports, and statements" (M) grants the powers given under "Tax matters" on the Nolo form and also gives your attorney-in-fact authority to file documents required by the Social Security Administration or other similar government agency.

Two powers on the Minnesota form, however, don't appear on the Nolo form:

Gift transactions (H). This authorizes the attorney-in-fact to make gifts to your spouse, children and other descendants (and their spouses), and organizations (charitable or otherwise) to which you've made gifts. The attorney-in-fact may not give more than $10,000 in one year to himself or to anyone he has a legal obligation to support.

Fiduciary transactions (I). This formally acknowledges that the attorney-in-fact is a "fiduciary"—someone who has a legal responsibility to act in your best interests and has legal authority to sign all kinds of documents, such as checks, releases or waivers, on your behalf.

Durability

Here you should state that you want the power of attorney to be durable—that is, to continue if you become incapacitated. Type an x in the first line.

Gifts to the Attorney-in-Fact

Here, indicate whether or not you want the attorney-in-fact to be able to give himself or herself your property. You may already have granted this power by giving the attorney-in-fact power over "gift transactions" (item H); under that power, the attorney-in-fact may fall into one of the categories of people (spouse, children, etc.) to whom gifts can be made.

If your attorney-in-fact isn't a close relative covered by that clause, it's best not to give the attorney-in-fact authority to transfer your property to himself or herself, to avoid a potential tax problem. If the attorney-in-fact's authority over your property is extremely broad, there's a minor risk that the value of that property would be included in the attorney-in-fact's taxable estate, if the attorney-in-fact died before you (not likely, but it could happen).

Additional Clauses

On the blank lines, you can add clauses to customize your durable power. (See Section B, above.) The list below shows the clauses you should consider copying from the Nolo form in Chapter 5 and adding to the Minnesota form. The Part number after the name of each clause shows you where to find it in the Nolo form.

The most important of these are the first two. It's always a good idea to name an alternate attorney-in-fact. And you must include the clause in Part 4 if you want a springing durable power of attorney.

Unless you add it, your durable power of attorney will take effect as soon as you sign it.

CLAUSES NOT INCLUDED IN THE MINNESOTA SHORT FORM

✓ Alternate Attorney-in-Fact (Part 1)

✓ Effective Date (Part 4)

Determination of Incapacity (Part 5)

Reimbursement and Compensation of Attorney-in-Fact (Part 8)

Nomination of Conservator or Guardian (Part 9)

Personal Benefit by Attorney-in-Fact (Part 10)

Commingling by Attorney-in-Fact (Part 11)

Liability to Attorney-in-Fact (Part 13)

Signature and Notarization

Sign the form in the presence of a notary public; the procedure is explained in *Chapter 7, Making It Legal.*

The Minnesota form also includes spaces for your attorney-in-fact's signature, but it's not required; the purpose is to have the attorney-in-fact's signature on record so that people the attorney-in-fact deals with later can verify it.

MINNESOTA STATUTORY SHORT FORM OF GENERAL POWER OF ATTORNEY

NOTICE: THE POWERS GRANTED BY THIS DOCUMENT ARE BROAD AND SWEEP-
ING. THEY ARE DEFINED IN SECTION 523.24. IF YOU HAVE ANY QUESTIONS ABOUT
THESE POWERS, OBTAIN COMPETENT ADVICE. THE USE OF ANY OTHER OR
DIFFERENT FORM OR POWER OF ATTORNEY DESIRED BY THE PARTIES IS ALSO
PERMITTED. THIS POWER OF ATTORNEY MAY BE REVOKED BY YOU IF YOU LATER
WISH TO DO SO. THIS POWER OF ATTORNEY AUTHORIZES THE ATTORNEY-IN-
FACT TO ACT FOR YOU BUT DOES NOT REQUIRE THAT HE OR SHE DO SO.

Know All Men by These Presents, which are intended to constitute a STATUTORY SHORT
FORM POWER OF ATTORNEY pursuant to Minnesota Statutes, section 523.23;

That I _Beatrice M. Steiner, 54 Lakeshore St., St. Paul, MN_

_____ (insert name and address of the principal) do hereby appoint _Samuel I._
_Cohen, 54 Lakeshore St., St. Paul, MN_____ (insert name and address of the
attorney-in-fact, or each attorney-in-fact, if more than one is designated) my attorney(s)-in-fact to act (jointly):

(NOTE: If more than one attorney-in-fact is designated and the principal wishes each attorney-
in-fact alone to be able to exercise the power conferred, delete the word "jointly." Failure to delete the
word "jointly" will require the attorneys-in-fact to act unanimously.)

First: in my name, place and stead in any way which I myself could do, if I were personally
present, with respect to the following matters as each of them is defined in section 523.24:

(To grant to the attorney-in-fact any of the following powers, make a check or "x" in the line in front of
each power being granted. To delete any of the following powers, do not make a check or "x" in the line in
front of the power. You may, but need not, cross out each power being deleted with a line drawn through it
(or in similar fashion). Failure to make a check or "x" in the line in front of the power will have the effect of
deleting the power unless the line in front of the power of (o) is checked or x-ed.)

Check or "x"

_____	(A)	real property transactions;
_____	(B)	tangible personal property transactions;
_____	(C)	bond, shares and commodity transactions;
_____	(D)	banking transactions;
_____	(E)	business operating transactions;
_____	(F)	insurance transactions;
_____	(G)	beneficiary transactions;
_____	(H)	gift transactions;
_____	(I)	fiduciary transactions;
_____	(J)	claims and litigation;
_____	(K)	family maintenance;
_____	(L)	benefits from military service;
_____	(M)	records, reports, and statements;
_____	(N)	all other matters;
___x___	(O)	all of the powers listed in (A) through (N) above.

Page 1

Second: (You must indicate below whether or not this power of attorney will be effective if you become incompetent. Make a check or "x" in the line in front of the statement that expresses your intent.)

    __x__   This power of attorney shall continue to be effective if I become incompetent. It shall not be affected by my later disability or incompetency.

    _____   This power of attorney shall not be effective if I become incompetent.

Third: (You must indicate below whether or not this power of attorney authorizes the attorney-in-fact to transfer your property directly to himself or herself. Make a check or "x" in the line in front of the statement that expresses your intent.)

    __x__   This power of attorney authorizes the attorney-in-fact to transfer property directly to himself or herself.

    _____   This power of attorney does not authorize the attorney-in-fact to transfer property directly to himself or herself.

If Samuel I. Cohen does not or ceases to serve as attorney-in-fact, I appoint Stephanie Cohen-Black, 390 Harris St., Minneapolis, MN, to serve as attorney-in-fact.

_____

_____

_____

_____

In Witness Whereof I have hereunto signed my name this _3d_ day of _December_ , 19_92_ .

Beatrice M Steiner
(Signature of principal)

ACKNOWLEDGMENT OF NOTARY PUBLIC

State of _Minnesota_

County of _Ramsey_

On _Dec. 3,_ , 19_92_ , before me, _Emmylou Koenig_ , a notary public, personally appeared _Beatrice M. Steiner_ , personally known to me or proved to me on the basis of satisfactory evidence to be the person whose name is subscribed to this instrument, and acknowledged that he or she executed it.

[NOTARY SEAL]

Emmylou Koenig
signature of notary public

Specimen Signature of Attorney(s)-in-Fact

Samuel I. Cohen

_____

Page 2

K.   New Jersey

New Jersey doesn't have an entire short form power of attorney, but it does have a standard way to give your attorney-in-fact authority to deal with banks. If you live in New Jersey, it's best to use the Nolo power of attorney form in Chapter 5, with a modification that incorporates the New Jersey banking power.

Follow the directions in Chapter 5, with this change: In Part 6 of the form, don't initial the blank in front of "e. banking and other financial institution transactions." (You can also cross it out if you wish.) Add the following language to Part 7:

"I hereby grant my attorney-in-fact the authority to conduct banking transactions as set forth in section 2 of New Jersey P.L. 1991, c. 95 (C. 46:2B-11)."

This gives your attorney-in-fact broad authority to deal with banks on your behalf. The attorney-in-fact can, among other things, modify or terminate any of your accounts, open accounts in your name, remove the contents of your safe deposit box or rent a new one, sign checks, withdraw funds, prepare financial statements and borrow money.

Banking institutions are required by law to allow your attorney-in-fact to exercise these powers if the attorney-in-fact shows the bank the original, signed power of attorney document, unless the bank believes, in good faith, that the document is not genuine.

L.   New Mexico

The New Mexico short form durable power of attorney contains its own instructions and is largely self-explanatory. A completed sample is shown below.

Attorney-in-Fact

Chapter 5, Section C, Part 1.
Chapter 3, *Choosing Your Attorney-in-Fact*.

In the first blank on the form, type your name. In the second, fill in the name of the county you live in. In the next blank, type in the name of the person (or persons) you've chosen and who has agreed to serve as your attorney-in-fact for finances.

Choosing your attorney-in-fact is the most important decision you make when preparing your durable power of attorney.

Successor Attorney-in-Fact

Chapter 3, *Choosing Your Attorney-in-Fact*, Section F.

In the next paragraph, name an alternate attorney-in-fact, who will take over if your first choice cannot serve.

More Than One Attorney-in-Fact

Chapter 3, *Choosing Your Attorney-in-Fact*, Section D.

If you named more than one person to serve as attorney-in-fact, you must check and initial the next paragraph if you want each one to have the authority to act separately on your behalf. If you don't, they will have to act jointly, which means that each attorney-in-fact will have to sign all documents and approve all decisions made on your behalf.

Powers

Chapter 4, *The Attorney-in-Fact's Responsibilities*, Section B.

Next, decide what powers to give your attorney-in-fact. You must choose from the list of powers on the form.

- If you, like most people, want to give your attorney-in-fact every power on the list, place your initials on every line.

- To give your attorney-in-fact only certain powers, place your initials on the line in front of each one.

Most of the powers listed on the New Mexico form correspond to the powers explained in Chapter 4. Three powers on the New Mexico form, however, don't appear on the Nolo form:

Records, reports, and statements (10). This gives your attorney-in-fact authority to file federal, state and local tax returns for you and handle any other tax matters that arise. It also authorizes the attorney-in-fact to file documents required by the Social Security Administration or other similar government agency.

Decisions relating to medical treatment (11 and 12). We don't recommend it, but you can use this document to give your attorney-in-fact authority to make medical decisions, including decisions about the use of life-prolonging treatments, on your behalf. But it's usually better to cover your medical and financial matters in separate documents. (See Chapter 1, *Using a Durable Power of Attorney*, Section D.)

Additional Powers

After the list of powers is a space (item 15) for you to write in any additional powers you want to give your attorney-in-fact.

If you don't want to give your attorney-in-fact authority over some but not all of your real estate or stocks, you can also specify which stocks or real property the attorney-in-fact has power over.

Effective Date

 Chapter 2, *How Durable Powers of Attorney Work*, Section B.

Next you must specify whether you want your durable power of attorney to become effective as soon as you sign it, or only if you become incapacitated (a springing durable power). When you use the New Mexico short form, affidavits (notarized statements) from two qualified health care professionals are required for a springing durable power of attorney to go into effect. If you're not sure when you want your power of attorney to take effect, reread the discussion in Chapter 2.

- If you want the durable power to become effective only if you become incapacitated, check and initial the last paragraph of the document above the signature line.
- If you want it to take effect immediately, don't do anything to this paragraph.

Additional Clauses

Here you can add clauses to customize your durable power. (See Section B, above.) The list below shows the clauses you should consider copying from the Nolo form in Chapter 5 and adding to the New Mexico form. The Part number after the name of each clause shows you where to find it in the Nolo form.

CLAUSES NOT INCLUDED IN THE NEW MEXICO SHORT FORM

Compensation and Reimbursement of Attorney-in-Fact (Part 8)

Nomination of Conservator or Guardian (Part 9)

Personal Benefit by Attorney-in-Fact (Part 10)

Commingling to Attorney-in-Fact (Part 11)

Liability of Attorney-in-Fact (Part 13)

Gifts to Attorney-in-Fact (Part 14)

Signature and Notarization

Sign the completed document in front of a notary public, who will fill out the "Acknowledgement" at the bottom of the form. Instructions are in Chapter 7, *Making It Legal*.

THE POWERS GRANTED BY THIS DOCUMENT ARE BROAD AND SWEEPING. THIS FORM, THE NEW MEXICO STATUTORY SHORT FORM UNDER SECTION 45-5-502 NMSA 1978, DOES NOT PROHIBIT THE USE OF ANY OTHER FORM.

POWER OF ATTORNEY

NEW MEXICO STATUTORY SHORT FORM

I, <u>Michael J. Rodriquez</u> reside in <u>Taos</u> County, New Mexico.
    (Name)

I appoint <u>Estella G. Rodriquez</u> to serve as my attorney(s)-in-fact.
         (Name(s))

If any attorney-in-fact appointed above is unable to serve, then I appoint <u>Elena S. Brown</u> _____ to serve as successor attorney-in-fact in place of the person who is unable to serve.

CHECK AND INITIAL THE FOLLOWING PARAGRAPH ONLY IF MORE THAN ONE PERSON IS APPOINTED TO ACT ON YOUR BEHALF AND YOU WANT ANY ONE OF THEM TO HAVE THE POWER TO ACT ALONE WITHOUT THE SIGNATURE OF THE OTHER(S). IF YOU DO NOT CHECK AND INITIAL THE FOLLOWING PARAGRAPH AND MORE THAN ONE PERSON IS NAMED TO ACT ON YOUR BEHALF THEN THEY MUST ACT JOINTLY.

(   )   If more than one person is appointed to serve as my attorneys-in-fact then they may act
_____ severally, alone and independently of each other.
initials

My attorney(s)-in-fact shall have the power to act in my name, place and stead in any way which I myself could do with respect to the following matters to the extent permitted by law:

INITIAL IN THE OPPOSITE BOX EACH AUTHORIZATION WHICH YOU DESIRE TO GIVE TO YOUR ATTORNEY(S)-IN-FACT. YOUR ATTORNEY(S)-IN-FACT SHALL BE AUTHORIZED TO ENGAGE ONLY IN THOSE ACTIVITIES WHICH ARE INITIALED.

1. real estate transactions; .... (MJR)
2. bond, share and commodity transactions; .... (MJR)
3. chattel and goods transactions; .... (MJR)
4. banking transactions; .... (MJR)
5. business operating transactions; .... (MJR)
6. insurance transactions; .... (MJR)
7. estate transactions; .... (MJR)
8. claims and litigation; .... (MJR)
9. government benefits; .... (MJR)
10. records, reports and statements; .... (MJR)
11. decisions regarding lifesaving and life prolonging medical treatment; .... (   )
12. decisions relating to medical treatment, surgical treatment, nursing care, medication,
    hospitalization, institutionalization in a nursing home or other facility and home health care;(   )
13. transfer of property or income as a gift to the principal's spouse for the purpose of
    qualifying the principal for governmental medical assistance; .... (MJR)
14. list other; .... (   )
    _____ (   )

Page 1

_____( )
_____( )
_____( )
15. list all other powers; ....( )
_____( )
_____( )
_____( )
_____( )

Specifically identified real estate or stocks and bonds for which my attorney-in-fact is authorized to act follow. If nothing is listed, then the attorney-in-fact is authorized to act with respect to any real estate or stocks and bonds and other securities that I own. A copy of this power of attorney must be recorded in the office of the county clerk where the real estate is located.

_____( )
_____( )
_____( )
_____( )

This power of attorney shall not be affected by my incapacity, but will terminate upon my death unless I have revoked it prior to my death.

CHECK AND INITIAL THE FOLLOWING PARAGRAPH IF YOU INTEND FOR THIS POWER OF ATTORNEY TO BECOME EFFECTIVE ONLY IF YOU BECOME INCAPACITATED. YOUR FAILURE TO DO SO WILL MEAN THAT YOUR ATTORNEY(S)-IN-FACT ARE EMPOWERED TO ACT ON YOUR BEHALF FROM THE TIME YOU SIGN THIS DOCUMENT UNTIL YOUR DEATH UNLESS YOU REVOKE THE POWER BEFORE YOUR DEATH.

(x)   This power of attorney shall become effective only if I become incapacitated. My attorney(s)-
MJR   in-fact shall be entitled to rely on notarized statements from two qualified health care profes-
initials   sionals as to my incapacity. By incapacity I mean that among other things, I am unable to effectively manage my personal care, property or financial affairs.

_____

_____
                                    Michael J Rodriguez
                                         (Signature)
                          Dated: _August 11,_ ____, 19 _92_

ACKNOWLEDGEMENT

STATE OF NEW MEXICO
                              } ss
COUNTY OF __Taos__

The foregoing instrument was acknowledged before me this _11th_ day of _August_ ____,
19_92_, by _Michael J. Rodriguez_ _____.

                    Robert C. Kwei
                         Notary Public
          My Commission Expires: _August 30, 1993_

Page 2

M. New York

The New York short form durable power of attorney truly is short and easy to fill out. A completed sample is shown below.

Attorney-in-Fact

Chapter 3, *Choosing Your Attorney-in-Fact*.

In the first blank on the form, type your name and address. In the next blank, type in the name and address of the person (or persons) you've chosen and who has agreed to serve as your attorney-in-fact for finances.

Choosing your attorney-in-fact is the most important decision you make when preparing your durable power of attorney.

If you named more than one person to serve as attorney-in-fact or successor attorney-in-fact, you must complete the sentence to state whether each one may act separately (independently) on your behalf or all of them must act jointly. If you require them to act jointly, each attorney-in-fact will have to sign all documents and approve all decisions made on your behalf.

*   If you want each agent to be able to act independently, type in the word "severally" at the end of the sentence.
*   If you want to require them to act jointly, type "jointly."

Powers

Chapter 4, *The Attorney-in-Fact's Responsibilities*, Section B.

Next, decide what powers to give your attorney-in-fact. You must choose from the list of powers on the form.

*   If you, like most people, want to give your attorney-in-fact every power on the list, you don't need to do anything in this section. All powers are granted unless you indicate otherwise.
*   If you don't want to grant a power, you must draw a line through it and initial the box opposite it. (This is the opposite of the way it's done on the Nolo form, where you must initial each power that you *do* want the attorney-in-fact to have.)

Most of the powers are explained in Chapter 4:

"Personal relationships and affairs" (item I) on the New York form corresponds to "personal and family maintenance" in Chapter 4.

"Records, reports, and statements" (K) grants the powers given under "Tax matters" on the Nolo form and also gives your attorney-in-fact authority to file documents required by the Social Security Administration or other similar government agency. The attorney-in-fact is also specifically authorized to file records, reports or statements necessary to safeguard your interests with regard to rent control.

"Authority to delegate powers" (L) is discussed in Chapter 5, Section C, Part 3.

Additional Clauses

After the list of powers, you can add clauses to customize your durable power. (See Section B, above.) The list below shows the clauses you should consider copying from the Nolo form in Chapter 5 and adding to the New York form. The Part number after the name of each clause shows you where to find it in the Nolo form.

The most important of these are the first two. It's always a good idea to name an alternate attorney-in-fact. And you must include the clause in Part 4 if you want a springing durable power of attorney. Unless you add it, your durable power of attorney will take effect as soon as you sign it.

CLAUSES NOT INCLUDED IN THE NEW YORK SHORT FORM

✓ Alternate Attorney-in-Fact (Part 1)

✓ Effective Date (Part 4)

   Determination of Incapacity (Part 5)

   Compensation and Reimbursement (Part 8)

   Nomination of Conservator or Guardian (Part 9)

   Personal Benefit by Attorney-in-Fact (Part 10)

   Commingling by Attorney-in-Fact (Part 11)

   Liability of Attorney-in-Fact (Part 13)

   Gifts to Attorney-in-Fact (Part 14)

Signature and Notarization

For the durable power to be valid, you must sign it in front of a notary public, who will fill out the "Acknowledgement" at the bottom of the form. Instructions are in Chapter 7, *Making It Legal.*

NEW YORK STATUTORY GENERAL POWER OF ATTORNEY

Notice: The powers granted by this document are broad and sweeping. They are defined in New York General Obligations Law, Article 5, Title 15, sections 5-1502A through 5-1503, which expressly permits the use of any other or different form of power of attorney desired by the parties concerned.

Know All Men by These Presents, which are intended to constitute a GENERAL POWER OF ATTORNEY pursuant to Article 5, Title 15 of the New York General Obligations Law:

That I ___Allison van Boorsten, 9234 W. Knox Ave., Ithaca, NY___
(insert name and address of the principal)

do hereby appoint ___Sarah Fukari, 332 Hopkins Ct., Ithaca, NY___
(insert name and address of the agent, or each agent, if more than one is designated)

my attorney(s)-in-fact TO ACT _____.

(a) If more than one agent is designated and the principal wishes each agent alone to be able to exercise the power conferred, insert in this blank the word "severally". Failure to make any insertion or the insertion of the word "jointly' will require the agents to act jointly.

In my name, place and stead in any way which I myself could do, if I were personally present, with respect to the following matters as each of them is defined in Title 15 of Article 5 of the New York General Obligations Law to the extent that I am permitted by law to act through an agent:

[Strike out and initial in the opposite box any one or more of the subdivisions as to which the principal does NOT desire to give the agent authority. Such elimination of any one or more of subdivisions (A) to (L), inclusive, shall automatically constitute an elimination also of subdivision (M).]

To strike out any subdivision the principal must draw a line through the text of that subdivision AND write his initials in the box opposite.

(A) real estate transactions; ....[   ]
(B) chattel and goods transactions; ....[   ]
(C) bond, share and commodity transactions ....[   ]
(D) banking transactions; ....[   ]
(E) business operating transactions; ....[   ]
(F) insurance transactions; ....[   ]
(G) estate transactions; ....[   ]
(H) claims and litigation; ....[   ]
(I) personal relationships and affairs; ....[   ]
(J) benefits from military service; ....[   ]
(K) records, reports and statements; ....[   ]
(L) full and unqualified authority to my attorney(s)-in-fact to delegate any or all of the
     foregoing powers to any person or persons whom any attorney(s)-in-fact shall select; ......[   ]
(M) all other matters ....[   ]

_____

_____

[Special provisions and limitations may be included in the statutory short form power of attorney only if they conform to the requirements of section 5-1503 of the New York General Obligations Law.]

TO INDUCE ANY THIRD PARTY TO ACT HEREUNDER, I HEREBY AGREE THAT ANY THIRD PARTY RECEIVING A DULY EXECUTED COPY OR FACSIMILE OF THIS INSTRUMENT MAY ACT HEREUNDER, AND THAT REVOCATION OR TERMINATION HEREOF SHALL BE INEFFECTIVE AS TO SUCH THIRD PARTY UNLESS AND UNTIL ACTUAL NOTICE OR KNOWLEDGE OF SUCH REVOCATION OR TERMINATION SHALL HAVE BEEN RECEIVED BY SUCH THIRD PARTY, AND I FOR MYSELF AND FOR MY HEIRS, EXECUTORS, LEGAL REPRESENTATIVES AND ASSIGNS, HEREBY AGREE TO INDEMNIFY AND HOLD HARMLESS ANY SUCH THIRD PARTY FROM AND AGAINST ANY AND ALL CLAIMS THAT MAY ARISE AGAINST SUCH THIRD PARTY BY REASON OF SUCH THIRD PARTY HAVING RELIED ON THE PROVISIONS OF THIS INSTRUMENT.

_____ If Sarah Fukari does not or ceases to serve as attorney-in-fact, Ethan White, 34 Park, Ithaca, NY shall serve as attorney-in-fact. _____

_____ This power of attorney is effective only if I become incapacitated or disabled and unable to manage my financial affairs. For purposes of this durable power of attorney, my incapacity or disability shall be determined by written declaration by a licensed physician. The declaration shall be made under penalty of perjury and shall state that in the physician's opinion I am substantially unable to manage my financial affairs. If possible, the declaration shall be made by Dr. Walter S. Khouri, Ithaca, NY. No licensed physician shall be liable to me for any action taken under this part which is done in good faith. _____

In Witness Whereof I have hereunto signed my name and affixed my seal this ___*17TH*___ day of ___*MARCH*___, 19_*92*_.

___*Allison van Boorsten*_____ (Seal)
(Signature of Principal)

State of New York

County of _*Tompkins*_ } ss

On _*March 19*_ 19_*92*_ before me, _*Nicholas Yu*_,
a notary public, personally appeared _*Allison van Boorsten*_,
personally known to me (or proved to me on the basis of satisfactory evidence) to be the person whose name is subscribed to this instrument, and acknowledged that he or she executed it.

___*Nicholas Yu*_____
[NOTARY SEAL]   Signature of notary public

Page 2

N.   North Carolina

If you use the North Carolina short form durable power of attorney, you'll probably want to add some clauses the form doesn't cover. A completed sample is shown below.

Attorney-in-Fact

Chapter 5, Section C, Part 1.
Chapter 3, *Choosing Your Attorney-in-Fact*.

At the top of the form, fill in the state and county. In the next sentence, type your name and then the name of the person (or persons) you've chosen and who has agreed to serve as your attorney-in-fact for finances. Choosing your attorney-in-fact is the most important decision you make when preparing your durable power of attorney.

Powers

Chapter 4, *The Attorney-in-Fact's Responsibilities*, Section B.

Next, decide what powers to give your attorney-in-fact. You must choose from the list of powers on the form.

- If you, like most people, want to give your attorney-in-fact every power on the list, you must initial the blank in front of each power listed.
- If you want to grant only some powers, initial just those lines.

The powers listed on the North Carolina form correspond to the powers explained in Chapter 4. ("Personal relationships and affairs" (item 9) on the North Carolina form is equivalent to "personal and family maintenance.")

Optional Clauses

After the list of powers are some more options. Because the form is rather poorly designed, to add some of these clauses you'll need to retype the language that's already on the form.

Power of substitution. If you want to give your attorney-in-fact the power to appoint someone else to serve as attorney-in-fact, in case your first choice can't serve, type this language on the form:

> "I also give to such person full power to appoint another to act as my attorney-in-fact and full power to revoke such appointment."

Termination date. If, for some unusual reason, you don't want the durable power of attorney to last until your death, fill in the date you want your attorney-in-fact's authority to end.

Effective date. If you want the power of attorney to take effect only if you become incapacitated, type in the following language:

"This power of attorney shall become effective after I become incapacitated or mentally incompetent."

You should also specify how your incapacity is to be determined. Copy the wording from Part 5 of the Nolo form in Chapter 5.

Additional Clauses

On the blank lines, you can add clauses to customize your durable power. (See Section B, above.) The list below shows the clauses you should consider copying from the Nolo form in Chapter 5 and adding to the North Carolina form. The Part number after the name of each clause shows you where to find it in the Nolo form.

The most important of these is the first one; it's always a good idea to name an alternate attorney-in-fact. And if you make a springing durable power of attorney, you should also specify how your incapacity is to be determined.

CLAUSES NOT INCLUDED IN THE NORTH CAROLINA SHORT FORM

✓ Alternate Attorney-in-Fact (Part 1)

Determination of Incapacity (Part 5)

Compensation and Reimbursement of Attorney-in-Fact (Part 8)

Nomination of Conservator or Guardian (Part 9)

Personal Benefit to Attorney-in-Fact (Part 10)

Commingling by Attorney-in-Fact (Part 11)

Liability of Attorney-in-Fact (Part 13)

Gifts by Attorney-in-Fact (Part 14)

Waiver of inventories and accountings. We have added this clause (the last one before your signature), which is authorized by state law, to the North Carolina short form. If it weren't there, state law would require your attorney-in-fact to file an inventory of all your property with the superior court if you become incapacitated.

- If for some reason you do want this requirement imposed on your attorney-in-fact, cross out the whole paragraph.

Signature and Notarization

Sign the completed document in front of a notary public, who will fill out the paragraph at the bottom of the form. The procedure is explained in *Chapter 7, Making It Legal.*

NORTH CAROLINA STATUTORY SHORT FORM OF GENERAL POWER OF ATTORNEY

NOTICE: THE POWERS GRANTED BY THIS DOCUMENT ARE BROAD AND SWEEP-
ING. THEY ARE DEFINED IN CHAPTER 32A OF THE NORTH CAROLINA GENERAL
STATUTES WHICH EXPRESSLY PERMITS THE USE OF ANY OTHER OR DIFFERENT
FORM OF POWER OF ATTORNEY DESIRED BY THE PARTIES CONCERNED.

State of _North Carolina_____

County of _Cumberland_____

I _____Ray C. Richardson_____, the undersigned, hereby
appoint _Elva Marie Richardson_____ my attorney-in-fact
for me and give such person full power to act in my name, place and stead in any way which I myself
could do if I were personally present with respect to the following matters as each of them is defined in
Chapter 32A of the North Carolina General Statutes to the event that I am permitted by law to act
through an agent. (DIRECTIONS: Initial the line opposite any one or more of the subdivisions as to
which the principal desires to give the attorney-in-fact authority.)

   (1) Real property transactions; ...._____
   (2) Personal property transactions; ...._____
   (3) Bond, share and commodity transactions; ...._____
   (4) Banking transactions; ...._____
   (5) Safe deposits; ...._____
   (6) Business operating transactions; ...._____
   (7) Insurance transactions; ...._____
   (8) Estate transactions; ...._____
   (9) Personal relationships and affairs; ...._____
  (10) Social security and unemployment; ...._____
  (11) Benefits from military service; ...._____
  (12) Tax; ...._____
  (13) Employment of agents; ...._____

(If power of substitution and revocation is to be given, add: 'I also give to such person full power
to appoint another to act as my attorney-in-fact and full power to revoke such appointment.')

I also give to such person full power to appoint another to act as
my attorney-in-fact and full power to revoke such appointment.

(If period of power of attorney is to be limited, add: 'This power terminates _____, 19 ___.')

_____

(If power of attorney is to be a durable power of attorney under the provision of Article 2 of Chapter 32A
and is to continue in effect after the incapacity or mental incompetence of the principal, add: 'This power of
attorney shall not be affected by my subsequent incapacity or mental incompetence.')

~~This power of attorney shall not be affected by my subsequent incapacity or mental incompetence.~~

(If power of attorney is to take effect only after the incapacity or mental incompetence of the principal, add: 'This power of attorney shall become effective after I become incapacitated or mentally incompetent.')

~~This power of attorney shall become effective after I become~~
~~incapacitated or mentally incompetent.~~
If Elva Marie Richardson cannot serve as attorney-in-fact, I appoint Lee S. Hunter to serve as attorney-in-fact.

For purposes of this durable power of attorney, my incapacity or
disability shall be determined by written declaration by a licensed physician. The declaration shall be made under penalty of
perjury and shall state that in the physician's opinion I am substantially unable to manage my financial affairs. If possible, the
delcaration shall be made by Dr. Ralph Chen. No licensed physician
shall be liable to me for any actions taken under this part which
are done in good faith.

I waive the requirement, set out in North Carolina Gen. Stat. § 32A-11, that the attorney-in-fact file this power of attorney with the clerk of the superior court and render inventories and accounts, after my incapacity or mental incompetence, to the clerk of the superior court.

Dated _June 19_, 19_92_

Ray C. Richardson (SEAL)
Signature

STATE OF ___North Carolina___   COUNTY OF ___Cumberland___

On this _19th_ day of _June_, _1992_, personally appeared before me, the said named ___Ray C. Richardson___ to me known and known to be the person described in and who executed the foregoing instrument and he (or she) acknowledged that he (or she) executed the same and being duly sworn by me, made oath that the statements in the foregoing instrument are true.

My Commission Expires: _December 1, 1992_

Mary Anne Doherty
(Signature of Notary Public)

Notary Public (Official Seal)

Page 2

O.   Pennsylvania

Pennsylvania hasn't come up with an entire durable power of attorney form, but it has set out a list of powers that can be granted to a Pennsylvania attorney-in-fact. Each of the powers is defined in the Pennsylvania statute. For example, if you give your attorney-in-fact power "to create a trust for my benefit" (one of the powers on the list), the statute itself contains many paragraphs explaining exactly what authority that confers on the attorney-in-fact.

The Pennsylvania list is not very thorough. It doesn't, for example, allow you to give your attorney-in-fact authority over your bank account or real estate, or allow your attorney-in-fact to represent you in dealing with the Social Security Administration or IRS. You can, however, use a different form. You'll probably want to use the Nolo form in Chapter 5, and supplement it with any of the special Pennsylvania powers you decide is important to add.

To add any of these powers to the Nolo form, add the following language to Part 7, Special Instructions:

> "I also grant my attorney-in-fact the following powers as set out in Section 5602 of the Pennsylvania Compiled Statutes:"

Then list the powers. An example is shown below.

Here are the powers, listed in the Pennsylvania statutes, that you may add to your durable power of attorney. If you want to include any of them, you need type only the words that appear in boldface type.

Either of the following clauses about gifts:

To make gifts. This allows your attorney-in-fact to give any amount of your property to himself or others.

To make limited gifts. This allows your attorney-in-fact to give your property only to your spouse or children, and only to give as much as is exempt from federal gift tax—currently, $10,000 per year per recipient.

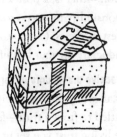

To create a trust for my benefit. This allows your attorney-in-fact to create a trust (the statute doesn't say what kind of trust) and transfer some or all of your property to it. The property in the trust, and the income it produces can be distributed only to you or to the guardian of your estate, if one has been appointed by a court.

To make additions to an existing trust for my benefit. If you already have a trust—a revocable living trust designed to avoid probate, for example—this authorizes your attorney-in-fact to add more of your property to it.

To claim an elective share of the estate of my deceased spouse. This allows your attorney-in-fact to go to court and demand a certain share of your spouse's property after his or her death. The attorney-in-fact must get court permission first, however.

Such demands are quite rare—they are made only when someone doesn't leave the legal minimum to a surviving spouse, and the surviving spouse objects. (Making such a demand is also known as "taking against the will," because you're challenging the terms of the deceased spouse's will.)

To disclaim any interest in property. This allows your attorney-in-fact to release any interest in property to which you may be entitled.

To renounce fiduciary positions. This allows your attorney-in-fact to offer your resignation from any "fiduciary" position—that is, a position in which you have a legal responsibility to act on someone else's behalf in their best interests. (Your attorney-in-fact, remember, is a fiduciary on your behalf.)

To withdraw and receive the income or corpus of a trust. This allows your attorney-in-fact to withdraw money that you are entitled to from a trust—for example, from a revocable living trust you set up to avoid probate or a trust that someone created for your benefit.

To authorize my admission to a medical, nursing, residential or similar facilities and to enter into agreements for my care. and **(9) To authorize medical and surgical procedures.** We don't recommend it, but you can give your attorney-in-fact the authority to consent to treatment or to your admission to a medical facility. It's usually better to cover medical and financial matters in separate documents. (See Chapter 1, *Using a Durable Power of Attorney,* Section D.)

P. Tennessee

Tennessee hasn't come up with an entire durable power of attorney form, but it has set out an extensive list of powers that can be granted to an attorney-in-fact.

Our form for Tennessee incorporates the language of the Tennessee statute and other aspects of Tennessee's law with respect to durable powers of attorney.

To complete the form, follow the instructions in Chapter 5. Two of the powers listed in Part 6 of the form are peculiar to Tennessee and aren't explained in that chapter:

Advance funeral and burial arrangements (n). You can authorize your attorney-in-fact to make burial and funeral arrangements for you, if you haven't already done so. But remember that because the attorney-in-fact's authority ends at your death, such arrangements must be made while you are still alive.

Personal records (o). This gives your attorney-in-fact access to any of your legal or medical records and the right to disclose that information as he or she sees fit.

DURABLE POWER OF ATTORNEY FOR FINANCIAL MANAGEMENT: TENNESSEE

THE POWERS GRANTED BY THIS DOCUMENT ARE BROAD AND SWEEPING. IF YOU HAVE ANY QUESTIONS ABOUT THESE POWERS, GET COMPETENT LEGAL ADVICE. THIS DOCUMENT DOES NOT AUTHORIZE ANYONE TO MAKE MEDICAL OR OTHER HEALTH CARE DECISIONS FOR YOU.

YOU MAY REVOKE THIS POWER OF ATTORNEY IF YOU LATER WISH TO DO SO.

1. Attorney-in-Fact

I, __Nicholas S. Ericsson_____ of
___Nashville_____, Tennessee, appoint _____Monica L. Skinner_____
_____ as my attorney-in-fact to act for me in any lawful way with respect to the powers delegated in Part 6 below. If that person or persons does not serve or ceases to serve as attorney-in-fact, I appoint _____David L. Ericsson_____ to serve as attorney-in-fact.

2. More Than One Attorney-in-Fact

a. Authorization

If more than one attorney-in-fact is designated, they are authorized to act:

☐ jointly. ☐ independently.

b. Resolution of Disputes

☐ If my attorneys-in-fact cannot agree on a decision or action under the authority delegated to them in this durable power of attorney, that dispute shall be resolved by binding arbitration. The arbitration shall be carried out by a single arbitrator, who shall be _____, if available. The arbitration shall begin within five days of written notice by any attorney-in-fact to the arbitrator that a dispute has arisen. The details of the arbitration shall be determined by the arbitrator. The written decision of the arbitrator shall be binding on all my my attorneys-in-fact.

3. Delegation of Authority

My attorney-in-fact ☒ may ☐ may not delegate, in writing, any authority granted under this durable power of attorney to a person he or she selects. Any such delegation shall state the period during which it is valid and specify the extent of the delgation.

4. Effective Date

This power of attorney is effective:
☐ immediately, and shall continue in effect if I become incapacitated or disabled.
☒ only if I become incapacitated or disabled and unable to manage my financial affairs.

5. Determination of Incapacity

For purposes of this durable power of attorney, my incapacity or disability shall be determined by written declarations by ☒ one ☐ two licensed physician(s). Each declaration shall be made under penalty of perjury and shall state that in the physician's opinion I am substantially unable to manage my financial affairs. If possible, the declaration(s) shall be made by ___Dr. Ellen_ ___Silverman, Nashville, TN_____. No licensed physician shall be liable to me for any actions taken by them under this part which are done in good faith.

6. Powers of Attorney-in-Fact

I hereby grant to my attorney-in-fact power to act on my behalf in the following matters, as indicated by my initials by each granted power. Powers that are not initialed are not granted. The Tennessee Code sections noted below are hereby incorporated by reference.

INITIALS

_____NSE___ a. ALL POWERS (b THROUGH o) LISTED BELOW.
      [Tenn. Code Ann. § 34-6-109(1)]
_____ b. Real estate transactions. [Tenn. Code Ann. § 34-6-109(3)]
_____ c. Tangible personal property transactions.
_____ d. Stock and bond, commodity and option transactions.
_____ e. Banking and other financial institution transactions.
      [Tenn. Code Ann. §§ 34-6-109(2), (7), (11), (12), (13)]
_____ f. Business operating transactions. [Tenn. Code Ann. § 34-6-109(14)]
_____ g Insurance and annuity transactions. [Tenn. Code Ann. § 34-6-109(5)]
_____ h. Estate, trust, and other beneficiary transactions.
      [Tenn. Code Ann. § 34-6-109(16)]
_____ i. Claims and litigation. [Tenn. Code Ann. § 34-6-109(17)]
_____ j. Personal and family maintenance.[Tenn. Code Ann. § 34-6-109(6), (15)]
_____ k. Benefits from social security, medicare, medicaid, or other governmental
      programs, or civil or military service. [Tenn. Code Ann. § 34-6-109(8)]
_____ l. Retirement plan transactions. [Tenn. Code Ann. § 34-6-109(19)]
_____ m. Tax matters. [Tenn. Code Ann. § 34-6-109(4), (20)]
_____ n. Advance funeral and burial arrangements. [Tenn. Code Ann. § 34-6-109(22)]
_____ o. Personal records. [Tenn. Code Ann. § 34-6-109 (21)]

7. Special Instructions to the Attorney-in-Fact

_____

_____

_____

8. Compensation and Reimbursement of the Attorney-in-Fact

☒ The attorney-in-fact shall not be compensated for services, but shall be entitled to reimbursement, from the principal's assets, for reasonable expenses. Reasonable expenses include reasonable fees for information or advice from accountants, lawyers or investment experts relating to the attorney-in-fact's responsibilities under this power of attorney.

☐ The attorney-in-fact shall be entitled to reimbursement for reasonable expenses and reasonable compensation for his or her services. Reasonable compensation shall be determined exclusively by the attorney-in-fact.

☐ The attorney-in-fact shall be entitled to reimbursement for reasonable expenses and compensation for his or her services of $_____ per _____ .

9. Nomination of Conservator or Guardian

If, in a court proceeding, it is ever resolved that I need a conservator, guardian or other person to administer and supervise my estate or person, I nominate my attorney-in-fact to serve in that capacity. If my attorney-in-fact cannot serve, I nominate the sucessor attorney-in-fact named in Part 1 to serve.

10. Personal Benefit to Attorney-in-Fact

☒ My attorney-in-fact may buy any assets of mine or engage in any transaction he or she deems in good faith to be in my interest, no matter what the interest of or benefit to my attorney-in-fact.

☐ My attorney-in-fact may not be personally involved in or benefit personally from any transaction he or she engages in on my behalf, except _____

_____ .

☐ My attorney-in-fact may not be personally involved in or benefit personally from any transaction he or she engages in on my behalf.

11. Commingling by Attorney-in-Fact

My attorney-in-fact ☒ may ☐ may not commingle any of my funds with any funds of his or hers.

12. Bond

The attorney-in-fact shall serve without bond.

13. Liability of Attorney-in-Fact

Neither my attorney-in-fact nor any successor attorney-in-fact shall incur any liability to me, my estate, my heirs, successors or assigns for acting or refraining from acting under this document, except for willful misconduct or gross negligence. Neither my attorney-in-fact nor any successors shall be required to make my assets productive of income, increase the value of my estate, diversify my investments or enter into transactions authorized by this document, as long as my attorney-in-fact or successor believes his or her actions are in my best interests or in the best interests of my estate and of those interested in my estate.

14. Gifts by Attorney-in-Fact

a. My attorney-in-fact shall have no incidents of ownership over any life insurance policy in which I may own an interest and which insures his or her life.

b. My attorney-in-fact may not (i) appoint, assign or designate any of my assets, interests or rights directly or indirectly to himself or herself, or estate, creditors, or the creditors of his or her estate, (ii) disclaim assets to which I would otherwise be entitled if the effect of the disclaimer is to cause such assets to pass directly or indirectly to my attorney-in-fact or his or her estate, or (iii) use my assets to discharge any of his or her legal obligations, including any obligation of support owed to others (excluding me and those whom I am legally obligated to support).

    c.   My attorney-in-fact shall not hold or exercise any powers I may have over assets he or she has given to me or over assets held in an irrevocable trust of which he or she is a grantor.

15. Reliance on this Power of Attorney

I agree that any third party who receives a copy of this document may act under it. Revocation of the power of attorney is not effective as to a third party until the third party has actual knowledge of the revocation. I agree to indemnify the third party for any claims that arise against the third party because of reliance on this power of attorney.

16. Severability

If any provision of this document is ruled unenforceable, the remaining provisions shall stay in effect.

I understand the importance of the powers I delegate to my attorney-in-fact in this document. I recognize that the document gives my attorney-in-fact broad powers over my assets, and that these powers shall become effective as of the date of my incapacity (or sooner if specified in this document) and shall continue indefinitely unless I revoke this durable power of attorney.

Signed this ___14 th___ day of ___JUNE___ 19 _72_ .

State of ___TENNESSEE___   County of ___DAVIDSON___

___Nicholas S. Ericsson___   ___234-51-6782___
    your signature   your social security number

CERTIFICATE OF ACKNOWLEDGMENT OF NOTARY PUBLIC

State of ___Tennessee___ }

County of ___Davidson___ } ss

On ___June 15___, 19 _72_ , before me, ___Jane Thill___, a notary public, personally appeared ___Nicholas S. Ericsson___, personally known to me or proved to me on the basis of satisfactory evidence to be the person whose name is subscribed to this instrument, and acknowledged that he or she executed it.

[NOTARY SEAL]   ___Jane Thill___
                                      signature of notary public

7

MAKING IT LEGAL

After you've done the hard part of putting together a durable power of attorney, you have some simple tasks left to make sure the document is legally valid and will be accepted by the people the attorney-in-fact may have to deal with. This chapter shows you what to do.

CHECKLIST: Making It Legal

After you've completed your durable power of attorney, follow these steps:

☐ 1. Show the durable power of attorney to banks, brokers, insurers and other financial institutions you expect your attorney-in-fact to deal with.

☐ 2. Sign the durable power of attorney in front of a notary public and, if you wish or state law requires, in the presence of witnesses.

☐ 3. Record the durable power of attorney in the county land records office, if necessary.

☐ 4. Distribute copies of the durable power of attorney to people the attorney-in-fact will deal with.

☐ 5. Store the durable power of attorney where your attorney-in-fact will have quick access to it.

A. Before You Sign

Before you finalize your power of attorney, you may want to show it to the banks, brokers, insurers and other financial institutions you expect your attorney-in-fact to deal with on your behalf.

Discussing your plans with people at these institutions now (and giving them a copy of the durable power of attorney, after you sign it, if you wish), can make your attorney-in-fact's job easier. An institution may ask that you include specific language in your durable power of attorney, authorizing the attorney-in-fact to do certain things on your

behalf. You may have to go along if you want cooperation later. If you don't want to change your durable power of attorney, find another bank that will accept the document as it is.

B. Sign and Notarize the Durable Power of Attorney

A durable power of attorney is a serious document, and to make it effective you must observe certain formalities when you sign the document. Fortunately, these requirements aren't difficult.

1. Notarization

You must sign your durable power of attorney in the presence of a notary public for your state. In some states, notarization is required by law to make the durable power of attorney valid. But even where law doesn't require it, custom does. A durable power of attorney that isn't notarized may not be accepted by people your attorney-in-fact tries to deal with.

The notary public watches you sign the durable power of attorney and then signs it, too and stamps it with an official seal. The notary will want proof of your identity, such as a driver's license that bears your photo and signature. The notary's fee is usually just a few dollars—probably $5 to $10 in most places. A notarized signature is shown below.

A NOTARIZED SIGNATURE

[text of document]

Signed this __21__ day of __October__, 19__93__

Francis Byrne
Signature

CERTIFICATE OF ACKNOWLEDGMENT OF NOTARY PUBLIC

State of __Michigan__)
) ss.
County of __Wayne__   )

On __October 21__, 19__93__ before me, __Hazel Ditka__, a notary public, personally appeared __Francis Byrne__, personally known to me (or proved to me on the basis of satisfactory evidence) to be the person whose name is subscribed to this instrument, and acknowledged that he or she executed it.

[NOTARY SEAL]   _Hazel Ditka_
                 Signature of notary public

My commission expires: __July 5, 1994__

Finding a notary public shouldn't be a problem; many advertise in the yellow pages. Or check with your bank, which may provide notarizations as a service to customers. Real estate offices and title companies also have notaries.

If you are gravely ill, you'll need to find a notary who will come to the your home or hospital room. To arrange it, call around to notaries listed in the yellow pages. Expect to pay a reasonable extra fee for a house call.

2.   Witnesses

Most states don't require the durable power of attorney to be signed in front of witnesses. (See the list below.) Nevertheless, it doesn't hurt to have a witness or two watch you sign, and sign the document themselves. Witnesses' signatures may make the power of attorney more acceptable to lawyers, banks, insurance companies and other entities the attorney-in-fact may have to deal with. (Part of the

Witnesses can serve another function, too. If you're worried that someone may challenge your capacity to execute a valid durable power of attorney later, it's prudent to have witnesses who can testify that in their judgment you knew what you were doing when you signed the document.

The witnesses must be present when you sign the document before the notary. Witnesses must be mentally competent adults, preferably ones who live nearby and will be easily available if necessary. The person who will serve as attorney-in-fact should *not* be a witness. (The attorney-in-fact does not have to sign the durable power of attorney document, but some states' forms have a place for the attorney-in-fact's signature, so other people will know it's genuine later.)

- If you used the Nolo power of attorney form (Chapter 5), the Appendix contains two different last pages (page 8) for the form. One has a place for witnesses to sign, the other doesn't. Choose the one you want.

- If you used a state-specific power of attorney form (Chapter 6), the form has a place for witnesses to sign if they're required by state law.

STATES THAT REQUIRE TWO WITNESSES

Connecticut

Georgia (if durable power is to be recorded)

Indiana

Louisiana

Michigan (if durable power is to be recorded)

Minnesota

South Carolina

Texas

C. Put the Durable Power of Attorney on Public Record

You may need to put a copy of your durable power of attorney on file in the county land records office, called the County Recorder's or Land Registry Office in most states. This is called "recording," or "registration" in some states.

1. When You Should Record Your Durable Power of Attorney

In North Carolina, South Carolina and Texas, you must record a power of attorney for it to be durable— that is, for it to remain in effect if you become incapacitated.

In other states, you should record the power of attorney if it gives your attorney-in-fact authority over your real estate. If you don't record the document, your attorney-in-fact won't be able to sell, mortgage or otherwise handle your real estate.

Recording makes it clear to all interested parties that the attorney-in-fact has power over the property. County land records are checked whenever real estate changes hands (or is mortgaged); if your attorney-in-fact goes to sell or mortgage your real estate, there must be something in the records that proves he or she has authority to do so.

There is no time limit on when you must record a durable power of attorney. So if you've created a springing durable power, which may not go into effect for many years (or ever), you may not want to record it immediately. Your attorney-in-fact can always record it later, if the document takes effect.

Even if recording is not legally required, you can go ahead and record your durable power of attorney; officials in some financial institutions may be reassured later on by seeing that you took that step.

NOTE FOR NORTH CAROLINA READERS

In your state, a durable power of attorney must be:

• recorded with the Register of Deeds; and

• filed with the clerk of the superior court within 30 days after recording, <u>unless</u> the durable power of attorney waives the requirement that the attorney-in-fact file inventories and accountings with the court. The North Carolina form in this book waives that requirement.

---

2.   Where To Record Your Power of Attorney

In most states, each county has its own county recorder's (or registry of deeds) office. Take the durable power of attorney to the local office—if you're recording to give the attorney-in-fact authority over real estate—in the county where the real estate is located. If you want your attorney-in-fact to have authority over more than one parcel of real estate, record the power of attorney in each county where you own property.

3.   How To Record a Document

Recording a document is easy. You may even be able to do it by mail, but it's safer to go in person. The clerk will make a copy (usually on microfilm these days) for the public records. It will be assigned a reference number, often in terms of books and pages—for example, "Book 14, Page 1932 of the Contra Costa County, California records." In most places, it costs just a few dollars per page to record a document.

D.   What To Do With the Signed Document

If the power of attorney is to take effect immediately, give the original, signed and notarized document to the attorney-in-fact. He or she will need it as proof of authority to act on your behalf.

If the durable power of attorney doesn't become effective until you are incapacitated (a springing durable power of attorney), keep the notarized, signed original yourself. Store it in a safe, convenient place that the attorney-in-fact has quick access to. A fireproof box in your home or office is fine. The attorney-in-fact will need the original document to carry out your wishes.

A safe deposit box isn't the best place to store a springing durable power of attorney, unless the attorney-in-fact is a co-tenant with access to the box. It's better just to keep the document wherever you file other important legal papers. Just make sure that the attorney-in-fact knows where it is.

E.   Distribute Copies of the Durable Power of Attorney

If you wish, you can give copies of your durable power to the people your attorney-in-fact will need to deal with—in banks or government offices, for example. If the durable power is in their records, it may eliminate hassles for your attorney-in-fact later.

If you're making a springing durable power of attorney, however, it may seem premature to contact people and institutions about a document that may never go into effect. It's up to you.

Be sure to keep a list of everyone to whom you give a copy. If you later revoke your durable power of attorney, notify each institution of the revocation.

**REMINDER: REVIEW YOUR
POWER OF ATTORNEY PERIODICALLY**

You should review, and perhaps revise, your durable power of attorney for finances every five to seven years. See Chapter 2, *How Financial Durable Powers of Attorney Work*, Section G.

REVOKING A DURABLE
POWER OF ATTORNEY

After you grant a power of attorney, you can revoke it at any time, as long as you are of sound mind. But to make the revocation legally effective, you must carefully follow all the procedures set out in this chapter.

CHECKLIST: REVOKING A POWER OF ATTORNEY

☐ 1. Prepare a Notice of Revocation.

☐ 2. Sign the Notice of Revocation in front of a notary public (and in the presence of witnesses, if you wish).

☐ 3. Record the Notice of Revocation at the county land records office, if necessary.

☐ 4. Deliver a copy of the Notice of Revocation to the attorney-in-fact and each institution and person who has dealt or might deal with the former attorney-in-fact.

A. Who Can Revoke a Power of Attorney

Only you, or someone a court appoints to act for you, can revoke your power of attorney.

1. The Principal

You can revoke your durable power of attorney as long as you are mentally competent and physically able to do so. The competency requirement is not difficult to satisfy. If someone challenged the revocation, a court would look only at whether or not you understood, when you signed it, the consequences of your act. (The competency requirement is the same as that required to create a valid power of attorney in the first place; see Chapter 2, *How Durable Powers of Attorney Work*, Section A.)

If you revoke a springing durable power of attorney that hasn't taken effect yet, you shouldn't run into any problems. You simply sign the Notice of Revocation (explained later in this chapter), and it's as if you had never prepared the original power of attorney.

If, however, your springing durable power of attorney has already taken effect, it means that one or two physicians (the ones you named in your power of attorney document) have stated, in writing, that you are incapacitated and unable to handle your financial affairs. Your attorney-in-fact may feel that you are not legally competent to revoke the durable power of attorney. If the attorney-in-fact doesn't accept the validity of the revocation, and keeps control over your financial matters, there may have to be court proceedings to resolve the conflict.

> **Example:** In a springing durable power of attorney, Arthur authorizes Jim to be his attorney-in-fact. Two years later, Arthur has a stroke. A doctor signs a statement saying that Arthur cannot manage his financial affairs, and Jim begins to act as Arthur's attorney-in-fact for finances.
>
> Arthur slowly recovers and eventually feels able to handle his own affairs again. But Jim thinks that Arthur is irrational and shouldn't be allowed to make his own decisions. He continues acting for Arthur, concluding that his authority is unchanged because Arthur isn't competent to revoke the durable power of attorney.
>
> If Arthur insists, Jim will have to accede to his wishes, or one of them will have to request a court proceeding, where a judge will determine whether or not Arthur is competent to revoke the durable power of attorney and manage his own affairs.

An attorney-in-fact who refuses to accept a revocation can create serious problems. If you get into such a dispute with your attorney-in-fact, consult a lawyer.

2.   A Conservator or Guardian

If your attorney-in-fact is satisfactorily handling your financial affairs while you can't, it's very unlikely that a court will need to appoint a conservator for you. After all, your affairs are being handled—the attorney-in-fact is depositing your checks, paying your bills and looking after your property. (Conservators are discussed in Chapter 1, *Using a Durable Power of Attorney*, Section B.)

If, however, you or a family member objected to the attorney-in-fact's actions, a court might appoint a conservator. In a few states, appointment of a conservator automatically revokes a durable power of attorney. In that case, the conservator would become solely responsible for your property and financial matters.

In many states, the conservator would have the legal authority to revoke your durable power of attorney. Someone appointed to take physical care of you (usually called a "guardian" or "guardian of the person"), not your property, may also, depending on state law, have the power to revoke a financial power of attorney. Each state's rules are listed below.

This is nothing to worry about. Again, keep in mind that a conservator will probably never be appointed. But to be cautious, you can control matters in advance, by stating that you want the attorney-in-fact named as conservator if one is ever appointed. This statement is a part of your durable power of attorney. (See Chapter 5, *Preparing the Durable Power of Attorney*, Section C, Part 9.)

POWER OF CONSERVATOR OR GUARDIAN TO REVOKE POWER OF ATTORNEY

Alabama	Curator or guardian of the estate can revoke power of attorney
Alaska	Conservator can revoke power of attorney
Arizona	Conservator can revoke power of attorney
Arkansas	Conservator or guardian of the estate can revoke power of attorney
California	Conservator can revoke power of attorney only if authorized by court
Colorado	Conservator can revoke power of attorney
Connecticut	Power of attorney automatically revoked if conservator of the estate appointed
Delaware	Power of attorney revoked to the extent that the attorney-in-fact's powers are specifically granted to the guardian of the person or of the estate. Guardian can revoke power of attorney only if authorized by court.
Dist. of Columbia	Conservator or guardian of the estate can revoke power of attorney
Florida	Power of attorney automatically suspended if a guardianship proceeding begun; revoked if guardian appointed
Georgia	Power of attorney automatically revoked if guardian or receiver appointed
Hawaii	Guardian of the property can revoke power of attorney
Idaho	Conservator or guardian of the estate can revoke power of attorney
Illinois	Guardian can revoke power of attorney only if ordered by court
Indiana	Guardian can revoke power of attorney only if ordered by court
Iowa	Conservator can revoke power of attorney
Kansas	Conservator or guardian of the estate can revoke power of attorney
Kentucky	Power of attorney automatically revoked if fiduciary appointed
Louisiana	Power of attorney automatically terminated if curator qualified
Maine	Conservator or guardian can revoke power of attorney
Maryland	Guardian can revoke power of attorney
Massachusetts	Conservator or guardian of the estate can revoke power of attorney
Michigan	Conservator can revoke power of attorney
Minnesota	Conservator or guardian can revoke power of attorney
Mississippi	Power of attorney automatically revoked if general guardian, guardian of the estate or conservator appointed
Missouri	Conservator can revoke power of attorney only with court approval
Montana	Conservator can revoke power of attorney

Nebraska	Conservator or guardian of the estate can revoke power of attorney
Nevada	Guardian can revoke power of attorney
New Hampshire	Guardian or conservator can revoke power of attorney
New Jersey	Guardian can revoke power of attorney
New Mexico	Conservator can revoke power of attorney
New York	Committee or conservator can revoke power of attorney
North Carolina	Conservator, guardian of the estate or guardian of the person can revoke power of attorney
North Dakota	Conservator or guardian of the estate can revoke power of attorney
Ohio	Guardian can revoke power of attorney
Oklahoma	Conservator or guardian of the estate can revoke power of attorney
Oregon	Conservator can revoke power of attorney
Pennsylvania	Guardian can revoke power of attorney
Rhode Island	Conservator or guardian can revoke power of attorney
South Carolina	Attorney-in-fact's powers revoked as to matters within scope of the guardianship or conservatorship, unless the power of attorney provides otherwise
South Dakota	Guardian of the estate can revoke power of attorney
Tennessee	Conservator or guardian of the estate can revoke power of attorney
Texas	Power of attorney automatically revoked when guardian appointed
Utah	Conservator can revoke power of attorney
Vermont	Guardian can revoke power of attorney
Virginia	Guardian or committee can revoke power of attorney only if authorized by court
Washington	Guardian can revoke power of attorney
West Virginia	Conservator or guardian of the estate can revoke power of attorney
Wisconsin	Conservator or guardian of the estate can revoke power of attorney
Wyoming	Conservator can revoke power of attorney

B.   When To Revoke a Power of Attorney

If you've prepared a springing durable power of attorney, years may elapse between the time you sign the durable power of attorney and the time it takes effect (if ever). During that interval—or even after the durable power of attorney goes into effect, as long as you are mentally competent—you may well decide you need to revoke the durable power of attorney. Here are the most common situations in which you should revoke a power of attorney and start over.

1.   You Want To Change the Terms of the Power of Attorney

There is no accepted way to amend a power of attorney. If you want to change or amend a durable power of attorney, the safe course is to revoke the existing document and prepare a new one. Don't go back and modify your old document with pen, typewriter or correction fluid—you could throw doubt on the authenticity of the whole thing.

> **Example:** Tom signed a durable power of attorney several years ago. Now he is in declining health and wants to add to the authority he gave his attorney-in-fact, Sarah, giving her the specific power to sell Tom's real estate if necessary.
>
> Tom should revoke his old durable power of attorney and create a new one, granting the additional authority.

Similarly, you should revoke your durable power of attorney if you change your mind about whom you want to name as attorney-in-fact. If you create a springing durable power of attorney, the person you named to be your attorney-in-fact may become unavailable before he or she is needed. Or you may simply change your mind. If that's the case, you can revoke the durable power of attorney before it ever takes effect.

2.   You Move to Another State

If you move to a different state, your attorney-in-fact may run into some trouble getting others to accept the validity of a power of attorney signed in your old state. (See Chapter 2, *How Durable Powers of Attorney Work*, Section E.) You may want to revoke your power of attorney and prepare a new one, especially if your new state has its own durable power of attorney form. (See Chapter 6, *State-Specific Durable Power of Attorney Forms.*)

3.   You Lose the Power of Attorney Document

If you conclude that you've really lost your signed power of attorney document, it's wise to formally revoke it, destroy any copies and create a new one. Very few people are likely to accept your attorney-in-fact's authority if they can't look at the document it's based on. By officially revoking the lost version, you minimize chances that the old power of attorney might someday appear and confuse matters.

4.   You Get Married or Divorced

If you get married after signing a durable power of attorney, you'll probably want to designate your new spouse to be your attorney-in-fact, if he or she wasn't the person you named originally.

If you name your spouse as your attorney-in-fact and later divorce, you should revoke the power of attorney and create a new one, naming someone else as the attorney-in-fact.

In California, Illinois, Indiana and Missouri, the designation is automatically ended if you divorce the attorney-in-fact. In that case, the alternate you named (if any) would serve as attorney-in-fact. You still may want to create a new power of attorney, one that doesn't mention your former spouse and lets you name another alternate attorney-in-fact.

5.   Your Durable Power Is Old

If you make a springing durable power of attorney, it's a good idea to review it every five to seven years. A durable power of attorney never expires, but if the document was signed many years before it goes into effect, the attorney-in-fact may have trouble getting banks, insurance companies or people in government agencies to accept its authority, just because people don't trust documents that are 15 years old. You may want to revoke it and sign a new one.

It's especially important to review your durable power of attorney if significant changes occur in your life. For example, if the person you named as your attorney-in-fact moves far away, becomes ill or is no longer closely involved with your life, you should appoint someone else to serve. To do that, revoke the old power of attorney and prepare a new one.

If after you sign your durable power of attorney, your state adopts an official form for creating durable financial powers of attorney, you may want to revoke your old durable power of attorney and use the new form. You can always find your state's current form in the law library. (See Chapter 9, *Lawyers and Legal Research*.)

If you use an official form and it is later changed (this is common), you're probably all right—you don't need to revoke the old one and use the new form, although it wouldn't hurt. Usually, when a legislature changes a form, it "grandfathers" in old forms that were prepared before the changes took effect. But don't use an old form if you know a newer one is available.

Example: Alan makes a durable power of attorney for finances, using the official Illinois short form. Three years later, the Illinois legislature makes some minor changes in the form, but declares that powers of attorney made using the old form, before the law creating the new one took effect, are still valid. Alan doesn't need to create a new power of attorney.

C.   How To Revoke a Power of Attorney

There are two ways to revoke your power of attorney:

- Prepare and sign a document called a Notice of Revocation.
- Destroy *all* existing copies of the power of attorney document.

The first method is always preferable, because it creates proof that you really revoked the power of attorney.

NOTE FOR ALASKA READERS

Alaska law allows you to revoke your power of attorney by preparing a new one. It's still advisable, however, to prepare a separate notice of revocation and notify everyone who needs to know about the revocation.

---

1.   Prepare a Notice of Revocation

The "Notice of Revocation" is called that because its purpose is to notify the attorney-in-fact, and those he or she may have been dealing with, that you have revoked the durable power of attorney.

Two kinds of Notice of Revocation forms are included in this book. If you didn't record your durable power of attorney in the county land records office (Chapter 7, *Making It Legal*), use the first one. If you did record the original durable power of attorney, you must also record the revocation; use the second form.

Samples are shown below. A blank tear-out copy of each form is included in the Appendix.

REVOCATION FORM 1: FOR UNRECORDED POWER OF ATTORNEY

NOTICE OF REVOCATION OF DURABLE POWER OF ATTORNEY

I, _____Ramona Linwood_____, of
____54 Sunburst Lane_____, City of _____Plymouth_____,
County of _____Cook_____, State of _____Illinois_____, give notice
that I hereby revoke the durable power of attorney dated _____Feb. 17, 1990____ empowering
_____Jeremy S. Brown_____ to act as my
attorney-in-fact for certain financial matters. I revoke and withdraw all power and authority granted
under that power of attorney.

Dated: _August 2, 1992_____   _Ramona Linwood_____
                                            (Signature of Principal)

                              ____Ramona Linwood_____, Principal

State of _____Illinois_____

County of ____Hancock_____ } ss

On _August 2_____, 19_92_, before me, __Radmilla Socheck____
_____, a notary public, personally appeared __Ramona Linwood___
_____, known to me or proved on the basis of satisfactory evidence to be the person
whose name is subscribed to this instrument as principal and acknowledged and executed the same.

                    ____Radmilla Socheck_____
                    Notary Public for the State of __Illinois__

[notarial seal]   My commission expires: _Feb 16, 1994_

REVOCATION FORM 2: FOR RECORDED POWER OF ATTORNEY

RECORDING REQUESTED BY
AND WHEN RECORDED MAIL TO

David L. Hernandez

463 Arlington St. N.E.

Portland, Oregon 97510

NOTICE OF REVOCATION OF RECORDED POWER OF ATTORNEY

I, David L. Hernandez , of

463 Arlington St. N.E. , City of Portland , County of

Multnomah , State of Oregon , give notice that I

hereby revoke the durable power of attorney dated Sept 1, 1991 empowering

Francis M. Rowland to act as my attorney-in-fact for certain financial

matters. I revoke and withdraw all power and authority granted under that power of attorney.

That power of attorney was recorded on Sept. 8 , 19 91 in Book 379 ,

at Page 2436 of the Official Records, County of Multnomah ,

State of Oregon .

Dated: Jan 7, 1993   *David L. Hernandez*
                              (Signature of Principal)

                    David L. Hernandez , Principal

State of Oregon

County of Multnomah } ss

On January 8 , 19 93 , before me, Evelyn Kramer

, a notary public, personally appeared David L. Hernandez

, known to me or proved on the basis of satisfactory evidence to be the person

whose name is subscribed to this instrument as principal and acknowledged and executed the same.

                    Evelyn Kramer
                    Notary Public for the State of Oregon

[notarial seal]   My commission expires: Aug. 1, 1994

2.   Sign and Notarize the Revocation

You must sign and date the Notice of Revocation. It needn't be witnessed, but witnessing may be a prudent idea, especially if you have reason to believe that someone might later raise questions regarding your mental competence to execute the revocation. If you want witnesses' signatures, you'll have to retype the Notice of Revocation. (Witnesses are discussed in Chapter 7, *Making It Legal*, Section B.)

Sign the Notice of Revocation in front of a notary public. Finding a notary shouldn't be a problem; many advertise in the yellow pages. Or check with a bank, real estate office or attorney's office. (For more on notarization, see Chapter 7, *Making It Legal*, Section B.)

3.   Record the Notice of Revocation

If you recorded the original durable power of attorney at your local recorder of deeds office, you must also record the revocation. (How to record documents is explained in Chapter 7, *Making It Legal*, Section C.)

But even if the original durable power of attorney was not recorded, you can record a revocation if you fear that the former attorney-in-fact might try to act without authorization. If the revocation is part of the public records, people who check those records (as anyone should if real estate is involved) will (or should) know that the former attorney-in-fact is no longer authorized to act on your behalf.

NOTE FOR NORTH CAROLINA READERS

When you register the revocation in the office of the register of deeds, it must be accompanied by a document showing that a copy of the revocation notice has been served on the former attorney-in-fact. This document is called a "proof of service." (N.C. Gen. Stat. § 32A-13.)

The revocation must be served on the attorney-in-fact by the county sheriff or someone else authorized by law to serve legal papers. (N.C. Rules of Civ. Proc. § 1A-1, Rule 4.)

---

4.   Notify Anyone Who Deals With the Former Attorney-in-Fact

It's not enough to sign a revocation, or even to record it, for it to take effect; there's one more crucial step. You must notify the former attorney-in-fact and all institutions and people who have dealt or might deal with the former attorney-in-fact. Each of them must receive a copy of the Notice of Revocation. (If you're naming the same person as your attorney-in-fact in again—for example, if you're preparing a new durable power because you moved to a different state—this may not be necessary.)

If you don't give this written notification, people or institutions who don't know the durable power of attorney has been revoked might still enter into transactions with the (former) attorney-in-fact. If they do this in good faith, they are legally protected. You may well be held legally liable for the acts of your attorney-in-fact, even though you have revoked his or her authority. In other words, once you create a durable power of attorney, the legal burden is on you to be sure everyone knows you have revoked it.

Example: When Michael undergoes a serious operation, his springing durable power of attorney goes into effect. After his convalescence, Michael revokes the power of attorney, in writing. He sends a copy of the revocation to

Colette, his attorney-in-fact, but neglects to send a copy to his bank. Colette, fraudulently acting as Michael's attorney-in-fact, removes money from Michael's accounts and spends it. The bank isn't responsible to Michael for his loss.

When you're ready to send out revocation notices, try to think of everyone with whom the attorney-in-fact has had, or may have, dealings. Some examples: banks, insurance companies, Social Security offices, pension funds, the post office, hospitals, doctors, stockbrokers, your landlord, lawyer or accountant.

LAWYERS AND LEGAL RESEARCH

Lawyer: One skilled in circumvention of the law.

—Ambrose Bierce

If you prepare your own durable power of attorney with this book, you probably won't need to see a lawyer. If, however, you have specific questions or unusual circumstances—a very large amount of property, potential family squabbles, or special worries about the attorney-in-fact's powers, for example—you may need legal advice.

If you do need more legal information or advice, you can hire a lawyer or look for your answers yourself in a law library. If you need clerical help typing your document, you may find help from a legal typing service.

A.   Legal Typing Services

Even if you need "legal" help, you may not need a lawyer. People who operate legal typing services, also known as independent paralegals or legal technicians, are experts at preparing and filing legal

documents. They are not lawyers and do not give legal advice. But if you know what you want, a typing service can help you prepare the legal paperwork at an affordable price. For example, if you want to modify and retype a state-specific durable power of attorney form, and are concerned about getting all the required legal warnings in the proper size and typeface (bold type is required in some states), a typing service might be able to help.

For the name of the legal typing service nearest you, call the National Association for Independent Paralegals at 800-542-0034.

B.   Legal Advice Over the Phone

You don't have to sign up as a lawyer's client to get advice from a lawyer; legal advice is now available over the phone. A group of lawyers in the Los Angeles area have formed a company, TeleLawyer, that offers legal advice for $3/minute ($180/hour). It may sound expensive, but compared to the conventional way of buying legal advice from a lawyer, it can be a bargain.

TeleLawyer's staff includes lawyers who specialize in many different areas, including estate planning. You're charged only for the time you spend talking to the lawyer on the phone. So if you have a concrete question that can be answered fairly quickly, it won't cost much. A lawyer who can't answer your question will find out the answer and call you back.

TeleLawyer offers only advice. Its lawyers do not accept cases, and it does not give referrals to lawyers—which means its lawyers have no financial incentive to recommend more legal services than you need. All conversations are confidential.

To contact TeleLawyer, call 800-835-3529 (charged to your credit card) or 900-776-7000 (charged on your phone bill).

C.   How To Choose a Lawyer

If you decide that you want to talk about your situation face to face with a lawyer, do a little shopping around. The trick isn't just finding (or being found by) any lawyer, but finding one who is trustworthy, competent and charges fairly.

Look for a lawyer who has experience with estate planning and preparing financial durable powers of attorney. Lawyers who concentrate on other kinds of law—divorce, tax or insurance, for example—may not know nearly as much as you do about the intelligent use of durable powers of attorney for finances. A specialist's fee may be 10 to 30% higher than that of a general practitioner, but a good specialist will probably produce results more efficiently and save you money in the long run.

Here are some suggestions on how to go about finding a good lawyer.

1.   Look Into a Group Legal Plan

Some unions, employers and consumer organizations offer group legal plans to their members or employees. Good group plans offer comprehensive legal assistance for free or at low rates. If you are a member of such a plan, check with it first. Your problem may be covered free of charge. If it is, and you are satisfied that the lawyer you are referred to is knowledgeable in estate planning, this route is probably a good choice.

Some plans, however, give you only a slight reduction in a lawyer's fee. In that case, you may be referred to a lawyer whose main virtue is the willingness to reduce fees in exchange for a high volume of referrals. Be wary.

2.   Check Out a Prepaid Legal Plan

For basic advice, you may want to consider joining a prepaid legal plan that offers advice, by phone or in person, at no extra charge. The plans cost about $100 a year. They are sold by companies such as Montgomery Ward and Amway, and are often offered to credit card holders or sold door-to-door.

The attraction of these plans is that initial membership fee is reasonable, compared to the cost of hiring a lawyer by the hour. You can join a plan for a specific period, get the help you need, and then not renew.

But before you sign up, consider that there's no guarantee that the lawyers available through these plans are of the best caliber. The lawyer you see probably receives at most $2 or $3 a month for dealing with you—obviously, not enough to cover costs. In most prepaid plans, lawyers agree to work for this minimal amount in the hope of finding clients who will pay for extra legal services not covered by the monthly premium. This set-up gives the lawyers a financial incentive to complicate, rather than simplify, your problem. So if a plan lawyer recommends an expensive legal procedure, get a second opinion.

One prepaid legal plan, LawPhone (4501 Forbes Blvd., Lanham, MD 20706) follows a better system. It uses a two-part system under which lawyers who advise clients aren't allowed to perform more complicated and expensive services for those clients.

3.   Ask Businesspeople and Friends

Personal contacts are the traditional, and probably the best, means for locating a good lawyer. Ask people you know in any social or other organization in which you are involved. They may well know of a good lawyer whose attitudes are similar to yours. Senior citizens' centers and other groups that advise and assist older people may have a list of well regarded local lawyers who specialize in estate planning.

Anyone who owns a small business probably has an ongoing relationship with a lawyer. Ask around to find someone you know who is a satisfied client. If that lawyer does not handle estate planning, he or she will likely know someone who does. And because of the continuing relationship with your friend, the lawyer has an incentive to recommend someone who is competent.

4.   Consult a Legal Clinic

Law firms with lots of small offices across the country, such as Hyatt Legal Services and Jacoby & Meyers, trumpet their low initial consultation fees. It's true that a basic consultation is cheap, often about $20; anything beyond that isn't cheap at all. Generally, the rates average about the same as those charged by other lawyers in general practice.

If you do consult a legal clinic, often the trick is to quickly extract the information you need and resist attempts to convince you that you need more services. If the lawyer you talk to is experienced in estate planning, however, and you're comfortable with the person and the service, it may be worthwhile. Unfortunately, most of these offices have extremely high lawyer turnover, so you may see a different one every time you visit.

5.   Call an Attorney Referral Service

A lawyer referral service will give you the name of an attorney who practices in your area. Usually, you can get a referral to an attorney who claims to specialize in estate planning and will give you an initial consultation for a low fee.

Most county bar associations have referral services. In some states, independent referral services, run by or for groups of lawyers, also operate.

Never assume a bar association referral is a seal of approval. Few referral services thoroughly screen the attorneys they list, which means those who participate may not be the most experienced or competent. Often, lawyers who sign up with referral services simply need clients, because they are just starting out or for some other reason. (Experienced lawyers with good reputations usually get plenty of new clients from recommendations of their current ones.) It may be possible to find a skilled estate planning specialist through a referral service, but be sure to take the time to check out the credentials and experience of the person to whom you're referred.

D.   Working With a Lawyer

Before you talk to the lawyer you've made an appointment with, decide what kind of help you really need. Do you want someone to review your durable power of attorney to make sure it looks all right? Or do you want advice on a complete estate plan? If you don't clearly tell the lawyer what you want, you may find yourself agreeing to more than you'd planned.

If you just want a lawyer to review your durable power to reassure you that it looks fine, you may have a hard time finding a willing lawyer. Although you may think it's perfectly reasonable for the lawyer to take a quick glance and charge you a half-hour's fee, from the lawyer's point of view there are several problems. First, a conscientious lawyer may feel that it's impossible to give an intelligent opinion about the wisdom of your durable power of attorney without first talking to you about your finances and family.

A related factor is the fear of a malpractice lawsuit sometime down the road. A lawyer doesn't want to give you a bit of advice now, for a small fee, and get a phone call from you years later saying that something has gone wrong. Economically, the risk isn't worth it.

Before you see the lawyer, a good strategy is to write down your questions as specifically as you can. If the lawyer doesn't give you clear, concise answers, say thank you and try someone else. Preparing a solid durable power of attorney isn't an overly complicated job in most instances; a knowledgeable lawyer should be able to give you satisfactory answers on the spot.

If the lawyer acts wise but says little except to ask that the problem be placed in his or her hands—with a substantial fee, of course—watch out. You're either dealing with someone who doesn't know the answer and won't admit it (common) or someone who finds it impossible to let go of the "me expert, you plebeian" philosophy (even more common).

E.   Lawyers' Fees

Most lawyers charge $100 to $350 per hour. It depends on where you live, but generally, fees of $125 to $200 per hour are reasonable in urban areas, given the lawyer's overhead expense. In rural areas and smaller cities, $80 to $150 is more like it.

Price is not always related to quality. A fancy office, three-piece suit and solemn face are no guarantee (or even any indication) that a lawyer is competent, but they do guarantee a high price tag. Fortunately, many good lawyers operate more modestly and pass the savings onto their clients.

Whatever the fee arrangement, be sure you've settled it—preferably in writing—at the start of your relationship. In addition to the hourly fee, you should get a clear, written commitment from the lawyer about how many hours your problem should take to handle. (In California, state law requires a lawyer to prepare a written fee agreement if the fee is expected to exceed $1000.)

F.   Doing Your Own Legal Research

If you're willing to learn how to do your own legal research, the benefits are substantial. Not only will you save some money, you'll gain a sense of mastery over an area of law and a confidence that will spill over into your other dealings with legal matters.

Fortunately, the law governing durable powers of attorney is not particularly difficult to research. But first, of course, you've got to find a law library, where the laws books are. Your choices are:

- a public law library (usually located in the county courthouse)
- a public library with a good law collection
- a library at a public (or even private, if you ask permission) law school.

When you get to the library, you'll probably need the help of a good legal research guidebook (see "Finding the Law," below) and of a librarian. Law librarians are almost always helpful and courteous to non-lawyers who try to do their own legal research.

Statutes. The first thing to do is ask a librarian where to find the state statutes, which are called "codes," "laws" or "statutes," depending on the state. If you can, get an "annotated version," which contains both your state's statutes and excerpts from any relevant court cases and references to related articles and commentaries.

Once you've found your state's statutes, check the general index. Your best bets are these topics:

- Durable Powers of Attorney for Finances
- Durable Powers of Attorney for Property
- Agents
- Attorneys-in-Fact.

Each state groups its durable power of attorney laws together. Statutes are numbered sequentially, so once you get the correct numbers from the index, it should be easy to find the statute you need. If you have trouble, ask the law librarian for help. When you find it, make sure you're reading the most recent version of the statute by checking the back of the statute book to see if there's a "pocket part" (supplement) inserted inside the back cover. Pocket parts contain statutory changes (and related court decisions) made since the hardback book was printed.

Be warned that statutes are rarely easy to read. Commonly, they are written in dense prose, full of incredibly long sentences, obscure legal terms and cross-references to other statutes. Wade through them as best you can, and expect to read any section you're interested in several times.

After you've looked at the basic law, you'll probably want to check any recent court decisions mentioned in the "Annotation" section of the code immediately following the law itself.

Form books. Form books, which are how-to-do-it books written primarily for lawyers, can also be very helpful. There will likely be a form book that contains sample durable power of attorney forms

valid in your state. Ask a law librarian to help you find a form book.

FINDING THE LAW

If you decide to delve into legal research, consult *Legal Research: How To Find and Understand the Law*, by Stephen Elias and Susan Levinkind (Nolo Press). This hands-on guide to the law library addresses research methods in detail and should answer most questions that arise in the course of your research. (It also contains a good discussion of how to read and analyze statutes.)

For a guided tour through the basics of legal research, you may also be interested in *Legal Research Made Easy: A Roadmap Through the Law Library Maze*, an entertaining and informative 2-1/2 hour videotape (Nolo Press and Legal Star Communications).

GLOSSARY

Words in boldface are defined separately in the Glossary.

Acknowledgment: A statement signed in front of a person who is qualified to administer oaths (a **notary public**) that a person's signature is genuine.

Affidavit: A written statement signed under oath in front of a **notary public**.

Agent: Someone who is legally authorized to act for another person. An **attorney-in-fact** is a legal agent of the **principal**.

Alternate attorney-in-fact: The person you name to serve as attorney-in-fact if your first choice cannot or will not serve.

Annuity: A contract that entitles one person to a series of payments over a certain time. People often buy annuities to provide regular income after they retire.

Attorney-in-Fact: The person who is authorized, in a written power of attorney, to act on behalf of another person.

Bond: A document guaranteeing that a certain amount of money will be paid to those injured if a person occupying a position of trust does not carry out his or her legal and ethical responsibilities. Thus, if an **executor, trustee** or **guardian** who is bonded (covered by a bond) wrongfully deprives a beneficiary of his or her property (say by blowing it during a trip in Las Vegas), the bonding company (usually a division of an insurance company) will replace it, up to the limits of the bond.

Commodity: A tangible thing, such as corn or livestock, that is sold on the futures market, where one person agrees to sell at a certain price on a certain future date.

Committee: See **conservator**.

Community property: Nine states follow a system of marital property ownership generally called "community property." Very generally, all property acquired after marriage and before permanent separation is considered to belong equally to both spouses, except for gifts to and inheritances by one spouse, and, in some community property states, income from property owned by one spouse prior to marriage. Spouses can, however, enter into an agreement to the contrary.

Both spouses have authority to manage community property, but there are restrictions on one spouse's ability to sell community property without the other's consent.

Competent: Having the mental ability to understand the consequences of signing a legal document such as a **will** or **durable power of attorney.**

Conservatee: Someone for whom a court has appointed a **conservator,** who will manage the conservatee's property and finances.

Conservator: Someone appointed by a court to manage the affairs of a mentally incompetent person. Called guardian, **guardian of the estate,** committee or curator in some states.

Conventional power of attorney: A document that gives someone authority to handle your financial affairs for a defined reason or time. A conventional power of attorney might be used, for example, to give someone authority to make business decisions if you can't be reached while on a vacation. In most states, a conventional power of attorney ends if you (the **principal**) become incapacitated.

Curator: See **conservator**.

Declaration: A written statement signed under penalty of perjury.

Deed of trust: A document, used in many states, which is the functional equivalent of a **mortgage**. The trust deed transfers title of **real estate** to a trustee, who holds it as security for a loan. When the loan is paid off, title is transferred to the borrower.

Durable power of attorney: A power of attorney that remains valid even if the **principal** later becomes disabled or incapacitated. It ends only when the **principal** revokes it or dies. There are two kinds of durable powers of attorney:

- **Durable power of attorney for finances.** A durable power of attorney for finances (also called a durable power of attorney for property) is created to allow management of one's finances without court proceedings.

- **Durable power of attorney for health care.** This power of attorney is used to give a trusted person the right to make health care decisions on your behalf if you cannot.

Easement: The legal right to use another's land, usually for a limited purpose. For example, someone may own an easement that entitles them to use a corner of your property as a shortcut to their property.

Estate: Generally, all the property you own when you die. There are different kinds of estates: the taxable estate (property subject to estate taxation), the probate estate (property that must go through **probate**) or the net estate (the net value of the property).

Estate planning: Figuring out how to prosper when you're alive, die with the smallest taxable estate and probate estate possible, and pass property to loved ones with a minimum of fuss and expense.

Estate taxes: Taxes imposed on property as it passes from the dead to the living. The federal government exempts $600,000 of property and all property left to a surviving spouse who is a U.S. citizen. Some states also impose estate taxes.

Executor: The person named in a **will** to manage the deceased person's **estate**, deal with the probate court, collect assets and distribute them as the will specifies. In some states this person is called the "personal representative." If someone dies without a will, the probate court will appoint such a person, who is called the administrator of the estate.

Guardian of the estate: See **conservator**.

Guardian of the person: Someone appointed by a court to be responsible for the day-to-day physical well being of an **incompetent** person.

Incapacitated: Unable to handle one's own financial matters and/or health care decisions. Also called "disabled" in some states. Generally, incapacity isn't precisely defined by state law. The determination is usually made by a physician.

Incompetent: Lacking the mental ability to understand the consequences of signing a legal document such as a **will** or **durable power of attorney**. Someone who is incompetent cannot, legally, enter into a contract or create a valid power of attorney.

Joint tenancy: A way to own jointly owned **real** or **personal property**. When two or more people own property as joint tenants, and one of the owners dies, the other owners automatically become owners of the deceased owner's share. Thus, if a parent and child own a house as joint tenants, and the parent dies, the child automatically becomes full owner. Because of this "right of survivorship," a joint tenancy interest in property does not go through **probate**.

Lien: A claim on property for payment of a debt. For example, the government might place a tax lien on property if the owner has not paid taxes.

Living trust: A trust set up while a person is alive and which remains under the control of that person until death. Living trusts are an excellent way to minimize the value of property passing through **probate**. An **attorney-in-fact** for finances has no authority over property that has been transferred to a living trust.

Living will: A document, directed to your physicians, in which you state your wishes about having your life prolonged by technological means if you become gravely ill and cannot communicate your wishes.

Mortgage: A document that makes a piece of **real estate** the security (collateral) for the payment of a debt. If the owners don't pay back the loan on time, the lender can seize the house and have it sold to pay off the loan.

Notarization: A statement signed in front of a person who is qualified to administer oaths (a **notary public**) that a person's signature is genuine. Also called **acknowledgment.**

Notary public: Someone who is authorized by a state government to notarize signatures—that is, to verify that a signature is valid by watching the person sign and checking his or her identity. The notary then signs the document and stamps it with an official seal as evidence of the validity of the signature.

Personal property: All property other than land and buildings attached to land. Cars, bank accounts, wages, securities, a small business, furniture, insurance policies, jewelry, pets and season baseball tickets are all personal property.

Power of appointment: Having the legal authority to decide who shall receive someone else's property, usually property held in a trust.

Power of attorney: A legal document in which you authorize someone else to act for you. See **Durable power of attorney.**

Principal: The person who creates and signs a **power of attorney** document, authorizing someone to act on his or her behalf. If you sign a power of attorney, you're the principal.

Probate: The court proceeding in which: (1) the authenticity of your will (if any) is established; (2) your **executor** or administrator is appointed; (3) your debts and taxes are paid; (4) your heirs are identified; and (5) your property in your probate estate is distributed according to your will (if there is a will).

Recording: The process of filing a copy of a deed, **durable power of attorney** or other document with the county land records office.

Real estate: Same as **real property.**

Real property: All land and items attached to the land, such as buildings, houses, stationary mobile homes, fences and trees are real property or "real estate." All property that is not real property is **personal property.**

Revocable living trust: See **living trust.**

Separate property: In states which have community property, all property that is not community property. See **community property.**

Springing durable power of attorney. A **durable power of attorney** that becomes effective only if the **principal** becomes **incapacitated** at some future time. If the principal never becomes incapacitated, a springing durable power of attorney never goes into effect, and the principal keeps control over his or her assets. But if a doctor signs a statement stating that the principal has become incapacitated, the durable power of attorney "springs" into effect. In other words, the principal creates a legally valid method for handling his or her affairs during any future period of incapacity.

Successor attorney-in-fact: See **alternate attorney-in-fact**.

Tenancy by the entirety: A form of property ownership allowed in some states. It is similar to **joint tenancy**, but is allowed only for property owned by a husband and wife.

Trustee: The people or institutions who manage trust property under the terms of a trust document.

Will: A legal document in which a person directs what is to be done with his or her property after death.

APPENDIX FORMS

Nolo Durable Power of Attorney for Financial Management (witnessed)

    Alternate Pages 7 and 8 (no witnesses)

State-Specific Power of Attorney Forms

    Alaska

    California

    Colorado

    Connecticut

    Illinois

    Indiana

    Minnesota

    New Mexico

    New York

    North Carolina

    Tennessee

Physician's Determination of Incapacity

Designation of Authority

Resignation of Attorney-in-Fact

Notice of Revocation (Unrecorded Power of Attorney)

Notice of Revocation (Recorded Power of Attorney)

DURABLE POWER OF ATTORNEY FOR FINANCIAL MANAGEMENT

WARNING TO PERSON EXECUTING THIS DOCUMENT

This is an important legal document. It creates a durable power of attorney. Before executing this document, you should know these important facts:

This document may provide the person you designate as your attorney-in-fact with broad powers to manage, dispose, sell and convey your real and personal property and to borrow money using your property as security for the loan.

These powers will exist for an indefinite period of time unless you limit their duration in this document. These powers will continue to exist notwithstanding your subsequent disability or incapacity.

This document does not authorize anyone to make medical or other health care decisions for you.

You have the right to revoke or terminate this power of attorney.

If there is anything about this form that you do not understand, you should ask a lawyer to explain it to you.

1. Attorney-in-Fact

I, _____ of
_____, appoint _____
_____ as my attorney-in-fact to act for me in any lawful way with respect to the powers delegated in Part 6 below. If that person (or all of those persons, if more than one is named) does not serve or ceases to serve as attorney-in-fact, I appoint _____
_____ to serve as attorney-in-fact.

2. More Than One Attorney-in-Fact

a. Authorization

If more than one attorney-in-fact is designated, they are authorized to act:
☐ jointly. ☐ independently.

b. Resolution of Disputes

☐ If my attorneys-in-fact cannot agree on a decision or action under the authority delegated to them in this durable power of attorney, that dispute shall be resolved by binding arbitration. The arbitration shall be carried out by a single arbitrator, who shall be _____
_____, if available. The arbitration shall begin within five days of written notice by any attorney-in-fact to the arbitrator that a dispute between the attorneys-in-fact has arisen. The details of the arbitration shall be determined by the arbitrator. The written decision of the arbitrator shall be binding on all my attorneys-in-fact.

3. Delegation of Authority

My attorney-in-fact ☐ may ☐ may not delegate, in writing, any authority granted under this durable power of attorney to a person he or she selects. Any such delegation shall state the period during which it is valid and specify the extent of the delegation.

4. Effective Date

This power of attorney is effective:

☐ immediately, and shall continue in effect if I become incapacitated or disabled.

☐ only if I become incapacitated or disabled and unable to manage my financial affairs.

5. Determination of Incapacity

For purposes of this durable power of attorney, my incapacity or disability shall be determined by written declarations by ☐ one ☐ two licensed physician(s). Each declaration shall be made under penalty of perjury and shall state that in the physician's opinion I am substantially unable to manage my financial affairs. If possible, the declaration(s) shall be made by _____ _____. No licensed physician shall be liable to me for any actions taken under this part which are done in good faith.

6. Powers of Attorney-in-Fact

I hereby grant to my attorney-in-fact power to act on my behalf in the following matters, as indicated by my initials by each granted power or on line a, granting all the listed powers. Powers that are not initialed are not granted.

INITIALS

_____ a. ALL POWERS (b THROUGH m) LISTED BELOW.

_____ b. Real estate transactions.

_____ c. Tangible personal property transactions.

_____ d. Stock and bond, commodity and option transactions.

_____ e. Banking and other financial institution transactions.

_____ f. Business operating transactions.

_____ g Insurance and annuity transactions.

_____ h. Estate, trust, and other beneficiary transactions.

_____ i. Claims and litigation.

_____ j. Personal and family maintenance.

_____ k. Benefits from social security, Medicare, Medicaid, or other governmental programs, or civil or military service.

_____ l. Retirement plan transactions.

_____ m. Tax matters.

Note: These powers are defined in Part 17, below.

7. Special Instructions to the Attorney-in-Fact

_____

_____

_____

_____

_____

8. Compensation and Reimbursement of the Attorney-in-Fact

☐ The attorney-in-fact shall not be compensated for services, but shall be entitled to reimbursement, from the principal's assets, for reasonable expenses. Reasonable expenses include reasonable fees for information or advice from accountants, lawyers or investment experts relating to the attorney-in-fact's responsibilities under this power of attorney.

☐ The attorney-in-fact shall be entitled to reimbursement for reasonable expenses and reasonable compensation for his or her services. Reasonable compensation shall be determined exclusively by the attorney-in-fact.

☐ The attorney-in-fact shall be entitled to reimbursement for reasonable expenses and compensation for his or her services of $_____ per _____ .

9. Nomination of Conservator or Guardian

If, in a court proceeding, it is ever resolved that I need a conservator, guardian or other person to administer and supervise my estate or person, I nominate my attorney-in-fact to serve in that capacity. If my attorney-in-fact cannot serve, I nominate the successor attorney-in-fact nominated in Part 1 to serve.

10. Personal Benefit to Attorney-in-Fact

☐ My attorney-in-fact may buy any assets of mine or engage in any transaction he or she deems in good faith to be in my interest, no matter what the interest of or benefit to my attorney-in-fact.

☐ My attorney-in-fact may not be personally involved in or benefit personally from any transaction he or she engages in on my behalf, except _____

_____ .

☐ My attorney-in-fact may not be personally involved in or benefit personally from any transaction he or she engages in on my behalf.

11. Commingling by Attorney-in-Fact

My attorney-in-fact ☐ may ☐ may not mix (commingle) any of my funds with any funds of his or hers.

12. Bond

The attorney-in-fact shall serve without bond.

13. Liability of Attorney-in-Fact

My attorney-in-fact shall not incur any liability to me, my estate, my heirs, successors or assigns for acting or refraining from acting under this document, except for willful misconduct or gross negligence. My attorney-in-fact is not required to make my assets produce income, increase the value of my estate, diversify my investments or enter into transactions authorized by this document, as long as my attorney-in-fact believes his or her actions are in my best interests or in the best interests of my estate and of those interested in my estate. A successor attorney-in-fact shall not be liable for acts of a prior attorney-in-fact.

14. Gifts by Attorney-in-Fact

My attorney-in-fact may not (i) appoint, assign or designate any of my assets, interests or rights directly or indirectly to himself or herself, or estate, creditors, or the creditors of his or her estate, (ii) disclaim assets to which I would otherwise be entitled if the effect of the disclaimer is to cause such assets to pass directly or indirectly to my attorney-in-fact or his or her estate, or (iii) use my assets to discharge any of his or her legal obligations, including any obligation of support owed to others (excluding me and those whom I am legally obligated to support).

15. Reliance on this Power of Attorney

I agree that any third party who receives a copy of this document may rely on and act under it. Revocation of the power of attorney is not effective as to a third party until the third party has actual knowledge of the revocation. I agree to indemnify the third party for any claims that arise against the third party because of reliance on this power of attorney.

16. Severability

If any provision of this document is ruled unenforceable, the remaining provisions shall stay in effect.

17. Construction of Powers Granted to the Attorney-in-Fact

The powers granted in Part 6 above authorize the attorney-in-fact to do the following.

b. Real estate transactions

Act for the principal in any manner to deal with all or any part of any interest in real property that the principal owns at the time of execution or thereafter acquires, under such terms, conditions and covenants as the attorney-in-fact deems proper. The attorney-in-fact's powers include but are not limited to the power to:

(1) Accept as a gift, or as security for a loan, reject, demand, buy, lease, receive or otherwise acquire ownership of possession of any estate or interest in real property.

(2) Sell, exchange, convey with or without covenants, quitclaim, release, surrender, mortgage, encumber, partition or consent to the partitioning of, grant options concerning, lease, sublet or otherwise dispose of any interest in real property.

(3) Maintain, repair, improve, insure, rent, lease, and pay or contest taxes or assessments on any estate or interest in real property owned, or claimed to be owned, by the principal.

(4) Prosecute, defend, intervene in, submit to arbitration, settle and propose or accept a compromise with respect to any claim in favor of or against the principal based on or involving any real estate transaction.

c. Tangible personal property transactions

Act for the principal in any manner to deal with all or any part of any interest in personal property that the principal owns at the time of execution or thereafter acquires, under such terms as the attorney-in-fact deems proper. The attorney-in-fact's powers include but are not limited to the power to:

Lease, buy, exchange, accept as a gift or as security for a loan, acquire, possess, maintain, repair, improve, insure, rent, lease, sell, convey, mortgage, pledge, and pay or contest taxes and assessments on any tangible personal property.

d. Stock and bond, commodity, option and other securities transactions

Do any act which the principal can do through an agent, with respect to any interest in a bond, share, other instrument of similar character or commodity. The attorney-in-fact's powers include but are not limited to the power to:

(1) Accept as a gift or as security for a loan, reject, demand, buy, receive or otherwise acquire ownership or possession of any bond, share, instrument of similar character, commodity interest or any instrument with respect thereto, together with the interest, dividends, proceeds or other distributions connected with it.

(2) Sell (including short sales), exchange, transfer, release, surrender, pledge, trade in or otherwise dispose of any bond, share, instrument of similar character or commodity interest.

(3) Demand, receive and obtain any money or other thing of value to which the principal is or may become or may claim to be entitled as the proceeds of any interest in a bond, share, other instrument of similar character or commodity interest.

(4) Agree and contract, in any manner, and with any broker or other person and on any terms, for the accomplishment of any purpose listed in this section.

(5) Execute, acknowledge, seal and deliver any instrument the attorney-in-fact thinks useful to accomplish a purpose listed in this section, or any report or certificate required by law or regulation.

e. Banking and other financial institution transactions

Do any act that the principal can do through an agent in connection with any banking transaction that might affect the financial or other interests of the principal. The attorney-in-fact's powers include but are not limited to the power to:

(1) Continue, modify and terminate any deposit account or other banking arrangement, or open either in the name of the agent alone or in the name of the principal alone or in both their names jointly, a deposit account of any type in any financial institution, rent a safe deposit box or vault space, have access to a safe deposit box or vault to which the principal would have access, and make other contracts with the institution.

(2) Make, sign and deliver checks or drafts, withdraw by check, order or otherwise funds or property of the principal from any financial institution.

(3) Prepare financial statements concerning the assets and liabilities or income and expenses of the principal and deliver them to any financial institution, and receive statements, notices or other documents from any financial institution.

(4) Borrow money from a financial institution on terms the attorney-in-fact deems acceptable, give security out of the assets of the principal, and pay, renew or extend the time of payment of any note given by or on behalf of the principal.

f. Business operating transactions

Do any act that the principal can do through an agent in connection with any business operated by the principal that the attorney-in-fact deems desirable. The attorney-in-fact's powers include but are not limited to the power to:

(1) Perform any duty and exercise any right, privilege or option which the principal has or claims to have under any contract of partnership, enforce the terms of any partnership agreement, and

defend, submit to arbitration or settle any legal proceeding to which the principal is a party because of membership in a partnership.

(2) Exercise in person or by proxy and enforce any right, privilege or option which the principal has as the holder of any bond, share or instrument of similar character and defend, submit to arbitration or settle a legal proceeding to which the principal is a party because of any such bond, share or instrument of similar character.

(3) With respect to a business owned solely by the principal, continue, modify, extend or terminate any contract on behalf of the principal, demand and receive all money that is due or claimed by the principal and use such funds in the operation of the business, engage in banking transactions the attorney-in-fact deems desirable, determine the location of the operation, the nature of the business it undertakes, its name, methods of manufacturing, selling, marketing, financing, accounting, form of organization and insurance, and hiring and paying employees and independent contractors.

(4) Execute, acknowledge, seal and deliver any instrument of any kind that the attorney-in-fact thinks useful to accomplish any purpose listed in this section.

(5) Pay, compromise or contest business taxes or assessments.

(6) Demand and receive money or other things of value to which the principal is or claims to be entitled as the proceeds of any business operation, and conserve, invest, disburse or use anything so received for purposes listed in this section.

g. Insurance and annuity transactions

Do any act that the principal can do through an agent, in connection with any insurance or annuity policy, that the attorney-in-fact deems desirable. The attorney-in-fact's powers include but are not limited to the power to:

(1) Continue, pay the premium on, modify, rescind or terminate any policy of life, accident, health, disability or liability insurance procured by or on behalf of the principal before the execution of this power of attorney. The attorney-in-fact cannot name himself or herself as beneficiary of a renewal, extension or substitute for such a policy unless he or she was already the beneficiary before the principal signed the power of attorney.

(2) Procure new, different or additional contracts of health, disability, accident or liability insurance on the life of the principal, modify, rescind or terminate any such contract and designate the beneficiary of any such contract.

(3) Sell, assign, borrow on, pledge, or surrender and receive the cash surrender value of any policy.

h. Estate, trust, and other beneficiary transactions

Act for the principal in all matters that affect a trust, probate estate, guardianship, conservatorship, escrow, custodianship or other fund from which the principal is, may become or claims to be entitled, as a beneficiary, to a share or payment.

i. Claims and litigation

Act for the principal in all matters that affect claims of or against the principal and proceedings in any court or administrative body. The attorney-in-fact's powers include but are not limited to the power to:

(1) Assert any claim or defense before any court, administrative board or other tribunal.

(2) Submit to arbitration or mediation or settle any claim in favor of or against the principal or any litigation to which the principal is a party, pay any judgment or settlement and receive any money or other things of value paid in settlement.

j. Personal and family maintenance

To do all acts necessary to maintain the customary standard of living of the principal, the spouse and children and other persons customarily or legally entitled to be supported by the principal. The attorney-in-fact's powers include but are not limited to the power to:

(1) Pay for medical, dental and surgical care, living quarters, usual vacations and travel expenses, shelter, clothing, food, appropriate education and other living costs.

(2) Continue arrangements with respect to automobiles or other means of transportation, charge accounts, discharge of any services or duties assumed by the principal to any parent, relative or friend, contributions or payments incidental to membership or affiliation in any church, club, society or other organization.

k. Benefits from social security, Medicare, Medicaid, or other governmental programs, or civil or military service

Act for the principal in all matters that affect the principal's right to government benefits. The attorney-in-fact's powers include but are not limited to the power to:

(1) Prepare, execute, file, prosecute, defend, submit to arbitration or settle a claim on behalf of the principal to benefits or assistance, financial or otherwise.

(2) Receive the proceeds of such a claim and conserve, invest, disburse or use them on behalf of the principal.

l. Retirement plan transactions

Act for the principal in all matters that affect the principal's retirement plans. The attorney-in-fact's powers include but are not limited to the power to:

Select payment options under any retirement plan in which the principal participates, make contributions to those plans, exercise investment options, receive payment from a plan, rollover plan benefits into other retirement plans, designate beneficiaries under those plans and change existing designations.

m. Tax matters

Act for the principal in all matters that affect the principal's local, state and federal taxes. The attorney-in-fact's powers include but are not limited to the power to:

(1) Prepare, sign and file federal, state, local and foreign income, gift, payroll, Federal Insurance Contributions Act returns and other tax returns, claims for refunds, requests for extension of time, petitions, any power of attorney required by the Internal Revenue Service or other taxing authority, and other documents.

(2) Pay taxes due, collect refunds, post bonds, receive confidential information, exercise any election available to the principal and contest deficiencies determined by a taxing authority.

I understand the importance of the powers I delegate to my attorney-in-fact in this document. I recognize that the document gives my attorney-in-fact broad powers over my assets, and that these powers will become effective as of the date of my incapacity (or sooner if specified in this document) and continue indefinitely unless I revoke this durable power of attorney.

Signed this _____ day of_____ 19_____.

State of _____ County of _____

_____   _____
your signature   your social security number

Witnesses:

_____   _____
Name   Name

_____   _____
Address   Address

_____   _____

CERTIFICATE OF ACKNOWLEDGMENT OF NOTARY PUBLIC

State of _____ }

County of _____ } ss

On _____, 19 _____ , before me, _____,

a notary public, personally appeared _____, personally

known to me or proved to me on the basis of satisfactory evidence to be the person whose name is subscribed to this instrument, and acknowledged that he or she executed it.

_____

Notary Public for the State of _____

(NOTARY SEAL)   My commission expires: _____

(1) Assert any claim or defense before any court, administrative board or other tribunal.

(2) Submit to arbitration or mediation or settle any claim in favor of or against the principal or any litigation to which the principal is a party, pay any judgment or settlement and receive any money or other things of value paid in settlement.

j. Personal and family maintenance

To do all acts necessary to maintain the customary standard of living of the principal, the spouse and children and other persons customarily or legally entitled to be supported by the principal. The attorney-in-fact's powers include but are not limited to the power to:

(1) Pay for medical, dental and surgical care, living quarters, usual vacations and travel expenses, shelter, clothing, food, appropriate education and other living costs.

(2) Continue arrangements with respect to automobiles or other means of transportation, charge accounts, discharge of any services or duties assumed by the principal to any parent, relative or friend, contributions or payments incidental to membership or affiliation in any church, club, society or other organization.

k. Benefits from social security, Medicare, Medicaid, or other governmental programs, or civil or military service

Act for the principal in all matters that affect the principal's right to government benefits. The attorney-in-fact's powers include but are not limited to the power to:

(1) Prepare, execute, file, prosecute, defend, submit to arbitration or settle a claim on behalf of the principal to benefits or assistance, financial or otherwise.

(2) Receive the proceeds of such a claim and conserve, invest, disburse or use them on behalf of the principal.

l. Retirement plan transactions

Act for the principal in all matters that affect the principal's retirement plans. The attorney-in-fact's powers include but are not limited to the power to:

Select payment options under any retirement plan in which the principal participates, make contributions to those plans, exercise investment options, receive payment from a plan, rollover plan benefits into other retirement plans, designate beneficiaries under those plans and change existing designations.

m. Tax matters

Act for the principal in all matters that affect the principal's local, state and federal taxes. The attorney-in-fact's powers include but are not limited to the power to:

(1) Prepare, sign and file federal, state, local and foreign income, gift, payroll, Federal Insurance Contributions Act returns and other tax returns, claims for refunds, requests for extension of time, petitions, any power of attorney required by the Internal Revenue Service or other taxing authority, and other documents.

(2) Pay taxes due, collect refunds, post bonds, receive confidential information, exercise any election available to the principal and contest deficiencies determined by a taxing authority.

I understand the importance of the powers I delegate to my attorney-in-fact in this document. I recognize that the document gives my attorney-in-fact broad powers over my assets, and that these powers will become effective as of the date of my incapacity (or sooner if specified in this document) and continue indefinitely unless I revoke this durable power of attorney.

Signed this _____ day of_____ 19_____.

State of _____ County of _____

_____   _____
              your signature   your social security number

CERTIFICATE OF ACKNOWLEDGMENT OF NOTARY PUBLIC

State of _____

County of _____ } ss

On _____, 19 _____ , before me, _____,
a notary public, personally appeared _____, personally known to me or proved to me on the basis of satisfactory evidence to be the person whose name is subscribed to this instrument, and acknowledged that he or she executed it.

_____

Notary Public for the State of _____

(NOTARY SEAL)   My commission expires: _____

ALASKA GENERAL POWER OF ATTORNEY

THE POWERS GRANTED FROM THE PRINCIPAL TO THE AGENT OR AGENTS IN THE FOLLOWING DOCUMENT ARE VERY BROAD. THEY MAY INCLUDE THE POWER TO DISPOSE, SELL, CONVEY, AND ENCUMBER YOUR REAL AND PERSONAL PROPERTY, AND THE POWER TO MAKE YOUR HEALTH CARE DECISIONS. ACCORDINGLY, THE FOLLOWING DOCUMENT SHOULD ONLY BE USED AFTER CAREFUL CONSIDERATION. IF YOU HAVE ANY QUESTIONS ABOUT THIS DOCUMENT, YOU SHOULD SEEK COMPETENT ADVICE.

YOU MAY REVOKE THIS POWER OF ATTORNEY AT ANY TIME.

Pursuant to AS 13.26.338—13.26.353, I, _____ (Name of principal), of _____ (Address of principal), do hereby appoint _____ (Name and address of agent or agents), my attorney(s)-in-fact to act as I have checked below in my name, place, and stead in any way which I myself could do, if I were personally present, with respect to the following matters, as each of them is defined in AS 13.26.344, to the full extent that I am permitted by law to act through an agent:

THE AGENT OR AGENTS YOU HAVE APPOINTED WILL HAVE ALL THE POWERS LISTED BELOW UNLESS YOU DRAW A LINE THROUGH A CATEGORY; AND INITIAL THE BOX OPPOSITE THAT CATEGORY.

(A) real estate transactions .... (   )
(B) transactions involving tangible personal property, chattels, and goods .... (   )
(C) bonds, shares, and commodities transactions .... (   )
(D) banking transactions .... (   )
(E) business operating transactions .... (   )
(F) insurance transactions .... (   )
(G) estate transactions .... (   )
(H) gift transactions .... (   )
(I) claims and litigation .... (   )
(J) personal relationships and affairs .... (   )
(K) benefits from government programs and military service .... (   )
(L) health care services .... (   )
(M) records, reports, and statements .... (   )
(N) delegation .... (   )
(O) all other matters, including those specified as follows: .... (   )

_____

_____

IF YOU HAVE APPOINTED MORE THAN ONE AGENT, CHECK ONE OF THE FOLLOWING:

(   ) Each agent may exercise the powers conferred separately, without the consent of any other agent.

(   ) All agents shall exercise the powers conferred jointly, with the consent of all other agents.

TO INDICATE WHEN THIS DOCUMENT SHALL BECOME EFFECTIVE, CHECK ONE OF THE FOLLOWING:

(   ) This document shall become effective upon the date of my signature.

(   ) This document shall become effective upon the date of my disability and shall not otherwise be affected by my disability.

IF YOU HAVE INDICATED THAT THIS DOCUMENT SHALL BECOME EFFECTIVE ON THE DATE OF YOUR SIGNATURE, CHECK ONE OF THE FOLLOWING:

( ) This document shall not be affected by my subsequent disability.

( ) This document shall be revoked by my subsequent disability.

IF YOU HAVE INDICATED THAT THIS DOCUMENT SHALL BECOME EFFECTIVE UPON THE DATE OF YOUR SIGNATURE AND WANT TO LIMIT THE TERM OF THIS DOCUMENT, COMPLETE THE FOLLOWING:

This document shall only continue in effect for _____ ( ) years from the date of my signature.

YOU MAY DESIGNATE AN ALTERNATE ATTORNEY-IN-FACT. ANY ALTERNATE YOU DESIGNATE WILL BE ABLE TO EXERCISE THE SAME POWERS AS THE AGENT(S) YOU NAMED AT THE BEGINNING OF THIS DOCUMENT. IF YOU WISH TO DESIGNATE AN ALTERNATE OR ALTERNATES, COMPLETE THE FOLLOWING:

If the agent(s) named at the beginning of this document is unable or unwilling to serve or continue to serve, then I appoint the following agent to serve with the same powers:

First alternate or successor atttorney-in-fact:_____.

(Name and address of alternate)

Secondalternate or successor atttorney-in-fact:_____.

(Name and address of alternate)

YOU MAY NOMINATE A GUARDIAN OR CONSERVATOR. IF YOU WISH TO NOMINATE A GUARDIAN OR CONSERVATOR, COMPLETE THE FOLLOWING:

In the event that a court decides that it is necessary to appoint a guardian or conservator for me, I hereby nominate _____(name and address of person) to be considered by the court for appointment to serve as my guardian or conservator, or in any similar representative capacity.

_____

_____

_____

NOTICE OF REVOCATION OF THE POWERS GRANTED IN THIS DOCUMENT.

You may revoke one or more of the powers granted in this document. Unless otherwise provided in this document, you may revoke a specific power granted in this power of attorney by completing a special power of attorney that includes the specific power in this document that you want to revoke. Unless otherwise provided in this document, you may revoke all the powers granted in this power of attorney by completing a subsequent power of attorney.

NOTICE TO THIRD PARTIES

A third party who relies on the reasonable representations of an attorney-in-fact as to a matter relating to a power granted by a properly executed statutory power of attorney does not incur any liability to the principal or to the principal's heirs, assigns, or estate as a result of permitting the attorney-in-fact to exercise the authority granted by the power of attorney. A third party who fails to honor a properly executed statutory form power of attorney may be liable to the principal, the attorney-in-fact, the principal's heirs, assigns, or estate for a civil penalty, plus damages, costs, and fees associated with the failure to comply with the statutory form power of attorney. If the power of attorney is one which becomes effective upon the disability of the principal, the disability of the principal is established by an affidavit, as required by law.

IN WITNESS WHEREOF, I have hereunto signed my name this _____ day of

_____, _____.

_____

Signature of Principal

Subscribed and sworn to or affirmed before me at _____

on _____   _____

Signature of Officer or Notary

CALIFORNIA UNIFORM STATUTORY FORM POWER OF ATTORNEY
(California Civil Code § 2475)

NOTICE: THE POWERS GRANTED BY THIS DOCUMENT ARE BROAD AND SWEEPING. THEY ARE EXPLAINED IN THE UNIFORM STATUTORY FORM POWER OF ATTORNEY ACT (CALIFORNIA CIVIL CODE SECTIONS 2475-2499.5, INCLUSIVE). IF YOU HAVE ANY QUESTIONS ABOUT THESE POWERS, OBTAIN COMPETENT LEGAL ADVICE. THIS DOCUMENT DOES NOT AUTHORIZE ANY-ONE TO MAKE MEDICAL AND OTHER HEALTH CARE DECISIONS FOR YOU. YOU MAY REVOKE THIS POWER OF ATTORNEY IF YOU LATER WISH TO DO SO.

I, _____

_____ [your name

and address] appoint_____

_____ [name and address

of the person appointed, or of each person appointed if you want to designate more than one] as my agent (attorney-in-fact) to act for me in any lawful way with respect to the following initialed subjects:

TO GRANT ALL OF THE FOLLOWING POWERS, INITIAL THE LINE IN FRONT OF (N) AND IGNORE THE LINES IN FRONT OF THE OTHER POWERS.

TO GRANT ONE OR MORE, BUT FEWER THAN ALL, OF THE FOLLOWING POWERS, INITIAL THE LINE IN FRONT OF EACH POWER YOU ARE GRANTING.

TO WITHHOLD A POWER, DO NOT INITIAL THE LINE IN FRONT OF IT. YOU MAY, BUT NEED NOT, CROSS OUT EACH POWER WITHHELD.

INITIAL

_____   (A) Real property transactions.
_____   (B) Tangible personal property transactions.
_____   (C) Stock and bond transactions.
_____   (D) Commodity and option transactions.
_____   (E) Banking and other financial institution transactions.
_____   (F) Business operating transactions.
_____   (G) Insurance and annuity transactions.
_____   (H) Estate, trust, and other beneficiary transactions.
_____   (I) Claims and litigation.
_____   (J) Personal and family maintenance.
_____   (K) Benefits from social security, medicare, medicaid, or other governmental pro-grams, or civil or military service.
_____   (L) Retirement plan transactions.
_____   (M) Tax matters.
_____   (N) ALL OF THE POWERS LISTED ABOVE.

YOU NEED NOT INITIAL ANY OTHER LINES IF YOU INITIAL LINE (N).

SPECIAL INSTRUCTIONS:

ON THE FOLLOWING LINES YOU MAY GIVE SPECIAL INSTRUCTIONS LIMITING OR EXTENDING THE POWERS GRANTED TO YOUR AGENT. _____

_____
_____
_____
_____
_____
_____

UNLESS YOU DIRECT OTHERWISE ABOVE, THIS POWER OF ATTORNEY IS EFFECTIVE IMMEDIATELY AND WILL CONTINUE UNTIL IT IS REVOKED.

This power of attorney will continue to be effective even though I become incapacitated.

STRIKE THE PRECEDING SENTENCE IF YOU DO NOT WANT THIS POWER OF ATTORNEY TO CONTINUE IF YOU BECOME INCAPACITATED.

EXERCISE OF POWER OF ATTORNEY WHERE
MORE THAN ONE AGENT DESIGNATED

If I have designated more than one agent, the agents are to act _____.
IF YOU APPOINTED MORE THAN ONE AGENT AND YOU WANT EACH AGENT TO BE ABLE TO ACT ALONE WITHOUT THE OTHER AGENT JOINING, WRITE THE WORD "SEPARATELY" IN THE BLANK SPACE ABOVE. IF YOU DO NOT INSERT ANY WORD IN THE BLANK SPACE, OR IF YOU INSERT THE WORD "JOINTLY," THEN ALL OF YOUR AGENTS MUST ACT OR SIGN TOGETHER.

I agree that any third party who receives a copy of this document may act under it. Revocation of the power of attorney is not effective as to a third party until the third party has actual knowledge of the revocation. I agree to indemnify the third party for any claims that arise against the third party because of reliance on this power of attorney.

Signed this _____ day of _____, 19_____

_____   _____
     (your signature)   (your social security number)

State of _____, County of _____,

CERTIFICATE OF ACKNOWLEDGEMENT OF NOTARY PUBLIC

State of California

County of _____ } ss

On this _____ day of _____ , 19_____ before me, _____,
(name of notary public) personally appeared _____, (name of principal)
personally known to me (or proved to me on the basis of satisfactory evidence) to be the person whose name is subscribed to this instrument, and acknowledged that he or she executed it.

[NOTARY SEAL]   _____
                                (signature of notary public)

BY ACCEPTING OR ACTING UNDER THE APPOINTMENT, THE AGENT ASSUMES THE FIDUCIARY AND OTHER LEGAL RESPONSIBILITIES OF AN AGENT.

COLORADO STATUTORY POWER OF ATTORNEY

Notice: The powers granted by this document are broad and sweeping. They are explained in the Uniform Statutory Power of Attorney Act. If you have any questions about these powers, obtain competent legal advice. This document does not authorize anyone to make medical and other health-care decisions for you. You may revoke this power of attorney if you later wish to do so.

You may have other rights or powers under Colorado law not contained in this form.

I, _____ , (insert your name and address) appoint _____

_____ (insert the name and address of the person appointed) as my agent (attorney-in-fact) to act for me in any lawful way with respect to the following initialed subjects:

To grant one or more of the following powers, initial the line in front of each power you are granting.

To withhold a power, do not initial the line in front of it. You may, but need not, cross out each power withheld.

Initial

_____ (A) Real estate transactions (when properly recorded).

_____ (B) Tangible personal property transactions.

_____ (C) Stock and bond transactions.

_____ (D) Commodity and option transactions.

_____ (E) Banking and other financial institution transactions.

_____ (F) Business operating transactions.

_____ (G) Insurance and annuity transactions.

_____ (H) Estate, trust and other beneficiary transactions.

_____ (I) Claims and litigation.

_____ (J) Personal and family maintenance.

_____ (K) Benefits from social security, medicare, medicaid, or other governmental programs, or military service.

_____ (L) Retirement plan transactions.

_____ (M) Tax matters.

SPECIAL INSTRUCTIONS

On the following lines you may give special instructions limiting or extending the powers granted to your agent.

_____

_____

_____

_____

_____

_____

_____

_____

_____

_____

_____

Unless you direct otherwise above, this power of attorney is effective immediately and will continue until it is revoked.

This power of attorney will continue to be effective even though I become disabled, incapacitated, or incompetent.

Strike and initial the preceding sentence if you do not want this power of attorney to continue if you become disabled, incapacitated, or incompetent.

I agree that any third party who receives a copy of this document may act under it. Revocation of the power of attorney is not effective as to a third party until the third party learns of the revocation. I agree to indemnify the third party for any claims that arise against the third party because of reliance on this power of attorney.

Signed this _____ day of _____, 19 _____.

_____
(Your signature)

_____
(Your social security number)

State of _____

County of _____

This document was acknowledged before me on
_____ (Date) by

_____
(Name of principal)

_____
(Signature of notarial officer)

(Seal, if any)

_____
(Title (and rank))

(My commission expires: _____)

By accepting or acting under the appointment, the agent assumes the fiduciary and other legal responsibilities of an agent.

CONNECTICUT STATUTORY SHORT FORM DURABLE POWER OF ATTORNEY

Notice: The powers granted by this document are broad and sweeping. They are defined in Connecticut Statutory Short Form Power of Attorney Act, sections 1-42 to 1-56, inclusive, of the general statutes, which expressly permits the use of any other or different form of power of attorney desired by the parties concerned.

Know All Men by These Presents, which are intended to constitute a GENERAL POWER OF ATTORNEY pursuant to Connecticut Statutory Short Form Power of Attorney Act:

That I _____

(insert name and address of the principal) do hereby appoint _____

_____ (insert name and address of the agent, or each agent, if more than one is designated) my attorney(s)-in-fact TO ACT _____.

If more than one agent is designated and the principal wishes each agent alone to be able to exercise the power conferred, insert in this blank the word 'severally'. Failure to make any insertion or the insertion of the word 'jointly' shall require the agents to act jointly.

First: In my name, place and stead in any way which I myself could do, if I were personally present, with respect to the following matters as each of them is defined in the Connecticut Statutory Short Form Power of Attorney Act to the extent that I am permitted by law to act through an agent:

(Strike out and initial in the opposite box any one or more of the subdivisions as to which the principal does NOT desire to give the agent authority. Such elimination of any one or more of subdivisions (A) to (L), inclusive, shall automatically constitute an elimination also of subdivision (M).)

To strike out any subdivision the principal must draw a line through the text of that subdivision AND write his initials in the box opposite.

(A)   real estate transactions;...(   )
(B)   chattel and goods transactions; ....(   )
(C)   bond, share and commodity transactions; ....(   )
(D)   banking transactions; ....(   )
(E)   business operating transactions; ....(   )
(F)   insurance transactions; ....(   )
(G)   estate transactions; ....(   )
(H)   claims and litigation; ....(   )
(I)   personal relationships and affairs;...(   )
(J)   benefits from military service; ....(   )
(K)   records, reports and statements; ....(   )
(L)   health care decisions; ....(   )
(M)   all other matters; ....(   )

_____

_____

_____

_____

_____

_____

_____

_____

_____

_____

_____

_____

_____

(Special provisions and limitations may be included in the statutory short form power of attorney only if they conform to the requirements of the Connecticut Statutory Short Form Power of Attorney Act.)

Second: With full and unqualified authority to delegate any or all of the foregoing powers to any person or persons whom my attorney(s)-in-fact shall select;

Third: Hereby ratifying and confirming all that said attorney(s) or substitute(s) do or cause to be done.

In Witness Whereof I have hereunto signed my name and affixed my seal this _____ day of _____, 19_____.

_____ (Signature of Principal) (Seal)

On the date written above, _____ declared to us that this instrument was [his/her] durable power of attorney, and requested us to act as witnesses to it. [He/She] signed it in our presence, all of us being present at the same time. We now sign this instrument as witnesses.

_____, Witness   _____
witness signature   city and county

_____, Witness   _____
witness signature   city and county

ACKNOWLEDGMENT

State of _____ }

County of _____ } ss

On _____, 19 _____ , before me, _____ _____, a notary public for the State of _____, personally appeared _____, personally known to me or proved to me on the basis of satisfactory evidence to be the person whose name is subscribed to this instrument, and acknowledged that he or she executed it.

_____
signature of notary public

[NOTARY SEAL]

My commission expires: _____

ILLINOIS STATUTORY SHORT FORM POWER OF ATTORNEY FOR PROPERTY

(NOTICE: THE PURPOSE OF THIS POWER OF ATTORNEY IS TO GIVE THE PERSON YOU DESIGNATE (YOUR "AGENT") BROAD POWERS TO HANDLE YOUR PROPERTY, WHICH MAY INCLUDE POWERS TO PLEDGE, SELL OR OTHERWISE DISPOSE OF ANY REAL OR PERSONAL PROPERTY WITHOUT ADVANCE NOTICE TO YOU OR APPROVAL BY YOU. THIS FORM DOES NOT IMPOSE A DUTY ON YOUR AGENT TO EXERCISE GRANTED POWERS; BUT WHEN POWERS ARE EXERCISED, YOUR AGENT WILL HAVE TO USE DUE CARE TO ACT FOR YOUR BENEFIT AND IN ACCORDANCE WITH THIS FORM AND KEEP A RECORD OF RECEIPTS, DISBURSEMENTS AND SIGNIFICANT ACTIONS TAKEN AS AGENT. A COURT CAN TAKE AWAY THE POWERS OF YOUR AGENT IF IT FINDS THE AGENT IS NOT ACTING PROPERLY. YOU MAY NAME SUCCESSOR AGENTS UNDER THIS FORM BUT NOT CO-AGENTS. UNLESS YOU EXPRESSLY LIMIT THE DURATION OF THIS POWER IN THE MANNER PROVIDED BELOW, UNTIL YOU REVOKE THIS POWER OR A COURT ACTING ON YOUR BEHALF TERMINATES IT, YOUR AGENT MAY EXERCISE THE POWERS GIVEN HERE THROUGHOUT YOUR LIFETIME, EVEN AFTER YOU BECOME DISABLED. THE POWERS YOU GIVE YOUR AGENT ARE EXPLAINED MORE FULLY IN SECTION 3-4 OF THE ILLINOIS "STATUTORY SHORT FORM POWER OF ATTORNEY FOR PROPERTY LAW" OF WHICH THIS FORM IS A PART (SEE THE BACK OF THIS FORM). THAT LAW EXPRESSLY PERMITS THE USE OF ANY DIFFERENT FORM OF POWER OF ATTORNEY YOU MAY DESIRE. IF THERE IS ANYTHING ABOUT THIS FORM THAT YOU DO NOT UNDERSTAND, YOU SHOULD ASK A LAWYER TO EXPLAIN IT TO YOU.)

POWER OF ATTORNEY made this _____ day of _____(month) _____(year)

1. I, _____

_____ (insert name and address of principal) hereby

appoint: _____

_____ (insert name and address of agent) as my attorney-in-fact (my "agent") to act for me and in my name (in any way I could act in person) with respect to the following powers, as defined in Section 3-4 of the "Statutory Short Form Power of Attorney for Property Law" (including all amendments), but subject to any limitations on or additions to the specified powers inserted in paragraph 2 or 3 below:

(YOU MUST STRIKE OUT ANY ONE OR MORE OF THE FOLLOWING CATEGORIES OF POWERS YOU DO NOT WANT YOUR AGENT TO HAVE. FAILURE TO STRIKE THE TITLE OF ANY CATEGORY WILL CAUSE THE POWERS DESCRIBED IN THAT CATEGORY TO BE GRANTED TO THE AGENT. TO STRIKE OUT A CATEGORY YOU MUST DRAW A LINE THROUGH THE TITLE OF THAT CATEGORY.)

(a) Real estate transactions.
(b) Financial institution transactions.
(c) Stock and bond transactions.
(d) Tangible personal property transactions.

§3-4. Explanation of powers granted in the statutory short form power of attorney for property. This Section defines each category of powers listed in the statutory short form power of attorney for property and the effect of granting powers to an agent. When the title of any of the following categories is retained (not struck out) in a statutory property power form, the effect will be to grant the agent all of the principal's rights, powers and discretions with respect to the types of property and transactions covered by the retained category, subject to any limitations on the granted powers that appear on the face of the form. The agent will have authority to exercise each granted power for and in the name of the principal with respect to all of the principal's interests in every type of property or transaction covered by the granted power at the time of exercise, whether the principal's interests are direct or indirect, whole or fractional, legal, equitable or contractual, as a joint tenant or tenant in common or held in any other form; but the agent will not have power under any of the statutory categories (a) through (o) to make gifts of the principal's property, to exercise powers to appoint to others or to change any beneficiary whom the principal has designated to take the principal's interests at death under any will, trust, joint tenancy, beneficiary form or contractual arrangement. The agent will be under no duty to exercise granted powers or to assume control of or responsibility for the principal's property or affairs; but when granted powers are exercised, the agent will be required to use due care to act for the benefit of the principal in accordance with the terms of the statutory property power and will be liable for negligent exercise. The agent may act in person or through others reasonably employed by the agent for that purpose and will have authority to sign and deliver all instruments, negotiate and enter into all agreements and do all other acts reasonably necessary to implement the exercise of the powers granted to the agent.

(a) Real estate transactions. The agent is authorized to: buy, sell, exchange, rent and lease real estate (which term includes, without limitation, real estate subject to a land trust and all beneficial interests in and powers of direction under any land trust); collect all rent, sale proceeds and earnings from real estate; convey, assign and accept title to real estate; grant easements, create conditions and release rights of homestead with respect to real estate; create land trusts and exercise all powers under land trusts; hold, possess, maintain, repair, improve, subdivide, manage, operate and insure real estate; pay, contest, protest and compromise real estate taxes and assessments; and, in general, exercise all powers with respect to real estate which the principal could if present and under no disability.

(b) Financial institution transactions. The agent is authorized to: open, close, continue and control all accounts and deposits in any type of financial institution (which term includes, without limitation, banks, trust companies, savings and building and loan associations, credit unions and brokerage firms); deposit in and withdraw from and write checks on any financial institution account or deposit; and, in general, exercise all powers with respect to financial institution transactions which the principal could if present and under no disability.

(e) Safe deposit box transactions.
(f) Insurance and annuity transactions.
(g) Retirement plan transactions.
(h) Social Security, employment and military service benefits.
(i) Tax matters.
(j) Claims and litigation.
(k) Commodity and option transactions.
(l) Business operations.
(m) Borrowing transactions.
(n) Estate transactions.
(o) All other property powers and transactions.

(LIMITATIONS ON AND ADDITIONS TO THE AGENT'S POWERS MAY BE INCLUDED IN THIS POWER OF ATTORNEY IF THEY ARE SPECIFICALLY DESCRIBED BELOW.)

2. The powers granted above shall not include the following powers or shall be modified or limited in the following particulars (here you may include any specific limitations you deem appropriate, such as a prohibition or conditions on the sale of particular stock or real estate or special rules on borrowing by the agent):

_____

_____

3. In addition to the powers granted above, I grant my agent the following powers (here you may add any other delegable powers including, without limitation, power to make gifts, exercise powers of appointment, name or change beneficiaries or joint tenants or revoke or amend any trust specifically referred to below):

_____

_____

YOUR AGENT WILL HAVE AUTHORITY TO EMPLOY OTHER PERSONS AS NECESSARY TO ENABLE THE AGENT TO PROPERLY EXERCISE THE POWERS GRANTED IN THIS FORM, BUT YOUR AGENT WILL HAVE TO MAKE ALL DISCRETIONARY DECISIONS. IF YOU WANT TO GIVE YOUR AGENT THE RIGHT TO DELEGATE DISCRETIONARY DECISION-MAKING POWERS TO OTHERS, YOU SHOULD KEEP THE NEXT SENTENCE, OTHERWISE IT SHOULD BE STRUCK OUT.)

4. My agent shall have the right by written instrument to delegate any or all of the foregoing powers involving discretionary decision-making to any person or persons whom my agent may select, but such delegation may be amended or revoked by any agent (including any successor) named by me who is acting under this power of attorney at the time of reference.

(YOUR AGENT WILL BE ENTITLED TO REIMBURSEMENT FOR ALL REASONABLE EXPENSES INCURRED IN ACTING UNDER THIS POWER OF ATTORNEY. STRIKE OUT THE NEXT SENTENCE IF YOU DO NOT WANT YOUR AGENT TO ALSO BE ENTITLED TO REASONABLE COMPENSATION FOR SERVICES AS AGENT.)

5. My agent shall be entitled to reasonable compensation for services rendered as agent under this power of attorney.

(THIS POWER OF ATTORNEY MAY BE AMENDED OR REVOKED BY YOU AT ANY TIME

(c) Stock and bond transactions. The agent is authorized to: buy and sell all types of securities (which term includes, without limitation, stocks, bonds, mutual funds and all other types of investment securities and financial instruments); collect, hold and safekeep all dividends, interest, earnings, proceeds of sale, distributions, shares, certificates and other evidences of ownership paid or distributed with respect to securities; exercise all voting rights with respect to securities in person or by proxy, enter into voting trusts and consent to limitations on the right to vote; and, in general, exercise all powers with respect to securities which the principal could if present and under no disability.

(d) Tangible personal property transactions. The agent is authorized to: buy and sell, lease, exchange, collect, possess and take title to all tangible personal property; move, store, ship, restore, maintain, repair, improve, manage, preserve, insure and safekeep tangible personal property; and, in general, exercise all powers with respect to tangible personal property which the principal could if present and under no disability.

(e) Safe deposit box transactions. The agent is authorized to: open, continue and have access to all safe deposit boxes; sign, renew, release or terminate any safe deposit contract; drill or surrender any safe deposit box; and, in general, exercise all powers with respect to safe deposit matters which the principal could if present and under no disability.

(f) Insurance and annuity transactions. The agent is authorized to: procure, acquire, continue, renew, terminate or otherwise deal with any type of insurance or annuity contract (which terms include, without limitation, life, accident, health, disability, automobile casualty, property or liability insurance); pay premiums or assessments on or surrender and collect all distributions, proceeds or benefits payable under any insurance or annuity contract; and, in general, exercise all powers with respect to insurance and annuity contracts which the principal could if present and under no disability.

(g) Retirement plan transactions. The agent is authorized to: contribute to, withdraw from and deposit funds in any type of retirement plan (which term includes, without limitation, any tax qualified or nonqualified pension, profit sharing, stock bonus, employee savings and other retirement plan, individual retirement account, deferred compensation plan and any other type of employee benefit plan); select and change payment options for the principal under any retirement plan; make rollover contributions from any retirement plan to other retirement plans or individual retirement accounts; exercise all investment powers available under any type of self-directed retirement plan; and, in general, exercise all powers with respect to retirement plans and retirement plan account balances which the principal could if present and under no disability.

AND IN ANY MANNER. ABSENT AMENDMENT OR REVOCATION, THE AUTHORITY GRANTED IN THIS POWER OF ATTORNEY WILL BECOME EFFECTIVE AT THE TIME THIS POWER IS SIGNED AND WILL CONTINUE UNTIL YOUR DEATH UNLESS A LIMITATION ON THE BEGINNING DATE OR DURATION IS MADE BY INITIALING AND COMPLETING EITHER (OR BOTH) OF THE FOLLOWING:)

6. (   ) This power of attorney shall become effective on _____
_____ (insert a future date or event during your lifetime, such as court determination of your disability, when you want this power to first take effect)

7. (   )This power of attorney shall terminate on _____
_____ (insert a future date or event, such as court determination of your disability, when you want this power to terminate prior to your death)

(IF YOU WISH TO NAME SUCCESSOR AGENTS, INSERT THE NAME(S) AND ADDRESS(ES) OF SUCH SUCCESSOR(S) IN THE FOLLOWING PARAGRAPH.)

8. If any agent named by me shall die, become incompetent, resign or refuse to accept the office of agent, I name the following (each to act alone and successively, in the order named) as successor(s) to such agent: _____
_____

For purposes of this paragraph 8, a person shall be considered to be incompetent if and while the person is a minor or an adjudicated incompetent or disabled person or the person is unable to give prompt and intelligent consideration to business matters, as certified by a licensed physician.

(IF YOU WISH TO NAME YOUR AGENT AS GUARDIAN OF YOUR ESTATE, IN THE EVENT A COURT DECIDES THAT ONE SHOULD BE APPOINTED, YOU MAY, BUT ARE NOT REQUIRED TO, DO SO BY RETAINING THE FOLLOWING PARAGRAPH. THE COURT WILL APPOINT YOUR AGENT IF THE COURT FINDS THAT SUCH APPOINTMENT WILL SERVE YOUR BEST INTERESTS AND WELFARE. STRIKE OUT PARAGRAPH 9 IF YOU DO NOT WANT YOUR AGENT TO ACT AS GUARDIAN.)

9. If a guardian of my estate (my property) is to be appointed, I nominate the agent acting under this power of attorney as such guardian, to serve without bond or security.

10. I am fully informed as to all the contents of this form and understand the full import of this grant of powers to my agent.

_____
_____
_____
_____
_____
_____
_____

Signed _____
(principal)

(h) Social Security, unemployment and military service benefits. The agent is authorized to: prepare, sign and file any claim or application for Social Security, unemployment or military service benefits; sue for, settle or abandon any claims to any benefit or assistance under any federal, state, local or foreign statute or regulation; control, deposit to any account, collect, receipt for, and take title to and hold all benefits under any Social Security, unemployment, military service or other state, federal, local or foreign statute or regulation; and, in general, exercise all powers with respect to Social Security, unemployment, military service and governmental benefits which the principal could if present and under no disability.

(i) Tax matters. The agent is authorized to: sign, verify and file all the principal's federal, state and local income, gift, estate, property and other tax returns, including joint returns and declarations of estimated tax; pay all taxes; claim, sue for and receive all tax refunds; examine and copy all the principal's tax returns and records; represent the principal before any federal, state or local revenue agency or taxing body and sign and deliver all tax powers of attorney on behalf of the principal that may be necessary for such purposes; waive rights and sign all documents on behalf of the principal as required to settle, pay and determine all tax liabilities; and, in general, exercise all powers with respect to tax manners which the principal could if present and under no disability.

(j) Claims and litigation. The agent is authorized to: institute, prosecute, defend, abandon, compromise, arbitrate, settle and dispose of any claim in favor of or against the principal or any property interests of the principal; collect and receipt for any claim or settlement proceeds and waive or release all rights of the principal; employ attorneys and others and enter into contingency agreements and other contracts as necessary in connection with litigation; and, in general, exercise all powers with respect to claims and litigation which the principal could if present and under no disability.

(k) Commodity and option transactions. The agent is authorized to: buy, sell, exchange, assign, convey, settle and exercise commodities futures contracts and call and put options on stocks and stock indices traded on a regulated options exchange and collect and receipt for all proceeds of any such transactions; establish or continue option accounts for the principal with any securities or futures broker; and, in general, exercise all powers with respect to commodities and options which the principal could if present and under no disability.

(YOU MAY, BUT ARE NOT REQUIRED TO, REQUEST YOUR AGENT AND SUCCESSOR AGENTS TO PROVIDE SPECIMEN SIGNATURES BELOW. IF YOU INCLUDE SPECIMEN SIGNATURES IN THIS POWER OF ATTORNEY, YOU MUST COMPLETE THE CERTIFICATION OPPOSITE THE SIGNATURES OF THE AGENTS.)

Specimen signatures of agent
(and successors)

I certify that the signatures of my
agent (and successors) are correct.

_____
(agent)

_____
(principal)

_____
(successor agent)

_____
(principal)

_____
(successor agent)

_____
(principal)

(THIS POWER OF ATTORNEY WILL NOT BE EFFECTIVE UNLESS IT IS NOTARIZED, USING THE FORM BELOW.)

State of _____ }
County of _____ } ss

The undersigned, a notary public in and for the above county and state, certifies that _____
_____ , known to me to be the same person whose name is subscribed as principal to the foregoing power of attorney, appeared before me in person and acknowledged signing and delivering the instrument as the free and voluntary act of the principal, for the uses and purposes therein set forth (, and certified to the correctness of the signature(s) of the agent(s)).

Dated: _____ (SEAL)

_____
Notary Public

My commission expires _____

(THE NAME AND ADDRESS OF THE PERSON PREPARING THIS FORM SHOULD BE INSERTED IF THE AGENT WILL HAVE POWER TO CONVEY ANY INTEREST IN REAL ESTATE.)

This document was prepared by: _____

(l) Business operations. The agent is authorized to: organize or continue and conduct any business (which term includes, without limitation, any farming, manufacturing, service, mining, retailing or other type of business operation) in any form, whether as a proprietorship, joint venture, partnership, corporation, trust or other legal entity; operate, buy, sell, expand, contract, terminate or liquidate any business; direct, control, supervise, manage or participate in the operation of any business and engage, compensate and discharge business managers, employees, agents, attorneys, accountants and consultants; and, in general, exercise all powers with respect to business interests and operations which the principal could if present and under no disability.

(m) Borrowing transactions. The agent is authorized to: borrow money; mortgage or pledge any real estate or tangible or intangible personal property as security for such purposes; sign, renew, extend, pay and satisfy any notes or other forms of obligation; and, in general, exercise all powers with respect to secured and unsecured borrowing which the principal could if present and under no disability.

(n) Estate transactions. The agent is authorized to: accept, receipt for, exercise, release, reject, renounce, assign, disclaim, demand, sue for, claim and recover any legacy, bequest, devise, gift or other property interest or payment due or payable to or for the principal; assert any interest in and exercise any power over any trust, estate or property subject to fiduciary control; establish a revocable trust solely for the benefit of the principal that terminates at the death of the principal and is then distributable to the legal representative of the estate of the principal; and, in general, exercise all powers with respect to estates and trusts which the principal could if present and under no disability; provided, however, that the agent may not make or change a will and may not revoke or amend a trust revocable or amendable by the principal or require the trustee of any trust for the benefit of the principal to pay income or principal to the agent unless specific authority to that end is given, and specific reference to the trust is made, in the statutory property power form.

(o) All other property powers and transactions. The agent is authorized to: exercise all possible powers of the principal with respect to all possible types of property and interests in property, except to the extent the principal limits the generality of this category (o) by striking out one or more of categories (a) through (n) or by specifying other limitations in the statutory property power form.

DURABLE POWER OF ATTORNEY FOR FINANCIAL MANAGEMENT: INDIANA

THE POWERS GRANTED BY THIS DOCUMENT ARE BROAD AND SWEEPING. IF YOU HAVE ANY QUESTIONS ABOUT THESE POWERS, GET COMPETENT LEGAL ADVICE.

THIS DOCUMENT DOES NOT AUTHORIZE ANYONE TO MAKE MEDICAL OR OTHER HEALTH CARE DECISIONS FOR YOU.

YOU MAY REVOKE THIS POWER OF ATTORNEY IF YOU LATER WISH TO DO SO.

1. Attorney-in-Fact

I, _____ of

_____, Indiana, appoint _____

_____ as my attorney-in-fact to act for me in any

lawful way with respect to the powers delegated in Part 6 below. If that person (or all those persons, if

more than one is named) does not serve or ceases to serve as attorney-in-fact, I appoint

_____ to serve as attorney-in-fact.

2. More Than One Attorney-in-Fact

a. Authorization

If more than one attorney-in-fact is designated, they are authorized to act:

☐ jointly. ☐ independently.

b. Resolution of Disputes

☐ If my attorneys-in-fact cannot agree on a decision or action under the authority delegated to them in this durable power of attorney, that dispute shall be resolved by binding arbitration. The arbitration shall be carried out by a single arbitrator, who shall be _____,

if available. The arbitration shall begin within five days of written notice by any attorney-in-fact to the arbitrator that a dispute has arisen. The details of the arbitration shall be determined by the arbitrator. The written decision of the arbitrator shall be binding on all my my attorneys-in-fact.

3. Delegation of Authority

My attorney-in-fact ☐ may ☐ may not delegate, in writing, any authority granted under this durable power of attorney to a person he or she selects. Any such delegation shall state the period during which it is valid and specify the extent of the delgation.

4. Effective Date

This power of attorney is effective:

☐ immediately, and shall continue in effect if I become incapacitated or disabled.

☐ only if I become incapacitated or disabled and unable to manage my financial affairs.

5. Determination of Incapacity

For purposes of this durable power of attorney, my incapacity or disability shall be determined by written declarations by ☐ one ☐ two licensed physician(s). Each declaration shall be made under penalty of perjury and shall state that in the physician's opinion I am substantially unable to manage my financial affairs. If possible, the declaration(s) shall be made by _____ _____. No licensed physician shall be liable to me for any actions taken by them under this part which are done in good faith.

6. Powers of Attorney-in-Fact

I hereby grant to my attorney-in-fact power to act on my behalf in the following matters, as indicated by my initials by each granted power. Powers that are not initialed are not granted. The Indiana Code sections noted below are hereby incorporated by reference.

INITIALS

_____	a.	ALL POWERS (b THROUGH o) LISTED BELOW.
_____	b.	Real property transactions. (Ann. Ind. Code § 30-5-5-2)
_____	c.	Tangible personal property transactions. (Ann. Ind. Code § 30-5-5-3)
_____	d.	Bond, share and commodity transactions. (Ann. Ind. Code § 30-5-5-4)
_____	e.	Banking transactions. (Ann. Ind. Code § 30-5-5-5)
_____	f.	Business operating transactions. (Ann. Ind. Code § 30-5-5-6)
_____	g.	Insurance transactions. (Ann. Ind. Code § 30-5-5-7)
_____	h.	Beneficiary transactions. (Ann. Ind. Code § 30-5-5-8)
_____	i.	Gift transactions. (Ann. Ind. Code § 30-5-5-9)
_____	j.	Fiduciary transactions. (Ann. Ind. Code § 30-5-5-10)
_____	k.	Claims and litigation. (Ann. Ind. Code § 30-5-5-11)
_____	l.	Family maintenance. (Ann. Ind. Code § 30-5-5-12)
_____	m.	Benefits from military service. (Ann. Ind. Code § 30-5-5-13)
_____	n.	Records, reports, and statements. (Ann. Ind. Code § 30-5-5-14)
_____	o.	Estate transactions. (Ann. Ind. Code § 30-5-5-15)

7. Special Instructions to the Attorney-in-Fact

_____

_____

_____

_____

8. Compensation and Reimbursement of the Attorney-in-Fact

☐ The attorney-in-fact shall not be compensated for services, but shall be entitled to reimbursement, from the principal's assets, for reasonable expenses. Reasonable expenses include reasonable fees for information or advice from accountants, lawyers or investment experts relating to the attorney-in-fact's responsibilities under this power of attorney.

☐ The attorney-in-fact shall be entitled to reimbursement for reasonable expenses and reasonable compensation for his or her services. Reasonable compensation shall be determined exclusively by the attorney-in-fact.

☐ The attorney-in-fact shall be entitled to reimbursement for reasonable expenses and compensation for his or her services of $_____ per _____ .

9. Nomination of Conservator or Guardian

If, in a court proceeding, it is ever resolved that I need a conservator, guardian or other person to administer and supervise my estate or person, I nominate my attorney-in-fact to serve in that capacity. If my attorney-in-fact cannot serve, I nominate the sucessor attorney-in-fact named in Part 1 to serve.

10. Personal Benefit to Attorney-in-Fact

☐ My attorney-in-fact may buy any assets of mine or engage in any transaction he or she deems in good faith to be in my interest, no matter what the interest of or benefit to my attorney-in-fact.

☐ My attorney-in-fact may not be personally involved in or benefit personally from any transaction he or she engages in on my behalf, except _____

_____

_____ .

☐ My attorney-in-fact may not be personally involved in or benefit personally from any transaction he or she engages in on my behalf.

11. Commingling by Attorney-in-Fact

My attorney-in-fact ☐ may ☐ may not commingle any of my funds with any funds of his or hers.

12. Bond

The attorney-in-fact shall serve without bond.

13. Liability of Attorney-in-Fact

Neither my attorney-in-fact nor any successor attorney-in-fact shall incur any liability to me, my estate, my heirs, successors or assigns for acting or refraining from acting under this document, except for willful misconduct or gross negligence. Neither my attorney-in-fact nor any successors shall be required to make my assets productive of income, increase the value of my estate, diversify my investments or enter into transactions authorized by this document, as long as my attorney-in-fact or successor believes his or her actions are in my best interests or in the best interests of my estate and of those interested in my estate.

14. Gifts by Attorney-in-Fact

a. My attorney-in-fact shall have no incidents of ownership over any life insurance policy in which I may own an interest and which insures his or her life.

b. My attorney-in-fact may not (i) appoint, assign or designate any of my assets, interests or rights directly or indirectly to himself or herself, or estate, creditors, or the creditors of his or her estate, (ii) disclaim assets to which I would otherwise be entitled if the effect of the disclaimer is to cause such assets to pass directly or indirectly to my attorney-in-fact or his or her estate, or (iii) use my assets to discharge any of his or her legal obligations, including any obligation of support owed to others (excluding me and those whom I am legally obligated to support).

c. My attorney-in-fact shall not hold or exercise any powers I may have over assets he or she has given to me or over assets held in an irrevocable trust of which he or she is a grantor.

15. Reliance on this Power of Attorney

I agree that any third party who receives a copy of this document may act under it. Revocation of the power of attorney is not effective as to a third party until the third party has actual knowledge of the revocation. I agree to indemnify the third party for any claims that arise against the third party because of reliance on this power of attorney.

16. Severability

If any provision of this document is ruled unenforceable, the remaining provisions shall stay in effect.

I understand the importance of the powers I delegate to my attorney-in-fact in this document. I recognize that the document gives my attorney-in-fact broad powers over my assets, and that these powers shall become effective as of the date of my incapacity (or sooner if specified in this document) and shall continue indefinitely unless I revoke this durable power of attorney.

Signed this _____ day of _____, 19_____.

State of _____   County of _____

_____   _____
your signature   your social security number

CERTIFICATE OF ACKNOWLEDGMENT OF NOTARY PUBLIC

State of _____
County of _____ } ss

On _____, 19 ____ , before me, _____ ,
a notary public, personally appeared _____
_____, personally known to me or proved to me on the basis of satisfactory evidence to be the person whose name is subscribed to this instrument, and acknowledged that he or she executed it.

[NOTARY SEAL]   _____
                                            signature of notary public

NEW YORK STATUTORY GENERAL POWER OF ATTORNEY

Notice: The powers granted by this document are broad and sweeping. They are defined in New York General Obligations Law, Article 5, Title 15, sections 5-1502A through 5-1503, which expressly permits the use of any other or different form of power of attorney desired by the parties concerned.

Know All Men by These Presents, which are intended to constitute a GENERAL POWER OF ATTORNEY pursuant to Article 5, Title 15 of the New York General Obligations Law:

That I _____
(insert name and address of the principal)

do hereby appoint _____
(insert name and address of the agent, or each agent, if more than one is designated)

my attorney(s)-in-fact TO ACT _____.

(a) If more than one agent is designated and the principal wishes each agent alone to be able to exercise the power conferred, insert in this blank the word "severally". Failure to make any insertion or the insertion of the word "jointly' will require the agents to act jointly.

In my name, place and stead in any way which I myself could do, if I were personally present, with respect to the following matters as each of them is defined in Title 15 of Article 5 of the New York General Obligations Law to the extent that I am permitted by law to act through an agent:

[Strike out and initial in the opposite box any one or more of the subdivisions as to which the principal does NOT desire to give the agent authority. Such elimination of any one or more of subdivisions (A) to (L), inclusive, shall automatically constitute an elimination also of subdivision (M).]

To strike out any subdivision the principal must draw a line through the text of that subdivision AND write his initials in the box opposite.

(A) real estate transactions; ....[   ]
(B) chattel and goods transactions; ....[   ]
(C) bond, share and commodity transactions ....[   ]
(D) banking transactions; ....[   ]
(E) business operating transactions; ....[   ]
(F) insurance transactions; ....[   ]
(G) estate transactions; ....[   ]
(H) claims and litigation; ....[   ]
(I) personal relationships and affairs; ....[   ]
(J) benefits from military service; ....[   ]
(K) records, reports and statements; ....[   ]
(L) full and unqualified authority to my attorney(s)-in-fact to delegate any or all of the foregoing powers to any person or persons whom any attorney(s)-in-fact shall select; ......[   ]
(M) all other matters ....[   ]

_____

_____

[Special provisions and limitations may be included in the statutory short form power of attorney only if they conform to the requirements of section 5-1503 of the New York General Obligations Law.]

TO INDUCE ANY THIRD PARTY TO ACT HEREUNDER, I HEREBY AGREE THAT ANY THIRD PARTY RECEIVING A DULY EXECUTED COPY OR FACSIMILE OF THIS INSTRUMENT MAY ACT HEREUNDER, AND THAT REVOCATION OR TERMINATION HEREOF SHALL BE INEFFECTIVE AS TO SUCH THIRD PARTY UNLESS AND UNTIL ACTUAL NOTICE OR KNOWLEDGE OF SUCH REVOCATION OR TERMINATION SHALL HAVE BEEN RECEIVED BY SUCH THIRD PARTY, AND I FOR MYSELF AND FOR MY HEIRS, EXECUTORS, LEGAL REPRESENTATIVES AND ASSIGNS, HEREBY AGREE TO INDEMNIFY AND HOLD HARMLESS ANY SUCH THIRD PARTY FROM AND AGAINST ANY AND ALL CLAIMS THAT MAY ARISE AGAINST SUCH THIRD PARTY BY REASON OF SUCH THIRD PARTY HAVING RELIED ON THE PROVISIONS OF THIS INSTRUMENT.

_____

_____

_____

_____

_____

_____

_____

_____

_____

_____

In Witness Whereof I have hereunto signed my name and affixed my seal this _____ day of _____, 19 ____.

_____ (Seal)
(Signature of Principal)

State of New York

County of _____ } ss

On _____19 ____ before me, _____, a notary public, personally appeared _____, personally known to me (or proved to me on the basis of satisfactory evidence) to be the person whose name is subscribed to this instrument, and acknowledged that he or she executed it.

_____

[NOTARY SEAL]   Signature of notary public

NORTH CAROLINA STATUTORY SHORT FORM OF GENERAL POWER OF ATTORNEY

NOTICE: THE POWERS GRANTED BY THIS DOCUMENT ARE BROAD AND SWEEPING. THEY ARE DEFINED IN CHAPTER 32A OF THE NORTH CAROLINA GENERAL STATUTES WHICH EXPRESSLY PERMITS THE USE OF ANY OTHER OR DIFFERENT FORM OF POWER OF ATTORNEY DESIRED BY THE PARTIES CONCERNED.

State of _____

County of _____

I _____, the undersigned, hereby appoint _____ my attorney-in-fact for me and give such person full power to act in my name, place and stead in any way which I myself could do if I were personally present with respect to the following matters as each of them is defined in Chapter 32A of the North Carolina General Statutes to the event that I am permitted by law to act through an agent. (DIRECTIONS: Initial the line opposite any one or more of the subdivisions as to which the principal desires to give the attorney-in-fact authority.)

(1)   Real property transactions; .... _____

(2)   Personal property transactions; .... _____

(3)   Bond, share and commodity transactions; .... _____

(4)   Banking transactions; .... _____

(5)   Safe deposits; .... _____

(6)   Business operating transactions; .... _____

(7)   Insurance transactions; .... _____

(8)   Estate transactions; .... _____

(9)   Personal relationships and affairs; .... _____

(10)   Social security and unemployment; .... _____

(11)   Benefits from military service; .... _____

(12)   Tax; .... _____

(13)   Employment of agents; .... _____

(If power of substitution and revocation is to be given, add: 'I also give to such person full power to appoint another to act as my attorney-in-fact and full power to revoke such appointment.')

_____

_____

(If period of power of attorney is to be limited, add: 'This power terminates _____, 19 ___.')

_____

(If power of attorney is to be a durable power of attorney under the provision of Article 2 of Chapter 32A and is to continue in effect after the incapacity or mental incompetence of the principal, add: 'This power of attorney shall not be affected by my subsequent incapacity or mental incompetence.')

<u>This power of attorney shall not be affected by my subsequent incapacity or mental incompetence.</u>

(If power of attorney is to take effect only after the incapacity or mental incompetence of the principal, add: 'This power of attorney shall become effective after I become incapacitated or mentally incompetent.')

_____

_____

_____

_____

_____

_____

_____

_____

_____

_____

_____

_____

_____

_____

I waive the requirement, set out in North Carolina Gen. Stat. § 32A-11, that the attorney-in-fact file this power of attorney with the clerk of the superior court and render inventories and accounts, after my incapacity or mental incompetence, to the clerk of the superior court.

Dated _____, 19_____

_____ (SEAL)
Signature

STATE OF _____ COUNTY OF _____

On this _____ day of _____ , ____, personally appeared before me, the said named _____ to me known and known to be the person described in and who executed the foregoing instrument and he (or she) acknowledged that he (or she) executed the same and being duly sworn by me, made oath that the statements in the foregoing instrument are true.

My Commission Expires:_____

_____
(Signature of Notary Public)

Notary Public (Official Seal)

DURABLE POWER OF ATTORNEY FOR FINANCIAL MANAGEMENT: TENNESSEE

THE POWERS GRANTED BY THIS DOCUMENT ARE BROAD AND SWEEPING. IF YOU HAVE ANY QUESTIONS ABOUT THESE POWERS, GET COMPETENT LEGAL ADVICE. THIS DOCUMENT DOES NOT AUTHORIZE ANYONE TO MAKE MEDICAL OR OTHER HEALTH CARE DECISIONS FOR YOU.

YOU MAY REVOKE THIS POWER OF ATTORNEY IF YOU LATER WISH TO DO SO.

1. Attorney-in-Fact

I, _____ of _____, Tennessee, appoint _____ _____ as my attorney-in-fact to act for me in any lawful way with respect to the powers delegated in Part 6 below. If that person or persons does not serve or ceases to serve as attorney-in-fact, I appoint _____ to serve as attorney-in-fact.

2. More Than One Attorney-in-Fact

a. Authorization

If more than one attorney-in-fact is designated, they are authorized to act:

☐ jointly. ☐ independently.

b. Resolution of Disputes

☐ If my attorneys-in-fact cannot agree on a decision or action under the authority delegated to them in this durable power of attorney, that dispute shall be resolved by binding arbitration. The arbitration shall be carried out by a single arbitrator, who shall be _____, if available. The arbitration shall begin within five days of written notice by any attorney-in-fact to the arbitrator that a dispute has arisen. The details of the arbitration shall be determined by the arbitrator. The written decision of the arbitrator shall be binding on all my my attorneys-in-fact.

3. Delegation of Authority

My attorney-in-fact ☐ may ☐ may not delegate, in writing, any authority granted under this durable power of attorney to a person he or she selects. Any such delegation shall state the period during which it is valid and specify the extent of the delgation.

4. Effective Date

This power of attorney is effective:

☐ immediately, and shall continue in effect if I become incapacitated or disabled.

☐ only if I become incapacitated or disabled and unable to manage my financial affairs.

5. Determination of Incapacity

For purposes of this durable power of attorney, my incapacity or disability shall be determined by written declarations by ☐ one ☐ two licensed physician(s). Each declaration shall be made under penalty of perjury and shall state that in the physician's opinion I am substantially unable to manage my financial affairs. If possible, the declaration(s) shall be made by _____ _____. No licensed physician shall be liable to me for any actions taken by them under this part which are done in good faith.

6. Powers of Attorney-in-Fact

I hereby grant to my attorney-in-fact power to act on my behalf in the following matters, as indicated by my initials by each granted power. Powers that are not initialed are not granted. The Tennessee Code sections noted below are hereby incorporated by reference.

INITIALS

_____ a. ALL POWERS (b THROUGH o) LISTED BELOW.
             [Tenn. Code Ann. § 34-6-109(1)]

_____ b. Real estate transactions. [Tenn. Code Ann. § 34-6-109(3)]

_____ c. Tangible personal property transactions.

_____ d. Stock and bond, commodity and option transactions.

_____ e. Banking and other financial institution transactions.
             [Tenn. Code Ann. §§ 34-6-109(2), (7), (11), (12), (13)]

_____ f. Business operating transactions. [Tenn. Code Ann. § 34-6-109(14)]

_____ g   Insurance and annuity transactions. [Tenn. Code Ann. § 34-6-109(5)]

_____ h. Estate, trust, and other beneficiary transactions.
             [Tenn. Code Ann. § 34-6-109(16)]

_____ i. Claims and litigation. [Tenn. Code Ann. § 34-6-109(17)]

_____ j. Personal and family maintenance.[Tenn. Code Ann. § 34-6-109(6), (15)]

_____ k. Benefits from social security, medicare, medicaid, or other governmental
             programs, or civil or military service. [Tenn. Code Ann. § 34-6-109(8)]

_____ l. Retirement plan transactions. [Tenn. Code Ann. § 34-6-109(19)]

_____ m. Tax matters. [Tenn. Code Ann. § 34-6-109(4), (20)]

_____ n. Advance funeral and burial arrangements. [Tenn. Code Ann. § 34-6-109(22)]

_____ o. Personal records. [Tenn. Code Ann. § 34-6-109 (21)]

7. Special Instructions to the Attorney-in-Fact

_____

_____

_____

8. Compensation and Reimbursement of the Attorney-in-Fact

☐ The attorney-in-fact shall not be compensated for services, but shall be entitled to reimbursement, from the principal's assets, for reasonable expenses. Reasonable expenses include reasonable fees for information or advice from accountants, lawyers or investment experts relating to the attorney-in-fact's responsibilities under this power of attorney.

☐ The attorney-in-fact shall be entitled to reimbursement for reasonable expenses and reasonable compensation for his or her services. Reasonable compensation shall be determined exclusively by the attorney-in-fact.

☐ The attorney-in-fact shall be entitled to reimbursement for reasonable expenses and compensation for his or her services of $_____ per _____ .

9. Nomination of Conservator or Guardian

If, in a court proceeding, it is ever resolved that I need a conservator, guardian or other person to administer and supervise my estate or person, I nominate my attorney-in-fact to serve in that capacity. If my attorney-in-fact cannot serve, I nominate the sucessor attorney-in-fact named in Part 1 to serve.

10. Personal Benefit to Attorney-in-Fact

☐ My attorney-in-fact may buy any assets of mine or engage in any transaction he or she deems in good faith to be in my interest, no matter what the interest of or benefit to my attorney-in-fact.

☐ My attorney-in-fact may not be personally involved in or benefit personally from any transaction he or she engages in on my behalf, except _____

_____ .

☐ My attorney-in-fact may not be personally involved in or benefit personally from any transaction he or she engages in on my behalf.

11. Commingling by Attorney-in-Fact

My attorney-in-fact ☒ may ☐ may not commingle any of my funds with any funds of his or hers.

12. Bond

The attorney-in-fact shall serve without bond.

13. Liability of Attorney-in-Fact

Neither my attorney-in-fact nor any successor attorney-in-fact shall incur any liability to me, my estate, my heirs, successors or assigns for acting or refraining from acting under this document, except for willful misconduct or gross negligence. Neither my attorney-in-fact nor any successors shall be required to make my assets productive of income, increase the value of my estate, diversify my investments or enter into transactions authorized by this document, as long as my attorney-in-fact or successor believes his or her actions are in my best interests or in the best interests of my estate and of those interested in my estate.

14. Gifts by Attorney-in-Fact

a. My attorney-in-fact shall have no incidents of ownership over any life insurance policy in which I may own an interest and which insures his or her life.

b. My attorney-in-fact may not (i) appoint, assign or designate any of my assets, interests or rights directly or indirectly to himself or herself, or estate, creditors, or the creditors of his or her estate, (ii) disclaim assets to which I would otherwise be entitled if the effect of the disclaimer is to cause such assets to pass directly or indirectly to my attorney-in-fact or his or her estate, or (iii) use my assets to discharge any of his or her legal obligations, including any obligation of support owed to others (excluding me and those whom I am legally obligated to support).

c. My attorney-in-fact shall not hold or exercise any powers I may have over assets he or she has given to me or over assets held in an irrevocable trust of which he or she is a grantor.

15. Reliance on this Power of Attorney

I agree that any third party who receives a copy of this document may act under it. Revocation of the power of attorney is not effective as to a third party until the third party has actual knowledge of the revocation. I agree to indemnify the third party for any claims that arise against the third party because of reliance on this power of attorney.

16. Severability

If any provision of this document is ruled unenforceable, the remaining provisions shall stay in effect.

I understand the importance of the powers I delegate to my attorney-in-fact in this document. I recognize that the document gives my attorney-in-fact broad powers over my assets, and that these powers shall become effective as of the date of my incapacity (or sooner if specified in this document) and shall continue indefinitely unless I revoke this durable power of attorney.

Signed this _____ day of_____ 19_____.

State of _____ County of _____

_____   _____
your signature   your social security number

CERTIFICATE OF ACKNOWLEDGMENT OF NOTARY PUBLIC

State of _____ }
                                                          } ss
County of _____ }

On _____, 19 _____ , before me, _____, a notary public, personally appeared _____, personally known to me or proved to me on the basis of satisfactory evidence to be the person whose name is subscribed to this instrument, and acknowledged that he or she executed it.

[NOTARY SEAL]   _____
                                      signature of notary public

PHYSICIAN'S DETERMINATION OF INCAPACITY

I, _____, of the City of _____ , County of

_____, State of _____, declare under penalty of perjury

that:

    1. I am a physician licensed to practice in the state of _____.

    2. I examined _____ on _____, 19_____. It is my

professional opinion that _____ is currently incapacitated and unable to

mange his/her finances and property.

    Dated: _____

                                     _____

                                         (Signature of Physician)

                                 _____ , Principal

State of _____

                                  } ss.

County of_____

On _____ , 19___ , before me, _____ , a notary public, personally

appeared _____, known to me or proved on the basis of

satisfactory evidence to be the person whose name is subscribed to this instrument and

acknowledged and executed the same.

                                  _____

                                  Notary Public for the State of _____

[notarial seal]   My commission expires:_____

DESIGNATION OF AUTHORITY

I, _____ , of _____ ,
City of _____ , County of _____ ,
State of _____ , am currently serving as attorney -in-fact
for _____ under
the Durable Power of Attorney for Finances dated _____ .

I hereby give notice that under the power granted to me, I delegate the following authority to
_____ for the period
beginning _____ and ending _____ :

_____

_____

_____

_____

_____

_____

_____

_____

_____

Dated: _____   _____
                                     (Signature of Attorney-in-Fact)

                                     _____ , Attorney-in-Fact

State of _____
                                            } ss
County of _____

On _____ , 19___ , before me, _____ , a notary public,
personally appeared _____ , known to me or proved on the
basis of satisfactory evidence to be the person whose name is subscribed to this instrument as principal
and acknowledged and executed the same.

                                     _____

                                     Notary Public for the State of _____

[notarial seal]   My commission expires :_____

RESIGNATION OF ATTORNEY-IN-FACT

I, _____ , of
_____ , City of _____ ,
County of _____ , State of _____ , give notice
that I hereby resign as attorney-in-fact under the Durable Power of Attorney for Finances created by
_____ and dated _____ .

Dated: _____   _____
                                            (Signature of Attorney-in-Fact)

                                _____ , Attorney-in-Fact

State of _____
                                        } ss
County of _____

On _____ , 19_____ , before me, _____
_____ , a notary public, personally appeared _____
_____ , known to me or proved on the basis of satisfactory evidence to be the person
whose name is subscribed to this instrument as principal and acknowledged and executed the same.

                                _____

                                Notary Public for the State of _____

[notarial seal]   My commission expires: _____

RECORDING REQUESTED BY
AND WHEN RECORDED MAIL TO

_____

_____

_____

NOTICE OF REVOCATION OF RECORDED POWER OF ATTORNEY

I, _____, of

_____, City of _____, County of

_____, State of _____, give notice that I

hereby revoke the durable power of attorney dated _____ empowering _____

_____ to act as my attorney-in-fact for certain financial

matters. I revoke and withdraw all power and authority granted under that power of attorney.

That power of attorney was recorded on _____, 19_____ in Book _____,

at Page _____ of the Official Records, County of _____ , State

of _____ .

Dated: _____   _____
                                      (Signature of Principal)

                                      _____ , Principal

State of _____
                                }ss
County of _____

On _____, 19_____, before me, _____

_____, a notary public, personally appeared _____

_____, known to me or proved on the basis of satisfactory evidence to be the person

whose name is subscribed to this instrument as principal and acknowledged and executed the same.

                                      _____

                                      Notary Public for the State of _____

[notarial seal]   My commission expires: _____

INDEX

RECYCLE YOUR OUT OF DATE BOOKS
AND GET 25% OFF YOUR NEXT PURCHASE

OUT OF DATE = DANGEROUS

Using an old edition can be dangerous if information in it is wrong. Unfortunately, laws and legal procedures change often. Generally speaking, any book more than two years old is of questionable value. Books more than four or five years old are a menace.

To help you keep up-to-date, we extend this offer:

If you cut out and deliver to us the title portion of the cover of any old Nolo book, we'll give you a 25% discount off the retail price of any new Nolo book. For example, if you have a copy of *Tenants' Rights*, 4th edition, and want to trade it for the latest *California Marriage and Divorce Law*, send us the *Tenants' Rights* cover and a check for the current price of *California Marriage and Divorce*, less a 25% discount.

Information on current prices and editions is listed in the back of this book and in the catalog in the *Nolo News* (see offer at the back of this book).

This offer is to individuals only.

SELF-HELP LAW BOOKS & SOFTWARE

ESTATE PLANNING & PROBATE

Plan Your Estate With a Living Trust
Attorney Denis Clifford
National 2nd Edition
This book covers every significant aspect of estate planning and gives detailed specific, instructions for preparing a living trust, a document that lets your family avoid expensive and lengthy probate court proceedings after your death. *Plan Your Estate* includes all the tear-out forms and step-by-step instructions to let you prepare an estate plan designed for your special needs.
$19.95/NEST

Nolo's Simple Will Book
Attorney Denis Clifford
National 2nd Edition
It's easy to write a legally valid will using this book. The instructions and forms enable people to draft a will for all needs, including naming a personal guardian for minor children, leaving property to minor children or young adults and updating a will when necessary. Good in all states except Louisiana.
$17.95/SWIL

How to Probate an Estate
Julia Nissley
California 6th Edition
If you find yourself responsible for winding up the legal and financial affairs of a deceased family member or friend, you can often save costly attorneys' fees by handling the probate process yourself. This book also explains the simple procedures you can use to transfer assets that don't require probate, including property held in joint tenancy or living trusts or as community property.
$34.95/PAE

The Conservatorship Book
Lisa Goldoftas & Attorney Carolyn Farren
California 1st Edition
When someone becomes incapacitated due to illness or age, a conservator may need to take charge of their medical and financial affairs. *The Conservatorship Book* comes with complete instructions and all the forms necessary to file conservatorship documents, appear in court, be appointed conservator and end a conservatorship.
$24.95/CNSV

software

WillMaker
Nolo Press
Version 4.0
This easy-to-use software program lets you prepare and update a legal will—safely, quickly and without the expense of a lawyer. Leading you step-by-step in a question-and-answer format, *WillMaker* builds a will around your answers, taking into account your state of residence. *WillMaker* comes with a 200-page legal manual which provides the legal background necessary to make sound choices. Good in all states except Louisiana.
**IBM PC
(3-1/2 & 5-1/4 disks included) $69.95/WI4
MACINTOSH $69.95/WM4**

Nolo's Personal RecordKeeper
(formerly For the Record)

Carol Pladsen & Attorney Ralph Warner
Version 3.0
Nolo's Personal RecordKeeper lets you record the location of personal, financial and legal information in over 200 categories and subcategories. It also allows you to create lists of insured property, compute net worth, consolidate emergency information into one place and export to *Quicken®* home inventory and net worth reports. Includes a 320-page manual filled with practical and legal advice.
**IBM PC
(3-1/2 & 5-1/4 disks included) $49.95/FRI3
MACINTOSH $49.95/FRM3**

Nolo's Living Trust
Attorney Mary Randolph
Version 1.0
A will is an indispensable part of any estate plan, but many people need a living trust as well. By putting certain assets into a trust, you save your heirs the headache, time and expense of probate. *Nolo's Living Trust* lets you set up an individual or shared marital trust, make your trust document legal, transfer your property to the trust, and change or revoke the trust at any time. The 380-page manual guides you through the process step-by-step, and over 100 legal help screens and an on-line glossary explain key legal terms and concepts. Good in all states except Louisiana.
MACINTOSH $79.95/LTM1

GOING TO COURT

Everybody's Guide to Municipal Court
Judge Roderic Duncan
California 1st Edition
Everybody's Guide to Municipal Court explains how to prepare and defend the most common types of contract and personal injury law suits in California Municipal Court. Written by a California judge, the book provides step-by-step instructions for preparing and filing all necessary forms, gathering evidence and appearing in court.
$29.95/MUNI

Everybody's Guide to Small Claims Court
Attorney Ralph Warner
National 5th Edition
California 10th Edition
These books will help you decide if you should sue in Small Claims Court, show you how to file and serve papers, tell you what to bring to court and how to collect a judgment.
**National $15.95/NSCC
California $15.95/ CSCC**

Fight Your Ticket
Attorney David Brown
California 5th Edition
This book shows you how to fight an unfair traffic ticket—when you're stopped, at arraignment, at trial and on appeal.
$17.95/FYT

Collect Your Court Judgment
Gini Graham Scott, Attorney Stephen Elias & Lisa Goldoftas
California 2nd Edition
This book contains step-by-step instructions and all the forms you need to collect a court judgment from the debtor's bank accounts, wages, business receipts, real estate or other assets.
$19.95/JUDG

How to Change Your Name
Attorneys David Loeb & David Brown
California 5th Edition
This book explains how to change your name legally and provides all the necessary court forms with detailed instructions on how to fill them out.
$19.95/NAME

The Criminal Records Book
Attorney Warren Siegel
California 3rd Edition
This book shows you step-by-step how to seal criminal records, dismiss convictions, destroy marijuana records and reduce felony convictions.
$19.95/CRIM

LEGAL REFORM

Legal Breakdown: 40 Ways to Fix Our Legal System
Nolo Press Editors and Staff
National 1st Edition
Legal Breakdown presents 40 common-sense proposals to make our legal system fairer, faster, cheaper and more accessible. It advocates abolishing probate, taking divorce out of court, treating jurors better and a host of other fundamental changes.
$8.95/LEG

BUSINESS/WORKPLACE

The Legal Guide for Starting & Running a Small Business
Attorney Fred S. Steingold
National 1st Edition
This book is an essential resource for every small business owner, whether you are just starting out or are already established. Find out everything you need to know about how to form a sole proprietorship, partnership or corporation, negotiate a favorable lease, hire and fire employees, write contracts and resolve disputes.
$19.95 / RUNS

Sexual Harassment on the Job
Attorneys William Petrocelli & Barbara Kate Repa
National 1st Edition
This is the first comprehensive book dealing with sexual harassment in the workplace. It describes what harassment is, what the laws are that make it illegal and how to put a stop to it. This guide is invaluable both for employees experiencing harassment and for employers interested in creating a policy against sexual harassment and a procedure for handling complaints.
$14.95/HARS

Your Rights in the Workplace
Dan Lacey
National 1st Edition
Your Rights in the Workplace, the first comprehensive guide to workplace rights —from hiring to firing—explains the latest sweeping changes in laws passed to protect workers. Learning about these legal protections can help all workers be sure they're paid fairly and on time, get all employment benefits, and know how to take action if fired or laid off illegally.
$15.95/YRW

How to Write a Business Plan
Mike McKeever
National 4th Edition
If you're thinking of starting a business or raising money to expand an existing one, this book will show you how to write the business plan and loan package necessary to finance your business and make it work.
$19.95/SBS

Marketing Without Advertising
Michael Phillips & Salli Rasberry
National 1st Edition
This book outlines practical steps for building and expanding a small business without spending a lot of money on advertising.
$14.00/MWAD

The Partnership Book
Attorneys Denis Clifford & Ralph Warner
National 4th Edition
This book shows you step-by-step how to write a solid partnership agreement that meets your needs. It covers initial contributions to the business, wages, profit-sharing, buy-outs, death or retirement of a partner and disputes.
$24.95/PART

How to Form Your Own Nonprofit Corporation
Attorney Anthony Mancuso
National 1st Edition
This book explains the legal formalities involved and provides detailed information on the differences in the law among 50 states. It also contains forms for the Articles, Bylaws and Minutes you need, along with complete instructions for obtaining federal 501 (c) (3) tax exemptions and qualifying for public charity status.
$24.95/NNP

The California Nonprofit Corporation Handbook
Attorney Anthony Mancuso
California 6th Edition
This book shows you step-by-step how to form and operate a nonprofit corporation in California. It includes the latest corporate and tax law changes, and the forms for the Articles, Bylaws and Minutes.
$29.95/NON

How to Form Your Own Corporation
Attorney Anthony Mancuso
California 7th Edition
New York 2nd Edition
Texas 4th Edition
Florida 3rd Edition
These books contain the forms, instructions and tax information you need to incorporate a small business yourself and save hundreds of dollars in lawyers' fees.
California $29.95/CCOR
New York $24.95/NYCO
Texas $29.95/TCOR
Florida $24.95/FLCO

The California Professional Corporation Handbook
Attorney Anthony Mancuso
California 4th Edition
Health care professionals, lawyers, accountants and members of certain other professions must fulfill special requirements when forming a corporation in California. This book contains up-to-date tax information plus all the forms and instructions necessary to form a California professional corporation.
$34.95/PROF

The Independent Paralegal's Handbook

Attorney Ralph Warner

National 2nd Edition

The Independent Paralegal's Handbook provides legal and business guidelines for those who want to take routine legal work out of the law office and offer it for a reasonable fee in an independent business.
$19.95/ PARA

Getting Started as an Independent Paralegal

(Two Audio Tapes)

Attorney Ralph Warner

National 2nd Edition

If you are interested in going into business as an Independent Paralegal—helping consumers prepare their own legal paperwork in uncontested proceedings such as bankruptcy, divorce, small business incorporation, landlord-tenant actions and probate—you'll want these tapes. Approximately two hours in length, the tapes will tell you everything you need to know about what legal tasks to handle, how much to charge and how to run a profitable business.
$44.95/GSIP

Nolo's Partnership Maker

Attorney Tony Mancuso & Michael Radtke

Version 1.0

Nolo's Partnership Maker prepares a legal partnership agreement for doing business in any state. The program can be used by anyone who plans to pool energy, efforts, money or property with others to run a business, share property, produce a profit or undertake any other type of mutual endeavor. You can select and assemble the standard partnership clauses provided or create your own customized agreement. And the agreement can be updated at any time. Includes on-line legal help screens, glossary and tutorial, and a manual that takes you through the process step-by-step.
IBM PC
(3-1/2 & 5-1/4 disks included) $129.00/PAGI1

California Incorporator

Attorney Anthony Mancuso

Version 1.0 (good only in CA)

Answer the questions on the screen and this software program will print out the 35-40 pages of documents you need to make your California corporation legal. Comes with a 200-page manual which explains the incorporation process.
IBM PC
(3-1/2 & 5-1/4 disks included) $129.00/INCI

The California Nonprofit Corporation Handbook

(computer edition)

Attorney Anthony Mancuso

Version 1.0 (good only in CA)

This book/software package shows you step-by-step how to form and operate a nonprofit corporation in California. Included on disk are the forms for the Articles, Bylaws and Minutes.
IBM PC 5-1/4 $69.95/ NPI
IBM PC 3-1/2 $69.95/ NP3I
MACINTOSH $69.95/ NPM

How to Form Your Own New York Corporation & How to Form Your Own Texas Corporation

(computer editions)

Attorney Anthony Mancuso

These book/software packages contain the instructions and tax information and forms you need to incorporate a small business and save hundreds of dollars in lawyers' fees. All organizational forms are on disk. Both come with a 250-page manual.
New York 1st Edition
IBM PC 5-1/4 $69.95/ NYCI
IBM PC 3-1/2 $69.95/ NYC3I
MACINTOSH $69.95/ NYCM

Texas 1st Edition
IBM PC 5-1/4 $69.95/ TCI
IBM PC 3-1/2 $69.95/ TC3I
MACINTOSH $69.95/ TCM

THE NEIGHBORHOOD

Neighbor Law: Fences, Trees, Boundaries & Noise

Attorney Cora Jordan

National 1st Edition

Neighbor Law answers common questions about the subjects that most often trigger disputes between neighbors: fences, trees, boundaries and noise. It explains how to find the law and resolve disputes without a nasty lawsuit.
$14.95/NEI

Dog Law

Attorney Mary Randolph

National 1st Edition

Dog Law is a practical guide to the laws that affect dog owners and their neighbors. You'll find answers to common questions on such topics as biting, barking, veterinarians and more.
$12.95/DOG

MONEY MATTERS

Stand Up to the IRS

Attorney Fred Daily

National 1st Edition

Stand Up to the IRS gives detailed stategies on surviving an audit with the minimum amount of damage, appealing an audit decision, going to Tax Court and dealing with IRS collectors. It also discusses filing tax returns when you haven't done so in a while, tax crimes, concerns of small business people and getting help from the IRS ombudsman. This book also includes confidential forms, unavailable to taxpayers, used by the IRS during audits and collection interviewers.
$19.95 / SUIRS

Barbara Kaufman's Consumer Action Guide

Barbara Kaufman

California 1st Edition

This practical handbook is filled with information on hundreds of consumer topics. Barbara Kaufman, the Bay Area's award-winning consumer reporter and producer of KCBS Radio's *Call for Action,* gives consumers access to their legal rights, providing addresses and phone numbers of where to complain when things go wrong, and providing resources if more help is necessary.
$14.95/CAG

Money Troubles: Legal Strategies to Cope With Your Debts

Attorney Robin Leonard

National 1st Edition

Are you behind on your credit card bills or loan payments? If you are, then *Money Troubles* is exactly what you need. It covers everything from knowing what your rights are, and asserting them, to helping you evaluate your individual situation. This practical, straightforward book is for anyone who needs help understanding and dealing with the complex and often scary topic of debts.
$16.95/MT

How to File for Bankruptcy
Attorneys Stephen Elias, Albin Renauer &
Robin Leonard
National 3rd Edition
Trying to decide whether or not filing for
bankruptcy makes sense? *How to File for
Bankruptcy* contains an overview of the
process and all the forms plus step-by-step
instructions on the procedures to follow.
$24.95/HFB

Simple Contracts for Personal Use
Attorney Stephen Elias & Marcia Stewart
National 2nd Edition
This book contains clearly written legal
form contracts to buy and sell property,
borrow and lend money, store and lend
personal property, release others from
personal liability, or pay a contractor to do
home repairs. Includes agreements to
arrange childcare and other household
help.
$16.95/CONT

FAMILY MATTERS

Divorce & Money
Violet Woodhouse & Victoria Felton-Collins with
M.C. Blakeman
National 1st Edition
Divorce & Money explains how to
evaluate such major assets as family homes
and businesses, investments, pensions, and
how to arrive at a division of property that
is fair to both sides. Throughout, the book
emphasizes the difference between legal
reality—how the court evaluates assets,
and financial reality—what the assets are
really worth.
$19.95/DIMO

The Living Together Kit
Attorneys Toni Ihara & Ralph Warner
National 6th Edition
The Living Together Kit is a detailed guide
designed to help the increasing number of
unmarried couples living together understand the laws that affect them. Sample
agreements and instructions are included.
$17.95/LTK

The Guardianship Book
Lisa Goldoftas & Attorney David Brown
California 1st Edition
The Guardianship Book provides step-by-
step instructions and the forms needed to
obtain a legal guardianship without a
lawyer.
$19.95/GB

A Legal Guide for Lesbian and
Gay Couples
Attorneys Hayden Curry & Denis Clifford
National 6th Edition
Laws designed to regulate and protect
unmarried couples don't apply to lesbian
and gay couples. This book shows you
step-by-step how to write a living-together
contract, plan for medical emergencies,
and plan your estates. Includes forms,
sample agreements and lists of both
national lesbian and gay legal
organizations and AIDS organizations.
$17.95/LG

How to Do Your Own Divorce
Attorney Charles Sherman
(Texas Ed. by Sherman & Simons)
California 17th Edition & Texas 4th Edition
These books contain all the forms and
instructions you need to do your own
uncontested divorce without a lawyer.
California $18.95/CDIV
Texas $17.95/TDIV

Practical Divorce Solutions
Attorney Charles Sherman
California 2nd Edition
This book is a valuable guide to the
emotional aspects of divorce as well as an
overview of the legal and financial
decisions that must be made.
$12.95/PDS

California Marriage & Divorce Law
Attorneys Ralph Warner, Toni Ihara &
Stephen Elias
California 11th Edition
This book explains community property,
pre-nuptial contracts, foreign marriages,
buying a house, getting a divorce, dividing
property, and more.
$19.95/MARR

How to Adopt Your Stepchild in California
Frank Zagone & Attorney Mary Randolph
California 3rd Edition
There are many emotional, financial and
legal reasons to adopt a stepchild, but
among the most pressing legal reasons is
the need to avoid confusion over
inheritance or guardianship. This book
provides sample forms and step-by-step
instructions for completing a simple
uncontested adoption by a stepparent.
$19.95/ADOP

JUST FOR FUN

29 Reasons Not To Go to Law School
Attorneys Ralph Warner & Toni Ihara
National 3rd Edition
Filled with humor and piercing
observations, this book can save you three
years, $70,000 and your sanity.
$9.95/29R

Devil's Advocates:
The Unnatural History of Lawyers
by Andrew & Jonathan Roth
National 1st Edition
This book is a painless and hilarious
education, tracing the legal profession.
Careful attention is given to the world's
worst lawyers, most preposterous cases and
most ludicrous courtroom strategies.
$12.95/DA

Poetic Justice: The Funniest, Meanest
Things Ever Said About Lawyers
Edited by Jonathan & Andrew Roth
National 1st Edition
A great gift for anyone in the legal
profession who has managed to maintain a
sense of humor.
$8.95/PJ

PATENT, COPYRIGHT & TRADEMARK

Trademark: How To Name Your
Business & Product
Attorneys Kate McGrath and Stephen Elias,
With Trademark Attorney Sarah Shena
National 1st Edition
This is by far the best comprehensive do-
it-yourself trademark book designed for
small businesses. It explains step-by-step
how to protect names used to market
services and products, and shows how to:
choose a name or logo that others can't
copy, conduct a trademark search, register
a trademark with the U.S. Patent and
Trademark Office and protect and
maintain the trademark.
$29.95 / TRD

Patent It Yourself
Attorney David Pressman
National 3rd Edition
From the patent search to the actual
application, this book covers everything
including the use and licensing of patents,
successful marketing and how to deal with
infringement.
$34.95/PAT